# THE CIVIL WAR
# AND RECONSTRUCTION

# THE CIVIL WAR
# and
# RECONSTRUCTION

## Ray B. Browne and
## Lawrence A. Kreiser, Jr.

American Popular Culture Through History

GREENWOOD PRESS
Westport, Connecticut • London

**Library of Congress Cataloging-in-Publication Data**

Browne, Ray Broadus.

    The Civil War and Reconstruction / Ray B. Browne and Lawrence A. Kreiser, Jr.
      p. cm.—(American popular culture through history)
    Includes bibliographical references and index.
    ISBN 0–313–31325–3 (alk. paper)
    1. United States—Civilization—19th century. 2. United States—History—Civil War,
1861–1865—Social aspects. 3. Reconstruction—Social aspects. 4. United States—
Social life and customs—19th century. 5. Popular culture—United States—History—
19th century. I. Kreiser, Lawrence A., 1922– II. Title. III. Series.
E167.B78 2003
973.7—dc21     2002035206

British Library Cataloguing in Publication Data is available.

Library of Congress Catalog Card Number: 2002035206
ISBN: 0–313–31325–3

First published in 2003

Greenwood Press, 88 Post Road West, Westport, CT 06881
An imprint of Greenwood Publishing Group, Inc.
www.greenwood.com

Printed in the United States of America

The paper used in this book complies with the
Permanent Paper Standard issued by the National
Information Standards Organization (Z39.48–1984).

10 9 8 7 6 5 4 3 2 1

# Contents

Series Foreword *by Ray B. Browne*                                          vii

Introduction                                                                 ix

Timeline of Popular Culture Events                                          xiii

## Part One   Life and Youth During the Civil War and Reconstruction        1

1   Everyday Life                                                             3

2   The World of Youth                                                       19

## Part Two   Popular Culture During the Civil War and Reconstruction       35

3   Advertising                                                             37

4   Architecture                                                           53

5   Clothing and Fashion                                                   65

6   Food                                                                    73

7   Leisure Activities                                                      89

8   Literature                                                             103

9   Music                                                                  119

# Contents

| | | |
|---|---|---|
| 10 | Performing Arts and Entertainment | 135 |
| 11 | Travel and Transportation | 149 |
| 12 | Visual Arts | 163 |
| Comparative Values of Money | | 181 |
| Notes | | 183 |
| Suggested Reading | | 201 |
| Index | | 209 |

# Series Foreword

Popular culture is the system of attitudes, behavior, beliefs, customs, and tastes that define the people of any society. It is the entertainments, diversions, icons, rituals, and actions that shape the everyday world. It is what we do while we are awake and what we dream about while we are asleep. It is the way of life we inherit, practice, change, and then pass on to our descendants.

Popular culture is an extension of folk culture, the culture of the people. With the rise of electronic media and the increase in communication in American culture, folk culture expanded into popular culture—the daily way of life as shaped by the popular majority of society. Especially in a democracy like the United States, popular culture has become both the voice of the people and the force that shapes the nation. In 1782, the French commentator Hector St. Jean de Crevecour asked in his *Letters from an American Farmer,* "What is an American?" He answered that such a person is the creation of America and is in turn the creator of the country's culture. Indeed, notions of the American Dream have been long grounded in the dream of democracy—that is, government by the people, or popular rule. Thus, popular culture is tied fundamentally to America and the dreams of its people.

Historically, culture analysts have tried to fine-tune culture into two categories: "elite"—the elements of culture (fine art, literature, classical music, gourmet food, etc.) that supposedly define the best of society—and "popular"—the elements of culture (comic strips, bestsellers, pop music, fast food, and so on) that appeal to society's lowest common denominator. The so-called educated person approved of elite culture and scoffed at popular culture. This schism first began to develop in Western Europe in the fifteenth century when the privileged classes tried to discover and develop differences in societies based on class, money, privilege, and lifestyles. Like many aspects of European society, the debate between elite and popular cultures came to the United States. The upper class in America, for example, supported museums and galleries that would exhibit the "finer things in life," that would elevate people. As the twenty-first century emerges, however, the distinctions between popular culture and elitist culture have blurred. The blues songs (once denigrated as "race music") of Robert Johnson are now revered by musicologists; architectural students study buildings in Las Vegas as examples of what Robert Venturi called the "kitsch of high capitalism"; sportswriter Gay Talese and heavyweight boxing champ Floyd Patterson were co-panelists at a 1992 SUNY New Paltz symposium on literature and sport. The examples go on and on, but the one commonality that emerges is the role of popular culture as a model for the American Dream, the dream to pursue happiness and a better, more interesting life.

To trace the numerous ways in which popular culture has evolved throughout American history, we have divided the volumes in this series into chronological periods—historical eras until the twentieth century, and decades between 1900 and 2000. In each volume, the author explores the specific details of popular culture that reflect and inform the general undercurrents of the time. Our purpose, then, is to present historical and analytical panoramas that reach both backward into America's past and forward to her collective future. In viewing these panoramas, we can trace a very fundamental part of American society. The American Popular Culture through History series presents the multifaceted parts of a popular culture in a nation that is both grown and still growing.

*Ray B. Browne*
*Secretary-Treasurer*
*Popular Culture Association*
*American Culture Association*

# Introduction

The Civil War and Reconstruction period is difficult to pin down precisely. The beginning date of the conflict is definite enough, with the firing on Fort Sumter on April 12, 1861. So, too, is the end of Reconstruction, dating to the end of Ulysses S. Grant's presidency during 1877. But both dates are somewhat imprecise when considering the nation culturally. The clouds of regionalism and conflict had hovered over the nation for years like storm clouds before the lightning struck. Essentially, the new United States was a tentative nation of three entities divided or loosely connected in their history, culture, and interests. All three entities were motivated by what they considered their best interests, their attitudes toward other groups of peoples, and their named and unidentified rights. The conflicting interests drove a fierce war that would not die.

The North had developed in essentially a religious and commercial atmosphere. From this background had grown certain attitudes toward the importance of the individual and ways of looking at life, and a feeling of being right in this approach to life had matured concurrently. The group of northern states constituted politically and philosophically a closely knit union, willing to have individual states unite into a larger group for the advancement of all. But dissidents of all kinds, varying greatly in the slant and degree of their convictions, were numerous and had their say.

The South, on the other hand, had a fiery dedication to what were loosely called states' rights and a fiercer insistence on the rights and obligations of the individual.

Somewhere between these two generally opposing points of view was a third group. The border states and western territories consisted of many who straddled the fences necessary for the states to remain nominally uncommitted, at least at the beginning of the conflict, with citizens and interests on both sides of the dividing line.

Slavery in the South was fundamentally restricted to flat lands and large plantations. Therefore, people in the mountainous areas, descended from poor and independent stock and having no commercial interests in slavery, envied and resented the more affluent Southerners. They were not inclined to favor what they came to call the rich man's war and the poor man's fight. Mountainous sections were filled with small communities that were indifferent or hostile to the Confederacy, and at least one section—the state of West Virginia—demonstrated that hostility by seceding from the Confederacy at the height of the conflict in 1863.

The Civil War and Reconstruction, and what they mean, simply will not fade away. Many studies of American social and cultural history use the trauma of the war as both the beginning point and the bottleneck through which American culture had to pass and by which it was transformed radically. During and after the war, cries reasserting state and individual rights rose from many corners of the South. Perhaps one of the strongest statements was a postwar song written at least half in fun by the nephew of Confederate General J. E. B. Stuart called "The Unreconstructed Rebel." The singer shouts, "I'm a good old Southern Soldier, and that's just what I am / And for this Yankee nation, I do not give a damn." Today such sentiment is still voiced by a hardcore minority and, though partially in jest and good humor, the cry arises that "the South shall rise again." One manifestation of the high seriousness with which is taken the resurrection of the idealized South is found in a recent book, *Confederate Symbols in the Contemporary South* (2000). The editors reexamine the Confederacy's monuments and gravestones and conclude that Americans who view the Old South either negatively or positively have some justification for their point of view.

The exploding development in nearly all aspects of American life during the Civil War and Reconstruction created all kinds of new and challenging cultural elements. These elements fused into the comprehensive general American culture, which became raw-edged and forward-leaning. At no other time, with the possible exception of the digital age at the end of the twentieth century, has American popular culture grown with such pell-mell speed and with such profound effect on Americans and the world. The lists of firsts in the Civil War are almost incredible. Historian Burke Davis lists more than four dozen, including railroad artillery, land-mine fields, naval torpedoes, anti-aircraft fire (against balloons), telescopic sights for rifles, the income and tobacco taxes, creation of the U.S. Secret Service, the Medal of Honor, commissioned army chaplains, and lunatic inventions by the dozens, most of which died with the end of the war. Others, in one form or another, are still being used in modern warfare.

The everyday culture of the Civil War and Reconstruction era must be characterized in all its elements and shadings in order to be understood. It is so complex that a book like the present one can only generalize and give a few examples of its complexity. These, then, are suggestions of the complex culture of the people—their everyday miniature and major cultures and the resulting total overall patterns—during the years when the various developing elements of the United States fought to tear the nation into diverse parts and then, that battle lost, struggled to reunite it into one nation of diverse people—to become in truth, in the words on the Great Seal of the United States, *E pluribus unum,* "From many, one."

# Timeline of Popular Culture Events

## 1852

Harriet Beecher Stowe's anti-slavery novel, *Uncle Tom's Cabin,* is published. Two dramatic adaptations are staged, but unsuccessfully.

## 1853

A successful adaptation of *Uncle Tom's Cabin* runs for 200 consecutive days. By 1854, there were successful touring companies everywhere. By 1870, there are forty-nine companies.

## 1855

Yankee Robinson's Opera Pavilion of Rock Island, Illinois, is the first theater company to perform under canvas tents.

## 1856

Erasmus and Irwin Beadle join with Robert Adams to found the publishing firm of Beadle & Adams.

## 1857

The population of Chicago, which had been only 4,100 in 1837, reaches 93,000.

# 1858

June 16: "A house divided against itself cannot stand," says Abraham Lincoln in Springfield, Illinois, in accepting the nomination as Republican candidate for U.S. Senator.

# 1859

Petroleum production begins at Titusville, Pennsylvania.

Telegraph promoter Samuel F. B. Morse joins the North American Telegraph Association, forming a near-monopoly.

# 1860

Beadle & Adams publish a paperbound novel, *Malaeska, the Indian Wife of the White Hunter,* and sell 65,000 copies within a few months at ten cents each.

More than 1,000 steamboats ply the Mississippi River.

*Godey's Lady's Book* recommends cooking tomatoes for at least three hours.

Total U.S. population reaches 31.4 million, 4 million of whom are foreign-born.

South Carolina secedes from the Union.

# 1861

January 29: Kansas enters the Union as free state.

January–May: Mississippi, Florida, Alabama, Georgia, Louisiana, Texas, Virginia, Arkansas, and North Carolina secede from the Union. Representatives of the Confederate states meet in Montgomery, Alabama, and name Jefferson Davis president.

March 4: In his inaugural address, President Lincoln says, "This country, with its institutions, belongs to the people who inhabit it. Whenever they shall grow weary of the existing Government they can exercise their constitutional right of amending it, or their revolutionary right to dismember it or overthrow it."

The U.S. Army numbers 13,024 officers and men. Lincoln calls for 42,034 volunteers.

August 5: First national income tax levied to pay for the war.

The velocipede, the first true bicycle, is developed by Parisian coach maker Pierre Michaux.

Baltimore canner Isaac Solomon reduces processing time for canning foods from six hours to thirty minutes by adding calcium chloride to the water.

Dr. Dio Lewis introduces popular exercises for men, women, and children that stress flexibility and general fitness over strength.

Gilbert C. Van Camp is awarded an army contract to supply canned foods.

America's first commercial pretzel bakery opens in Lititz, Pennsylvania.

# 1862

April 16: Congress abolishes slavery in the District of Columbia. On June 19 emancipation is extended to all areas "in rebellion against the United States," with slaves to be free on and after January 1, 1863.

July: "Taps" is composed by Army of Potomac Chief of Staff General David Butterfield.

New York City's population numbers 800,000 citizens, 200,000 of whom are Irish.

# 1863

Lincoln signs a bill guaranteeing the Central Pacific and Union Pacific railroads $16,000 per mile for track laid on the plains, $32,000 per mile in intermountain stretches, and $48,000 per mile in the mountains.

October 3: Lincoln declares the last Thursday in November a day of national thanksgiving.

Draft riots break out in New York. A mob attacks the Colored Orphan Asylum, which is evacuated, but blacks are killed and wounded throughout the city.

November 19: Lincoln dedicates the National Cemetery at Gettysburg, Pennyslvania, where he delivers the Gettysburg Address.

December 3: The Capitol dome is capped in Washington, D.C.

As food shortages increase, Jefferson Davis urges Southerners to plant corn, peas, and beans instead of cotton and tobacco.

The British Cunard Line begins to transport immigrants at low fare.

# 1864

The Confederacy suffers from inflation.

# 1865

April 9: Robert E. Lee surrenders at Appomattox Court House, Virginia, effectively ending the Civil War.

April 14: Lincoln is assassinated by actor and Southern sympathizer John Wilkes Booth at Ford's Theatre in Washington, D.C. Andrew Johnson is sworn in as the seventeenth president the following day.

April 17: The side-wheeler *Sultana* explodes and burns on the Mississippi River, killing 1,700 passengers, most of them discharged Union soldiers.

May 5: First U.S. train robbery to employ derailing.

Northern "carpetbaggers" move into the South.

The Ku Klux Klan is organized in Pulaski, Tennessee.

A patent for a typewriter is issued to Christopher Sholes, Carlos G. Glidden, and Samuel W. Soule. The machine is eventually produced by Remington Firearms in 1874.

Philadelphia hat maker John Batterson Stetson creates the Stetson "Ten-Gallon" hat.

Cans are made of thinner steel with a rim on top that allows the use of a can opener.

Lawn croquet becomes popular.

Vassar College opens with the express purpose of admitting only women.

## 1866

New York, Baltimore, Boston, Memphis, New Orleans, Philadelphia, and Washington, D.C., experience epidemics of cholera, scarlet fever, smallpox, typhoid fever, typhus, and yellow fever.

*The Black Crook*, a scandalous burlesque featuring a scantily clad female chorus, opens in New York.

*Ragged Dick*, the first of Horatio Alger's rags-to-riches sagas, is published.

Cattle are driven for the first time on the Chisholm Trail to Abilene, Kansas.

Inflation reduces the value of the dollar to forty-six cents; the dollar will not regain its full value until 1878.

## 1867

Alaska is sold to the United States for $7.2 million, or 1.9 cents per acre.

Steel rail production begins in the United States

Baseball's first curveball is pitched by Brooklyn pitcher William Arthur Cummings.

First patented baby food is introduced by Justus von Liebig.

Louisa May Alcott's *Little Women* is published.

December 24: R. H. Macy's in New York becomes the first department store to stay open until midnight, setting a sales record in the process.

## 1868

Congress makes retention of black suffrage a "fundamental condition" for readmission of seven former rebel states.

The Fourteenth Amendment is ratified.

Congress passes an eight-hour workday for government employees.

Lydia Thompson tours the United States with her "British Blondes" burlesque troupe.

Eli Hamilton Janney invents a "knuckle" coupler that hooks railroad cars on contact, thus eliminating dangers of the old coupler. George Westinghouse invents an air brake, and Aaron French invents coil and elliptical railroad springs, leading to improved railroad safety and comfort. William Davis patents a refrigerated railcar to transport fish, meats, and fruits. First regularly scheduled U.S. dining car service is scheduled on the Chicago-Alton Railroad.

May 30: First observation of Memorial Day (Decoration Day).

# 1869

May 10: Union Pacific and Central Pacific railroads join at Promontory Point near Ogden, Utah, completing the transcontinental railroad.

September 24: Wall Street has its first "Black Friday." Jay Gould, James Fisk, and Ulysses S. Grant's brother-in-law try to corner the market on gold.

Ulysses S. Grant is sworn in as eighteenth president of the United States.

The Cardiff Giant, a hoax in the form of a "petrified" human figure, attracts thousands at Cardiff, New York.

The Cincinnati Red Stockings become the first baseball team to hire professional players.

Boston gets its first shipment of fresh meat from Chicago via refrigerated rail car.

The Great American Tea Company is renamed the Great Atlantic & Pacific Tea Company.

# 1870

The Fifteenth Amendment is ratified.

First through railroad service from the Pacific coast to New York City is established.

Smith Brothers Cough Drops are patented.

# 1871

First structure in Dodge City, Kansas, is a sod house built on the Santa Fe Trail five miles west of Fort Dodge to lodge buffalo hunters.

P. T. Barnum's "Greatest Show on Earth" opens in Brooklyn.

# 1872

The brigantine *Mary Celeste* sails out of New York never to be seen again, giving birth to numerous folktales.

The James gang robs its first train between Council Bluff and Des Moines, Iowa, getting away with only $3,000 of an expected $75,000 in gold.

Montgomery Ward & Co. is founded in Chicago.

Yellowstone National Park, the world's first national park, is established.

# 1873

United States adopts the gold standard.

Cable cars are introduced in San Francisco.

Barbed wire is introduced by Joseph Farmwell Glidden and Jacob Haish, who develop machines to produce endless rolls. The invention spells the end of the open range.

# 1874

Levi Strauss begins riveting denim jeans, which sell for $13.50 a dozen.

# 1875

Alexander Graham Bell invents the telephone.

The first Kentucky Derby is run at Churchill Downs.

R. H. Macy's is the first department store to introduce a toy section.

The first Harvard-Yale football game is played with new rules allowing running with the ball and tackling.

U.S. cigarette production reaches 50 million.

Luther Burbank establishes a plant nursery at Santa Rosa, California.

Hires Root Beer is introduced.

# 1876

The Centennial Exposition in Philadelphia marks the hundredth anniversary of the signing of Declaration of Independence and showcases American industry and technology.

The first American professional architectural magazine, *The American Architect and Building News,* is introduced.

Lydia E. Pinkham receives a label patent for her Vegetable Compound, a popular quack remedy she has been selling for a decade.

Alexander Graham Bell patents the improved telephone.

The player piano, which reproduces music via a moving perforated paper roll, is invented.

Wild Bill Hickok is murdered in Deadwood, Dakota Territory.

Central Park is completed in New York City.

B.V.D. underwear is introduced by Bradley, Vorhees, and Day of New York.

First Fred Harvey restaurant opens in the Santa Fe railroad station in Topeka, Kansas.

# 1877

Reconstruction ends.

First Bell telephone is sold in May, and 778 are in use by August.

Edison demonstrates the first phonograph.

# PART ONE

# Life and Youth During the Civil War and Reconstruction

# 1

# Everyday Life

The future of the United States appeared boundless by all measurable observation during the first half of the nineteenth century. Between 1800 and 1861, the nation had outpaced all others in the Western world in the growth of its population, territory, and economy. By 1861, Americans numbered 31 million people, a population total behind only Russia and France. The Union had grown by eighteen states between the admission of Ohio in 1803 and the admission of Kansas in 1861, with tens of thousands of miles of territories west of the Mississippi River remaining to be settled. The gross domestic product of the United States had increased seven times during the same years, one of the fastest rates of growth yet seen in the nation's history. Yet, despite the unprecedented quantitative growth of the United States, the sectional conflict between North and South over the westward expansion of slavery loomed over all. Whether the future of the nation lay toward slavery or freedom was a question that remained intractable to a peaceful solution, propelling Americans to the outbreak of civil war during the spring of 1861.[1]

## BATTLING OVER THE FUTURE OF THE NATION

The Civil War dominated everyday life in the United States during the mid-nineteenth century because of the scale and the cost of the fighting. At the outbreak of hostilities during 1861, the United States possessed a regular army of only 16,000 men. Most of these soldiers were stationed in scattered outposts along the western frontier, rarely coming together in units that numbered more than a few hundred men. The army had no mobilization plans to bolster its ranks, perhaps a moot point because nothing resembling a general staff yet existed.[2] By the end of the fighting in 1865, however, the Union had raised 2.1 million men and the Confederacy between 850,000 and 900,000 men. Almost all American families had a husband, father, son, or brother in the military, making the maneuvers and battles of the armies very closely watched affairs.[3]

In addition to the scale of the effort, the Civil War dominated everyday American life between 1861 and 1865 because of the financial and human cost of the fighting. The Union and the Confederacy spent some $20 billion waging the war. The outlay of money by both sides totaled eleven times the amount the federal government had spent since the ratification of the Constitution in 1788–89. More important to the nation because of the human suffering involved, the Union lost 360,000 soldiers to death from both battle and disease and the Confederacy lost 260,000 soldiers. Additionally, another 500,000 Union and Confederate soldiers suffered wounds during the fighting. Two percent of the American population had become casualties during the fighting, making the Civil War the bloodiest in the nation's history. By comparison, a similar casualty level in a war fought today, in percentage terms, would result in 5.5 million Americans killed and wounded, a nearly unthinkable cost.[4]

The recruitment of the Civil War armies that fought so hard and so long depended upon local efforts. Individual communities raised companies of 100 soldiers through patriotic rallies, speeches, and other public activities. In turn, state officials grouped ten companies from neighboring towns and villages into a regiment, the standard building block of American armies since the colonial era. Regiments received numerical designations in the order that they had mustered into service. Thus, the 22nd Massachusetts, the 7th Indiana, and the 19th Virginia all served during the war, among hundreds of other regiments. Members of each regiment elected their officers upon completing their recruitment, a long-standing practice among American volunteers at the time. Some officers had previous military experience, whether in the Mexican War, the nation's last major conflict, or at a military school, most notably West Point in the North and the Citadel and the Virginia Military Institute in the South. Many officers, however, were prominent community leaders, such as lawyers and merchants. These men had to learn their newfound trade through experience, with its accompanying cost in battlefield casualties.[5]

The local orientation of Civil War regiments reflected the nature of American life at mid-century. Northerners and Southerners grew up, lived, and died in communities large and small. They had learned the importance of self-government in local schools and had practiced it through holding public office. When the Civil War began, the strong local connections among Americans meant that they worked first to ready themselves along with other members of their neighborhoods, towns, and villages. By contrast, direct ties to the national government were weak in 1861. Americans living during the mid-nineteenth century paid no income taxes, and few of them had any contact with federal officials beyond the local postmaster. To the Union and the Confederacy alike, an army raised through national recruiting efforts would have been as unfamiliar as it would have been unnecessary.[6]

Civil War soldiers gave many reasons for volunteering, but ideology was the most important factor.[7] Union soldiers believed that they were fighting for their flag and country. One New Jersey volunteer explained that he had enlisted because the Civil War was a great "struggle for the Union, Constitution, and law.... We will be held responsible before God if we don't do our part in helping to transmit this boon of civil & religious liberty down to succeeding generations."[8] Another volunteer from Ohio argued that he was fighting to uphold the sacrifices and accomplishments of the Revolutionary War generation. "Our fathers made this country," he declared, "and we their children are to save it."[9] Similarly, Confederate soldiers believed that they were fighting for their country, but one free from northern rule. "Thank God!, we have a country at last," one Mississippian exulted, "to live for, to pray for, to fight for, and if necessary, to die for."[10] Another Confederate volunteer explained that he had enlisted because "If we should suffer ourselves to be subjugated by the tyrannical government of the North, our property would all be confiscated ... & our people reduced to the most abject bondage & utter degradation."[11]

Union and Confederate soldiers also volunteered from a sense of duty to their respective cause. "I performed but a *simple* duty," one northern soldier explained after enlisting, "a duty to my country and myself ... to give up *life* if need be ... in this battle for freedom & right, opposed to slavery & wrong."[12] A member of the 64th Ohio voiced a similar sentiment, declaring that "My country had a demand on me which made all my plans, calculations, hopes and expectations of minor consequence."[13] Confederate volunteers professed an equally strong sense of duty. As one prominent Civil War historian recently argues, however, many Confederate soldiers also intertwined a sense of honor, or the upholding of one's image in the eyes of his peers, with that of duty.[14] The emphasis upon honor among many Confederate volunteers reflected slight social differences in mid-nineteenth-century America, where Southerners often placed greater emphasis upon public reputation than Northerners. A soldier from South Carolina articulated the belief, arguing that a "man who will not offer up his life ... does dishonor to his wife and children."[15] A Mississippi sergeant agreed, declaring that "I [would] much [rather] be numbered amongst the slain than those that stay at home for it will be a brand upon their name as long as a southern[er] lives."[16]

In addition to prompting enlistments, ideology sustained soldiers throughout the fighting. Soldiers who had experienced combat knew full well the bloody realities of the battlefield, where the numbers of men killed and wounded often ran as high as one-third of the totals engaged. Yet the vast majority of Union and Confederate combat veterans remained in the ranks, continuing to fight bravely. "Sick as I am of this war and bloodshed [and] as much oh how much I want to be home with my dear wife and children," Alfred Hough, a Union officer, admitted to his family during late 1863, " ... every day I have a more religious feeling, that this war is a crusade for the good of mankind.... I [cannot] bear to think of what my children would be if we were to permit this hell-begotten conspiracy to destroy this country."[17] At the same time but from across the battle lines, Edward Cade, a Confederate officer, also admitted that he was tired of war. But, he quickly added, "were the contest again just commenced I would willingly undergo it again for the sake of ... our country's independence and [our children's] liberty."[18]

Why Union soldiers fought broadened by the end of the war to include the destruction of slavery. President Abraham Lincoln implemented his Emancipation Proclamation on January 1, 1863, declaring free all slaves in the Confederacy. Although initially voicing strong opposition, many Union soldiers came to support Lincoln's measure for several reasons.[19] Some men supported the Emancipation Proclamation as a means to militarily weaken the South. "Crippling the institution of slavery," Colonel Lucius Hubbard of the 5th Minnesota argued as early as the autumn of 1862, "is ... striking a blow at the heart of the rebellion."[20] A member of the 86th Indiana declared during late March 1863 that he and other members of his regiment "use all other kinds of rebel property and [we] see no reason why we should not use negroes. Every negro we get strengthens us and weakens the rebels."[21] Other Union soldiers supported the Emancipation Proclamation because they believed that freeing the slaves was the right and noble thing to do. A Pennsylvania officer railed against slavery from the start of the war, asserting that the conflict was not a struggle "between North & South; but a contest between human rights and human liberty on one side and eternal bondage on the other."[22] A Massachusetts officer spoke in favor of abolishing slavery after watching a slave owner attempt to reclaim a runaway slave during the winter of 1862. "I never will be instrumental in returning a slave to his master in any way shape or manner," he fumed, "I'll die first."[23]

The soldiers who served in the Union and Confederate armies reflected the societies from which they came. Men on both sides of the battle lines most often worked as farmers and farm laborers before the war, like four out of every ten American males in 1860. The Union had a greater percentage of skilled and unskilled laborers in the ranks, reflecting the more sizable urban population of the North by the mid-nineteenth century.[24] Both Union and Confederate soldiers were young, like the rest of American society. The largest age grouping in both armies was men between the ages of eighteen years old and twenty-nine years old. Most men who wore the blue uniforms of the Union and the gray uniforms of the Confederacy had yet to celebrate their twenty-fifth birthday.[25] Literacy rates among soldiers varied by army. In the Union army, 90 percent of soldiers could read and write, compared to 80 percent of soldiers in the Confederate army. Still, despite the discrepancy in literacy rates between the Union and the Confederacy, Civil War soldiers on the whole were among the most literate group of people in the world to that time.[26]

Union and Confederate soldiers came from each state across their respective lands, a national distribution that often fueled regional prejudices. In the Union army, nearly three-quarters of soldiers came from the eleven Midwest and Middle Atlantic states. The remainder of Union soldiers came from eleven New England and border states, with a sprinkling of soldiers from both the West Coast and various Confederate states. In the Confederate army, three-quarters of soldiers came from the nine states of the Upper South and the Lower South. The remaining one-quarter of Confederate soldiers came from the five Trans-Mississippi and border states.[27] Union and Confederate soldiers often expressed strong regional pride, despite fighting in common cause. Their sense of superiority generally centered around their individual field army, comprised overwhelmingly of soldiers from either the East or the West.[28] In a notable example, the predominantly eastern soldiers in the Confederate Army of Northern Virginia prided themselves both on their commander, Virginia-born General Robert E. Lee, and on their stunning record of battlefield successes. "If I live to be a hundred year's [sic] old," one of Lee's soldiers proudly declared, "I shall always be proud to know that I once belonged to the Army of N. Va."[29] Despite such pride, regional prejudices occasionally flared within individual armies. In the Union Army of the Potomac, an overwhelmingly eastern organization, Captain Henry Abbott of the 20th Massachusetts expressed dismay upon meeting soldiers from New York and Pennsylvania during the late summer of 1861. Abbott called the Middle Atlantic men "ragged" and "half-clad savages" because of their alleged shabby personal appearance, sentiments presumably warmly returned.[30]

In addition to attracting volunteers from every state, the Union bolstered its ranks through the recruitment of both foreign-born and African American soldiers. Although the exact percentage of ethnic soldiers in the Union army is uncertain, many historians place the figure at about one out of every four men.[31] The large numbers of foreign-born soldiers to wear Union blue reflected the massive waves of immigration that arrived in northern seaports throughout much of the mid-nineteenth century. German and Irish soldiers constituted the most numerous ethnic groups to serve in the Union army, at 350,000 men.[32] Members of both nationalities often went to war in their own regiments, an expression of ethnic pride. The Irish soldiers of the 63rd New York, the 69th New York, and the 88th New York composed the famed Irish Brigade, among the most hard-fighting units in the Federal army, in terms of casualties suffered.[33] Members of the Irish Brigade and other ethnic units expressed a strong ideological commitment toward the Union. "This is my country as much as the man that was born on the soil," a sergeant of the Irish 28th Massachusetts explained after enlisting, "and so it is with every man who comes to this country ... I have as much interest in the maintenance of the government and laws and the integrity of the nation as any other man."[34] Other ethnic regiments well known throughout the Union army included the 79th New York, comprising Scottish-born soldiers, and the 39th New York, comprising soldiers from southern and eastern Europe.[35]

African American soldiers served in the Union army after President Lincoln implemented the Emancipation Proclamation.[36] By the end of the fighting, 200,000 blacks had served in the Federal military. These numbers represented about 9 percent of the total Union manpower organized during the war. Blacks often suffered discrimination while in the military, most notably serving in segregated regiments under the command of white officers, working extensively in heavy-labor duties, and earning less pay per month than their white comrades.[37] Yet blacks proved that, when given the opportunity, they were as willing to fight for their country as any other Union soldier. The 54th Massachusetts was among the most well-known black regiments to serve in the Union army. Members of the unit won praise for their battlefield gallantry while leading a failed federal attempt to storm the Confederate stronghold at Battery Wagner, South Carolina, on July 18, 1863. The black soldiers gained Wagner's parapet for an hour before falling back under intense Confederate musket and artillery fire. The bravery of the 54th Massachusetts won wide praise throughout the North. "Through the cannon smoke of that dark night," the *Atlantic Monthly* extolled following the battle, "the manhood of the colored race shines before many eyes that would not see."[38] The acclaim, however, had come at high human cost. The 54th Massachusetts lost 227 men killed, wounded, and missing; during the fighting, nearly one-half of its numbers engaged.[39]

A few enterprising women served as soldiers in the Union and Confederate armies although, at least on paper, they were legally barred from doing so.[40] Many of the four-hundred or so women who served in the ranks ultimately were exposed.[41] For some, discovery came after a visit to the hospital for treatment of wounds and illness. "We discovered last week a soldier who turned out to be a girl," one Indiana volunteer described in amazement during the winter of 1863. "She had already been in service for 21 months and was twice wounded. Maybe she would have remained undiscovered for a long time if she hadn't fainted. She was given a warm bath which gave away the secret."[42] For other women soldiers, discovery came after nature had taken its course. One surprised Union general commented that he had learned that one of his soldiers had recently given birth, in "violation of all military law and or army regulations."[43]

Sarah Emma Edmonds was among the most famous women soldiers, enlisting in the 2nd Michigan during April 1861. Edmonds worked in the regiment as both a hospital steward and a mail carrier, under the alias "Franklin Thompson." Edmonds deserted her regiment two years later, fearful that an illness that she was suffering from might result in a hospital stay and, likely, exposure of her true gender. Edmonds served as a nurse for the remainder of the war, publishing her tale in *Nurse and Spy in the Union Army* (1865). She applied for and received a veterans' pension after the war, the only woman soldier to do so under her own name. The federal government later dropped the desertion charge against Edmonds, allowing her to receive full military honors at her burial after her death in 1898.[44]

Civil War soldiers spent the overwhelming majority of their time in camp, fighting boredom and loneliness. Military drill occupied several hours each day, but soldiers otherwise were left to entertain themselves. The men had ample time to fill, spending about fifty days in camp for every one in battle.[45] Many soldiers filled the time by writing letters, singing songs, thinking about food, and playing sports and games (all activities discussed in later chapters). Other bored and lonely soldiers sought pleasures of the flesh. Brothels flourished in large cities and towns, and around the encampments, where soldiers both on assignment and on leave passed to and from and wasted time.[46] "Complaints are daily made to me of the number of lewd women in this town," a Confederate officer stationed in Dalton, Georgia, fumed in disgust during early 1864, "and on the outskirts of the army. They are said to be impregnating this whole command ... "[47] A Union newspaper reporter was equally disturbed after passing through Washington, D.C., during 1862. He described the nation's capital as the "most pestiferous hole since the days of Sodom and Gomorrah. The majority of the women in the streets were openly disreputable."[48] Despite these reproaches, many Union and Confederate soldiers availed themselves of the opportunity to visit women of ill repute, at least according to available medical records. In the Union army, with more detailed medical reports than the Confederate army, between eight and nine out of every one hundred soldiers suffered from some form of venereal disease.[49]

Debauchery failed to triumph in Civil War encampments because many soldiers turned to religion for inner guidance and strength.[50] Union and Confederate soldiers overwhelmingly were Christian in their religious beliefs, like the rest of mid-nineteenth-century American society. Religious revivals occurred often in camp, where soldiers praised the Lord for surviving their most recent campaign and beseeched His protection for their next.[51] The encampment of the Union Army of the Potomac during the winter of 1863–64 witnessed among the largest religious revivals, in terms of numbers of men involved. "I have never witnessed anything like it," Colonel Robert McAllister marveled that April. "When our regiment is not on picket, our church is crowded for preaching and prayer every night. After the regular meeting is over, a large number still remains for conversation and more prayer."[52] Private Wilbur Fisk described the religious gatherings among members of his regiment. "The meetings commence at half past six," Fisk recorded, "and are held till the drum calls us to roll call at eight. One of the delegates preaches a short sermon, or rather makes a few practical remarks founded upon some text of Scripture, and then the time is occupied by any one who wishes to speak, sing or pray. Generally the time is fully occupied, and often two or more rise to speak at once. Many have risen at the invitation to manifest a desire for the others in their behalf, and some have spoken there that never spoke in meeting before."[53] The camp meetings only ended during early May 1864, when the Army of the Potomac moved into the field and undertook a new offensive.[54]

The Union and the Confederacy were only to win the war through fighting, and the experience of battle proved the ultimate test for soldiers.[55] Many new volunteers eagerly had anticipated what they termed "seeing the elephant," a nineteenth-century expression for any unusual but exciting experience.[56] A Michigan soldier expressed the fears of many other men in blue and gray when he worried during the summer of 1861 that the war "will be all over before we have a chance to do anything."[57] The terrifying realities of combat, however, quickly dashed such glorified expectations. The waiting to attack proved the most trying of battlefield moments for many soldiers, especially if under enemy fire. "We lay there about eight minutes and yet it seemed an age to me," an Illinois sergeant described of a federal assault upon Confederate defensive works at Vicksburg, Mississippi, on May 22, 1863, "for showers of bullets and grape were passing over me. ... Oh how my heart palpitated! It seemed to thump the ground (I lay on my face) as hard as the enemy's bullets. The sweat from off my face run [sic] in a stream from the tip ends of my whiskers.... Twice I exclaimed aloud...'*My God, why dont* [sic] *they order us to charge!*'"[58] The move forward brought temporary relief to many men, who found refuge in action. Yet, for some, the horrors of death became only too readily apparent. "Death from a bullet is ghastly," one Union soldier described, "but to see a man's brains dashed out at your side by a grape shot and another body severed by a screeching cannon ball is truly appalling."[59] A Confederate private declared that "I have seen enough of the glory of war.... I am sick of seeing dead men and men's limbs torn from their bodies."[60]

The aftermath of battle often proved as horrific as the fighting itself. Soldiers from the victorious army had to retrieve the wounded and bury the dead, a grim task. "I never had a clear conception of the horrors of war until that night and the morning," a Texas volunteer wrote to his wife following the Confederate triumph at the Battle of Gaines's Mill, Virginia, on June 27, 1862. "On going round on that battlefield with a candle searching for my friends I could hear on all sides the dreadful groans of the wounded and their heart piercing cries for water and assistance. Friends and foes all to-gether. ... Oh the awful scene witnessed on the battle field. May I never see any more such in life."[61] After the Union victory at the Battle of Antietam, Maryland, on September 17, 1862, Cyrus Stone scoured the battlefield with other members of his regiment looking for wounded men. "Oh what a smell," Stone described later "some of the men vomit as they went along."[62] Union and Confederate soldiers stationed in reserve from the fighting had to endure the horrors of field hospitals set up near their lines. In a particu-larly gruesome episode, a federal soldier detailed the goings-on outside a hospital constructed near his regiment during the Battle of Fredericksburg, Virginia, on December 13, 1862. "There was a Hospital [within] thirty yards of us," he wrote, " ... about the building you could see the Hogs belonging to the Farm eating arms and other portions of the body."[63]

While Union and Confederate soldiers fought the war, civilians on the homefronts supported their efforts. At way stations and refreshment sa-loons, civilians distributed food and clothing to soldiers traveling toward the front lines. The Cooper's Shop in Philadelphia, Pennsylvania, was among the most efficient, claiming to feed 1,000 men an hour when needed.[64] Religious societies published periodicals and leaflets, known by soldiers as tracts. The American Bible Society and the Confederate Bible Society also distributed Bibles and hymn books to northern and southern soldiers.[65] Union and Confederate women sewed socks, pants, and shirts for needy soldiers. Equally important, more than 3,000 women served as nurses in army hospitals, an otherwise traditionally male occupation. Fe-male nurses won praise from their soldier patients, despite enduring crit-icism from many doctors jealous of their professional territory.[66] The Union supplemented the medical work of its doctors and nurses, organizing the U. S. Sanitary Commission during June 1861. The commission attempted to reduce the incidence of disease among soldiers in camps and hospitals by advising them on matters of "sanitary and hygienic interests." The or-ganization also donated to soldiers $15 million of various supplies, from medicine to clothing; and from food to writing paper and stamps.[67]

Northern and southern families attempted to adjust as best as possible to the extended absences of husbands and fathers.[68] The task was, arguably, more difficult in the Confederacy. Southern women had to cope with the threat of both slave insurrection and northern invasion, all the while rais-ing their children and running their households. "We who stay behind," Kate Stone admitted after watching her brothers depart for the war, "may find it harder than they who go."[69] Many Confederate women rallied en-thusiastically behind the war effort, withstanding ever-present daily hard-ships and worry over the fate of their loved ones in uniform. Yet many other women questioned the need for continued self-sacrifice, especially as the Confederacy lurched closer and closer toward final military defeat. "Am I willing to give my husband to gain Atlanta for the Confederacy?" Gertrude

Thomas asked after Union forces captured the Georgia city during the fall of 1864, "No, No, No, a thousand times No!"[70] Another woman felt compelled to express her displeasure to President Jefferson Davis after her second son entered the military. "I need not tell you," she declared, "of my devotion to my country, of the sacrifices I have made, and of the many more I am willing to make. ... But I want my oldest boy at home."[71] A North Carolina mother wrote no less passionately to her son during the last winter of the war, "Tell [them] all to s[t]op fiting [sic] and come home to live...I want you all to come home."[72]

Soldiers who survived the four years of fighting eventually did return home, although to vastly different public reception. Union veterans generally met crowds and cheers, albeit some complained that they received too little fanfare. In the largest victory celebration, 150,000 Union soldiers paraded up Pennsylvania Avenue in Washington, D.C., on May 23–24, 1865.[73] Onlookers cheered the men at almost every step. "Any man in uniform was ... the rage today," one Union officer described in delight. "It certainly is pleasant to be made much of by pretty women, especially after four years of absence from female society." Another man declared that the "wild enthusiasm, the inspiring cheers, seemed sufficient recompense for all those years of blood."[74] By contrast, Confederate veterans returned to subdued welcomes. Many of the men arrived in their hometowns either individually or in groups of two or three, having had to walk from where they were when the fighting ended. The sight of men struggling across the countryside in tattered uniforms inspired compassion rather than celebration. "Often as I sit in the twilight and drift back into the past," one Alabama woman recalled years later of the end of the Confederate army, "it is not easy to restrain tears, as memory views those soldiers in their worn gray, marching home sad and depressed, with the cause they had so warmly espoused lost." [75] Yet, despite different homecoming experiences, Union and Confederate veterans and their families now shared together a nation already in the throes of profound and far-reaching change.

## A CHANGING AMERICA

Union victory in the Civil War marked a turning point in American history, as the country underwent profound economic, political, and social changes. Allan Nevins, a distinguished historian, noted as early as 1927 that the postwar era of Reconstruction marked the "emergence of modern America."[76] Between 1865 and 1877, the nation sped toward an economic system of industrial capitalism, in which national markets and free labor ruled supreme. The power of the federal government expanded greatly, touching more and more the daily lives and affairs of American citizens. And, most dramatic of the postwar era changes, 4 million African Americans made the journey from slave to citizen.[77] Contemporary Americans marveled at the many changes, some in despair and some in elation. One downcast Confederate veteran declared in 1865 that "Society has been completely changed by the war. The [French] Revolution of '89 did not produce a greater change ... than this has in our social life."[78] Four years later, George Ticknor, a retired Harvard professor, declared in amazement that the Civil War was the "great gulf between what happened before in our century and what has happened since, or what is likely to happen hereafter. It does not seem to me as if I were living in the country in which I was born."[79]

Everyday life changed along with the rest of American society during the postwar era. The expansion of American political rights to include African Americans formed among the most immediately visible changes in everyday life. Blacks gained the right to own property, marry, and serve on juries, under the Fourteenth Amendment, ratified in 1868. "The law no longer knows white nor black," one civil rights group triumphantly declared after the granting of equal citizenship, "but simply men."[80] Under the Fifteenth Amendment, ratified in 1870, black men won the right to vote, changing the political landscape of the South. By the end of Reconstruction in 1877, sixteen blacks had served in Congress, over six hundred blacks had served in state legislatures, and several hundred other blacks had served in various local offices.[81] "Nothing in all history," William Lloyd Garrison, a leading abolitionist figure of the day, proudly declared after the passage of the Fifteenth Amendment, equaled "this wonderful, quiet, sudden transformation of four millions of human beings from ... the auction-block to the ballot-box." Equally dramatic, the American Anti-Slavery Society, a leading organization in the fight against slavery, disbanded after black men won the right to vote, its members believing their long-struggle finally completed.[82]

Yet change proved illusory and southern whites moved quickly to nullify the political gains made by freedmen. In part, they did so by restricting the daily activities and freedoms of blacks under a series of laws known as Black Codes. African Americans had to sign work contracts each year, generally to farm cotton at miserably low wages. Any black person who quit his contract forfeited his pay to that date and was subject to arrest for vagrancy. Freedmen also lost the right to serve on a jury under the Black Codes and were banned from "insulting" whites.[83] One congressman visiting the South of the Black Codes declared that "The blacks eat, sleep, move, live, only by the tolerance of the whites, who hate them."[84] Equally important, southern whites used violence to restrict the citizenship rights of blacks. The most infamous terrorist group was the Ku Klux Klan (KKK), founded during the late 1860s. The KKK attempted to keep African Americans "in their place," through the use of underhand tactics, often including murder.[85] "We believe you are not familiar with the description of the Ku Klux Klans riding nightly over the country," one group of blacks described to Congress in 1871, "going from county to county, and in the county towns, spreading terror wherever they go by robbing, whipping, ravishing, and killing our people without provocation."[86] Whether through law or coercion, or a combination of both, southern whites had reduced blacks to the status of second-class citizens in everything but name by the end of Reconstruction.[87]

Many Americans were distracted from the political struggles in the South, their attention focused squarely upon ongoing economic expansion that occurred across much of the nation. By 1877, the industrial production of the United States had soared to 75 percent above its level at the end of the Civil War in 1865. The emergence of the modern steel industry accounted for much of the economic growth. The discovery of the Bessemer-Kelly process during the late 1850s allowed for the transformation of iron into steel. Named after the family names of its two inventors, the process called for blowing cold air onto red hot iron. The metal became white hot as the carbon ignited, thereby gaining tremendously in strength as impurities were eliminated. When combined with ample cheap labor and bountiful natural resources, the Bessemer-Kelly process caused American steel production to soar. By 1873, the United States produced 115,000 tons of steel per year, with production rising fast. By comparison, the nation had imported all its steel rails at the start of the Civil War, primarily from England.[88]

The boom in industrial production following the end of the Civil War raised the standard of living among many Americans. In general, wages were high. In 1870, common farm laborers earned $16.57 per month, with board. During the same year, unskilled town laborers earned $1.55 per day, without board, while skilled town workers earned about one dollar per day more, but also without board. By comparison, Union soldiers at the start of the Civil War earned only $13 per month.[89] The cost of living also dropped during the postwar era, after skyrocketing during the Civil War. Most important to the everyday life of many citizens, prices for both food and household furnishings fell dramatically during the first five years that followed the conclusion of the Civil War. The postwar economic boom faltered, and a nationwide economic depression that lasted between 1873 and 1877 caused wages to take a downward tumble. But prices also dropped during the depression, resulting from declining consumer demand.[90] Taken as a whole, economic boom and bust together, Americans living during the postwar era earned more at work and paid less to live than they had since the late 1850s and early 1860s.[91]

Americans received their wages in varied form. The federal government first issued a national system of paper money during the Civil War. Popularly known as "greenbacks," pieces of paper money came in denominations of $5, $10, $20, $50, $500, and $1,000. The federal government also coined money. In addition to the standard denominations of the early twenty-first century, two-cent pieces, three-cent pieces, and $2.50, $5, $10, and $20 gold pieces also circulated. Some of these coins produced during and after 1865 first bore the inscription "In God We Trust." Additionally, some companies issued scrip money to their workers. Printed on paper and in various denominations, scrip money only could be spent to purchase goods and supplies available in company stores, often at an outrageous price.[92]

Some groups of Americans benefited more than others from the economic prosperity of the postwar era. Most women remained at home during the late 1860s and early 1870s, working as wives and mothers. Yet, other women made notable strides in entering the workforce, especially with the invention and commercial distribution of the typewriter. By 1880, 644,208 women worked in factories, offices, and stores.[93] Many of these women worked as stenographers and typists, popularly known in the business world as "type girls." One national typewriter manufacturer boasted in 1875 that "no invention has opened for women so broad and easy an avenue to profitable and suitable employment.... More girls are now earning from $10 to $20 per week with the 'Type-Writer,' and we can at once secure good situations for one hundred expert writers on it."[94] The road to "suitable employment" was not always easy. Women engaged in clerical work often received harsh public criticism. The barbs aimed against working women ranged from charges that they suffered low morals to accusations that they neglected their husbands and families. Women continued to work in the office, however, because they welcomed the opportunity and because they received good pay. In Washington, D.C., for example, federal clerks earned an average salary of $900 per year. By comparison, women teachers in the nation's capital earned only between $400 and $800 per year.[95]

By contrast to women, unskilled and semiskilled laborers often missed the economic prosperity of the postwar years. Increased wages failed to offset increased living costs, especially in housing rents. One economic study conducted in 1866 found that workers in large cities struggled to make financial ends meet far more often than they had in 1861. Additionally, hours were long, often ten per day. In some trades, the day stretched even longer. In New York City, drivers of horse cars and stages labored between twelve to sixteen hours each day, six days a week, rain and shine. The drivers' hard hours won little appreciation from their customers, who often derisively referred to them as "Jehu," after the out of control Biblical charioteer.[96] The problem was different in other lines of work, where seasonal slowdowns occurred because of overproduction. Shoemakers suffered among the worst of the trend, because machines began to replace humans in many parts of the labor process. Production figures soared, but demand for year-round labor remained variable. "There has never been a year of steady work," one Massachusetts shoemaker complained in 1871. "At first a month only would be lost; now it has got so that we lose over four months' time every year." The men earned no pay if not at work, forcing them to scramble to make financial ends meet.[97]

There were more Americans than ever before to try to take advantage of the growing postwar economy. Between 1860 and 1880, the nation's population swelled from 31 million people to 50 million people. The nearly 40 percent increase in population was among the fastest rates of growth in the Western world. With more people, the United States was more crowded than ever before. By 1880, Americans numbered 16.9 people per square mile. By comparison, in 1790, when the federal government compiled the first census, Americans numbered only 4.5 people per square mile. Still, if judged by European standards, where crowded cities and countrysides were the norm, the population of the United States was refreshingly sparse.[98]

The growing American population occurred from both natural increase and immigration. Birthrates in the United States remained high by European standards throughout the late nineteenth century, albeit declining in overall numbers. Between 1800 and 1880, birth-rates per 1,000 white women fell from 55 births per year to 35 births per year. Between 1850 and 1880, birth-rates per 1,000 black women fell from 59 births per year to 52 births per year. Despite declining birth rates, the American population increased naturally during the mid- and late-nineteenth century because fewer infants died at birth and more adults lived into middle age. A word of caution is in order, however, because the census tabulated infant mortality and life expectancy for whites only until the early twentieth century. Still, given this limitation, infant mortality rates dropped from 217 deaths per 1,000 births to 176 deaths per 1,000 births between 1850 and 1870. During the same years, the average life expectancy at birth among Americans rose from 39 years to 44 years.[99]

In addition to natural increase, immigration swelled the American population during the mid-and late-nineteenth century. Between 1865 and 1890, 10 million people came to the United States from abroad. The arriving immigrants came overwhelmingly from England, Wales, Ireland, Germany, and Scandinavia, as they also had prior to the start of the Civil War in 1861.[100] Some immigrants came to work in America's burgeoning factory system. They were encouraged to do so by many American manufacturers who, in the words of one historian, sent representatives abroad to tout the "opportunities open to active men."[101] But more, if not most, immigrants came to work the land. The Homestead Act of 1862 gave farmers 160 acres of public land free of charge, if they worked it for at least five years. Arriving immigrants quickly seized the opportunity for land ownership, especially because many had lost farms in their native countries from drought, war, and other manmade and natural disasters. In a notable example because of the numbers involved, over 100,000 Swedes emigrated to the United States to farm the land between 1868 and 1873, after a series of crop failures had devastated the agricultural economy of their home country.[102]

Eastern cities and the western frontier experienced among the largest surges in population during the postwar era. Americans overwhelmingly were a rural people during the 1860s and 1870s, with nearly 75 percent of the nation's population living in the countryside (with rural defined in the 1870 census as towns and villages with fewer than 2,500 residents). Yet, the nation's cities grew rapidly in population, especially those east of the Mississippi River. Many Americans moved to the city to search for manufacturing and industrial work, but others came to take advantage of the perceived excitement and amenities of urban living. Either for work or for lifestyle, or for a combination of both, 9.9 million Americans resided in a city by 1870, an increase of 6 percent since 1860. Most cities were middle-sized in terms of population, with between 2,500 and 5,000 residents. But large cities also were present. The most populated urban centers were New York, with almost one million residents; Philadelphia, with nearly three-quarters of a million; Chicago, with 300,000; and Cincinnati, with slightly more than 200,000.[103]

Choosing against city life, many Americans instead headed for the western frontier. Nevada, Nebraska, and Colorado all joined the Union between 1864 and 1876. The surge westward by Americans increasingly pulled along the geographic center of the nation's population. By 1880, the center of the nation's population was in southwestern Ohio, almost directly across the Ohio River from Louisville, Kentucky. By comparison, the center of the nation's population in 1790 was near Baltimore, Maryland. Americans moved to the West to pursue various employment opportunities, but most notably to farm, ranch, and mine. Military and cultural clashes with the roughly 350,000 Native Americans also living in the West often followed. Given greater numbers and advanced military and industrial technology, American settlers and soldiers almost inevitably triumphed. By the late 1880s, Americans in the West had broken Indian military power, along with much of Indian culture and society, and had settled all but a few areas of the fast-disappearing frontier.[104]

Religion remained a constant to many Americans amid the otherwise rapid changes in everyday life. Americans overwhelmingly were Christian, with nearly 70,000 churches in all parts of the nation by 1870. "The first thing almost which strikes a newly arrived traveler in the United States," an English visitor observed, "is the immense number of churches.... The country is dotted over with wooden steeples, whose white painted sides, I must own, sparkle in the bright sunlight uncommonly like marble."[105] Protestants formed the largest religious community, led in numbers by Methodists, Baptists, and Presbyterians. Roman Catholics grew rapidly in strength, with four million members, although largely concentrated in northern cities. Joining white churchgoers, southern blacks established the

Colored Primitive Baptist Church and the Colored Methodist Episcopal Church by 1870. These two independent churches joined the African Methodist Episcopal Church and the Zion Church, both previously established by African Americans in the North.[106]

Despite an impressive presence in American life, the Christian Church came under mounting criticism following the conclusion of the Civil War. Some dissent came from inside the faith, where less well-to-do church members felt alienated by the social displays made by their more wealthy peers. "[How] can I afford to be a Christian," one frustrated churchgoer asked, "and hire a pew and dress up my family in such a style on Sunday that they won't be snubbed for their shabby appearance by genteel Christians?"[107]

Other attacks came from outside the Church, where proponents of evolution questioned religious teachings on the creation of both the universe and human life. The debate between science and religion raged throughout the postwar era, marred more often than not by intense hostility and bitterness.[108] The criticisms of the practices and teachings of the Church marked one of many transitions of American life during the late nineteenth century. What now needs to be explored is whether these changes filtered downward, from the world of adults to the world of youth.

# 2

# The World of Youth

The world of American youth had undergone many transformations by the outbreak of the Civil War in 1861. Most important, the spread of egalitarian principles in the United States during and after the Revolutionary War had made families increasingly child-centered. By the mid-nineteenth century, many parents recognized that children were individuals with needs of their own, rather than mere property. Additionally, families perceived children as sources of tremendous emotional satisfaction, taking care to participate as much as possible in their upbringing. Both of these changes were significant, but the world of youth underwent further transformation during the Civil War era. Children had to learn about war and its aftermath, often firsthand. The experience took many forms, all of them making the youth of the mid- and late-nineteenth century among a distinct generation in American history.[1]

## LEARNING ABOUT WAR

In order to understand how children living during the mid-nineteenth century learned about war, it first is necessary to define who constitutes "youth." The definition used in this chapter draws from both census data and from research recently conducted by James Marten, a prominent social historian. The U.S. census lists three age categories that fall under traditional headings of youth (five years of age and younger; five years of age through nine years of age; and ten years of age through fourteen years of age). Adding together the individual numbers in each of the three age categories used by the census yields 12.7 million Americans who were fourteen years of age and younger in 1860. This figure means that young people made up nearly one-half of the American population, at 41 percent of the total.[2] But defining youth is more encompassing than relying only upon age. James Marten recently argues in *The Children's Civil War* (1998) that youth also includes older teenagers living at home with one or both parents. These children worked occasionally, if at all, and attended at least some school.[3] Although many of these individuals were in their late teens and early twenties, their actions defined them as children, rather than as adults. Marten's definition of youth excludes boys who served as soldiers and drummer boys in the Union and Confederate armies. "Although certainly children in a chronological sense," Marten explains of underage Civil War soldiers, "their military service made them de facto adults; their experiences resembled the exploits of the men with whom they served more than those of the children who stayed home."[4]

The letters written home by fathers and older brothers serving in the army formed among the most immediate ways that children learned about the Civil War. Many military fathers were absent from their homes for months and years at a time, and they felt compelled to explain to their sons and daughters why they had volunteered.[5] Joshua Lawrence Chamberlain, who became one of the great Union battlefield heroes of the war, declared that he and his fellow soldiers had volunteered to "see if we cannot make those Rebels behave better, and stop their wicked works in trying to spoil our country and making us all so unhappy."[6] Another federal soldier told his children that he and his comrades had a duty to their fathers and grandfathers to enlist. He explained that preceding generations had given the nation "to *us entire,* and *we* must give it to you, entire and you must give it as you receive it, to those who come after you."[7] Josiah Patterson, a Georgia soldier, also wrote in terms of duty. He wrote to his sons that he had volunteered because he loved them "too dearly to permit the ruthless footsteps of the invader to crush out your liberty while I am enjoying an inglorious inactivity or ease at home."[8]

Other fathers struggled with what to tell their families about their daily life in the army. Some wrote relatively sanitized accounts of their military experiences, especially if their children were young. Henry Hitchcock asked his wife to tell his "darling boy" about his uniform and his horse. "I wear the 'soldier cap' that he liked, all the time," Hitchcock wrote, "and ... I have a nice dark brown horse, who is pretty gay, and whose name is 'Button.'"[9] Captain James Hall of Tennessee wrote to his children about the playful antics among the men in his regiment as they prepared to go to sleep. "We have a great deal of noise in camp at night," he described, "some of the boys sing some holler some bark like dogs, some crow like chickens and one whistles so much like a mocking bird that you would think it was a bird indeed."[10] Other men gave graphic descriptions of combat, perhaps too shocked by the horrors of the battlefield to restrain themselves. A Confederate soldier positioned behind the front lines at the Battle of Shiloh,

Tennessee, on April 6–7, 1862, graphically described what he saw. The "wounded passed all the time," he shuddered, "and I saw men pass that was shot from the top of their head to the bottom of their feat Some with one eye shot out, nose shot off mouth shot off side of their face shot off shot in the arms hand & legs." Several days later, the same man, still shaken by his recent battle experiences, asked his wife to tell his children that "I would like to have holt of them awhile certain."[11]

More than a few fathers sent their children various wartime souvenirs to remember them by. Soldiers mailed home song sheets, dolls, books, and toys. One Union soldier, taking gift-giving to its simplest extreme, sent home a bean that he had found in his boot to his young baby. He likely was delighted when his wife informed him that the baby played happily with the present. The most popular gifts, however, were souvenirs from the battlefield. Men sent their families spent bullets, bits of uniforms and flags, and other assorted odds and ends. One Union officer sent home a spent bullet that had struck him in the chest during the Battle of Fredericksburg, Virginia, on December 13, 1862. Another Union soldier sent home the shotgun that a Confederate soldier had fired at him during a battle in Tennessee. Confederate soldiers displayed a more practical, if not also somewhat morbid, bent to their gift giving. They sent home to their families shoes taken from Union soldiers captured, killed, and wounded in battle.[12]

Children's literature formed another venue through which northern and southern youth learned about the Civil War. Textbooks became among the most important media to attempt to both teach children why the war was being fought and inspire them with stories of patriotism and bravery. The struggle was most intense in the Confederacy, where children generally received instruction at private academies or at home, from parents and tutors. Confederate educators pushed immediately upon the outbreak of war for the publication of new textbooks, fearing that prewar editions reflected northern biases. Their worries seemingly were exaggerated. All but a few schoolbooks avoided mention of controversial political and social issues like slavery, hoping to avoid alienating southern consumers. Yet northern publishers dominated the textbook market, and that was enough.[13] "We hope the day is past," a local newspaper in Columbia, South Carolina, declared during the summer of 1861, "for the importation of books for our children from our enemies, who never omitted an opportunity … to inculcate their fanatical teachings against our institutions."[14] The effort to write and publish Confederate textbooks carried considerable momentum throughout the war. By the end of the fighting in 1865, schoolbooks constituted nearly three-quarters of the youth literature published in the Confederacy.[15]

Confederate schoolbooks displayed several themes distinct from prewar editions. The most notable difference in tone was an active defense of slavery. Confederate schoolbooks represented slavery as a positive good for both white and black. "Under the influence of slavery," one textbook boasted,

Children of the Civil War. *Left:* "The Little Soldier," *Carte de Visite*,
c. 1870. *Right:* "Young Lass with Accordion and Straw Bonnet,"
Ambrotype, c. 1870. *Bottom:* "The Little Union Sympathizer," Tintype with
patriotic brass mat, c. 1862. (Photographs from the private collection
of Colleen Warner, Bowling Green, Ohio. Used by permission.)

"which is the corner stone of her governmental fabric ... the Confederate
States has just commenced a career of greatness." Another schoolbook
claimed that black slaves in the Confederacy were well clothed and fed, and
that they were "better instructed than in their native country." Confederate
schoolbooks also included ample political criticism of Abraham Lincoln and
the Republican Party. "If the rulers of the United States had been good Christian men," Marinda Moore, the author of an elementary geography book,
argued, "the present war would not have come upon us. The people sent
bad men to Congress, and they were not willing to make just laws, but were
selfish, and made laws to suit themselves." Another Confederate educator
warned that a "despotism is a tyrannical, oppressive government. The ad-

ministration of Abraham Lincoln is a despotism."[16] Still other Confederate textbooks used the war to extol supposed Confederate martial prowess. The most famous to do so was L. Johnson's arithmetic text for beginners. Johnson asked students to solve story problems such as "A Confederate soldier captured 8 Yankees each day for 9 successive days; how many did he capture in all?"; and "If one Confederate soldier can whip 7 yankees, how many soldiers can whip 49 yankees?"[17]

Union counterparts to Confederate schoolbooks were few, because most northern texts remained based upon prewar editions. The *Union ABC* and *The Patriotic Speaker,* both published in 1864, were notable exceptions. Printed in red, white, and blue, the *Union ABC* used war-related images and themes to provide reading exercises to preschool and early grammar school children. The book began with "A is America, land of the free"; and ended with "Z is Zouave, who charged on the foe." Letters and images in between included "D is a Drummer Boy, called little Ben"; "H is for Hardtack, you scarcely can gnaw"; and "T is a Traitor, that was hung on a tree." By contrast, *The Patriotic Speaker* employed excerpts from speeches and writings from various sources to provide elocution lessons for older students. Most of the excerpts came from essays and poems authored by European writers. But other excerpts came from speeches and talks delivered by noted Union politicians. Among these included William Seward, Lincoln's Secretary of State; Charles Sumner, a Republican senator from Massachusetts; and William Lloyd Garrison, a nationally known leader of the abolitionist movement.[18]

Schoolbooks for newly freed slaves, intended for both children and adults, appeared late during the war. Among the most widely used were *The Freedman, The Freedman's Spelling Book, The Freedman's Primer, The Freedman's Second Reader,* and *The Freedman's Third Reader,* all published by the American Tract Society during 1864 and 1865. The five books attempted to teach basic educational skills, such as grammar and spelling. But the books also attempted to teach African Americans a greater understanding of their shared history. Stories about black Union soldiers were common, as well as biographies of historical figures such as Frederick Douglass and Phillis Wheatley. Additionally, religious instructions and stories intermixed throughout each of the books. The authors of *The Freedman's Third Reader,* for example, assured readers that the work "is thoroughly Christian, containing numerous selections from able and interesting writers on religious subjects, and from the Word of God."[19] The books tread more lightly on other issues, most notably avoiding overt discussion of voting rights and civil rights. Despite the absences, the *Freedman's* books received wide readership. Distribution of the *Freedman* alone ran to 648,000 copies during 1865–66, a sizable portion of the freed black community in the South.[20]

In addition to schoolbooks, children's magazines appeared during the war years. In the Union, leading children's magazines included *The Stu-*

*dent and Schoolmate, The Little Pilgrim, Our Young Folks,* and *The Little Corporal.* These four magazines and others like them employed similar organizational formats, with short stories, trivia games, and opinion pieces. The magazines also focused upon common political themes, especially hitting slavery as the cause of the war. "In a word, children," Uncle Rodman, a fictional character in *Our Children,* declared in one story, "slavery was the cause of the war; and God permitted the war in order that slavery might be destroyed."[21] In the Confederacy, children's magazines were fewer in number due to shortages in paper, ink, and printing equipment. Among the longest-running southern children's magazines was *Child's Index,* a Baptist religious publication. One article in the magazine declared that although readers "ought all to pray for peace," they should recognize that "we are fighting ... to drive wicked invaders from our land."[22] Pieces in other issues included comparing the Confederate cause in the Civil War to the American cause in the Revolutionary War and demonstrating the supposed biblical support for slavery.[23]

Games provided an additional way for children to learn about the fighting that raged between 1861 and 1865. Children played a variety of rule-based games that already were in existence by the early 1860s, including checkers, chess, and dominos. Many other existing games incorporated the war into their method of play. Various trivia games tested players' knowledge of generals and battles, while mazes printed with various naval and nautical obstacles allowed children to attempt to "run" the Union blockade of the Confederate coast. In decks of cards, eagles, shields, stars, and flags, replaced spades, hearts, diamonds, and clubs. Additionally, colonels replaced kings, the Goddess of Liberty replaced queens, and majors replaced jacks. Other toy manufacturers produced jigsaw puzzles that featured various wartime scenes, including Union recruiting rallies in Boston, Massachusetts, during 1861, and Confederate General Robert E. Lee's surrender at Appomattox Court House, Virginia, during 1865.[24]

Many children moved beyond games produced by toy companies and incorporated the war into their own play. Children commonly formed imaginary military companies, imitating soldiers in drill and parade.[25] Willie and Tad Lincoln, youngest sons of the president, were the most famous of the self-appointed soldiers. The two boys often formed military companies among their friends and led them on parade through the White House. Julia Taft, a sixteen-year-old friend of the presidential family, witnessed one march of "Mrs. Lincoln's Zouaves" early during the war. "They were reviewed," Taft later recounted, "with great ceremony by the President and Mrs. Lincoln who gave them a flag, but the company dwindled until, like the one Artemus Ward told about, it was all officers." In another episode, the Lincoln boys sentenced Jack, a doll, to death by firing squad for some imagined military transgression. After some debate over the harshness of the penalty, Willie and Tad asked and received a pardon for

Jack from their father. The doll later succumbed to an even less glorious fate, despite the reprieve. "The last time I saw poor Jack," Julia Taft again recalled, "he reposed on top of the cornice of one of the East Room windows, where he had been tossed by one of the boys."[26]

But all was not play, and Union and Confederate children often learned about war through the assumption of adult responsibilities. Many children attempted to shoulder, as much as possible, the workloads of their departed fathers.[27] Children throughout the Union and Confederacy went to work on family farms, tending to planting and harvesting, among other agricultural tasks. The work was demanding, as indicated by the advice given by Theodorick Montfort, a Confederate soldier, to David, his thirteen-year-old son. "Attend evry thing," Theodorick admonished, "see to it yourself, dont rely on any one else attending to it, but never go to sleep of a night until you see that evry thing is attended to."[28] Other children replaced industrial laborers departed for the army. The military arsenal in Washington, D.C., employed 250 self-described "boys" at war-related work, among the largest collection of youthful workers in the Union.[29] Many children enjoyed their newfound responsibilities in farm and factory, but more found them a seemingly never ending burden. "It was an incessant struggle," one Michigan youth later admitted, "to keep our land, to pay our taxes, and to live."[30]

Children in the Union and the Confederacy also assumed adult responsibilities through their public support of the war effort. Many children worked as individuals and small groups to raise supplies for soldiers. In Philadelphia, schoolchildren in the Eighteenth Ward collected food and linens to send to soldiers. In Richmond, children joined with adults in vowing to avoid eating meat on Fridays, to leave more for soldiers. Children also worked to support the war effort in conjunction with established relief organizations. Among the most elaborate were children's fund-raisers that operated alongside Sanitary Fairs in many cities across the Union. Children sold handicrafts, foodstuffs, pictures, and other items to raise money for various war-related causes. Nellie Grant, daughter of Ulysses S. Grant, the Union's highest-ranking general, was among the most famous participants in children's fund-raising. In a common theme at fund-raisers throughout the Union, Nellie played "the old women who lived in the shoe" at the 1864 Sanitary Fair in St. Louis. Posing as the famous fairy-tale character, Nellie raised money for the war effort by selling dolls and reading stories.[31]

Direct contact with various Union and Confederate armies formed a final way that mid-nineteenth-century children learned about war. Many children had the war literally land on their doorstep, with soldiers passing back and forth through their towns and villages during various battles and campaigns. Sue Chancellor, a fourteen-year-old Virginian, experienced among the most harrowing direct involvement with the war. Living in the house that gave name to the Battle of Chancellorsville, Virginia, during May 1–4, 1863, Sue recounted her ordeal in a memoir published during the early twentieth century. Sue huddled in the basement with family and friends for much of the fighting. "Such cannonading on all sides," she recalled of the ongoing battle, "such shrieks and groans, such commotion of all kinds!" Early during the fighting, the federals turned the Chancellor house into a hospital. They quickly filled the house with wounded and the surrounding yard, in Sue's words, with "rows and rows of dead bodies covered with canvas." Affairs took a turn for the worse for the Sue and the rest of the Chancellor family during the second to last day of the battle. Their home caught fire during the fighting, forcing their evacuation by Union soldiers. The Chancellor family and their soldier escorts made their way toward the Union rear lines while the battle raged all around. "The woods around the house were a sheet of fire," Sue vividly remembered, "the air was filled with shot and shell; horses were running, rearing, and screaming; the men were amass with confusion, moaning, cursing, and praying." The Chancellors completed their journey in safety, even coming to enjoy the company of their Union escorts. The Chancellor family later moved to Charlottesville, Virginia, where they lived for the remainder of the war.[32]

Unlike Sue Chancellor, who had the war come to her, many other children sought out the fighting. Southern youths had ample opportunities to witness combat, with most of the war occurring in the Confederacy. Opie Read bribed a Confederate bugler with brandy to carry him into a skirmish against Union cavalrymen. The swirl of the action delighted Read until his companion toppled over, dead from a gunshot wound. Read quickly rode from the battlefield and dismounted, cured from his sense of adventure.[33] In another episode, the two oldest sons of Cornelia MacDonald investigated a battle that unfolded outside their hometown of Winchester, Virginia. "They seemed not like the same boys," the youths' mother described after their return from the fighting, " … though there was no sign of fright or of excitement, they were very grave and sorrowful."[34] Northern children displayed similar curiosity to witness battle when the opportunity presented itself. Albertus McCreary tagged behind Union soldiers as they readied themselves for combat outside his hometown of Gettysburg, Pennsylvania, on July 1, 1863. McCreary's courage lasted only until the fighting started, when exploding Confederate artillery shells sent him scurrying back into town and to the safety of his family's basement. McCreary ventured back to the battlefield when the fighting ended two days later, watching in horrified fascination as Union surgeons operated upon wounded soldiers. "I must say," he later admitted, "I got pretty well hardened by such sights."[35]

Direct involvement of children in the war also occurred with various disruptions of family life. The death in battle of fathers-turned-soldiers represented the ultimate disruption of family life. Religious organizations and individual philanthropists in both the Union and the Confederacy attempted fill the breach as much as possible by providing fatherless children with at least some type of organizational support. Orphanages became a common solution, and their numbers during the 1860s equaled that of the past two decades combined. Many state governments throughout the Union also gave aid to soldiers' orphans, when available. Most important, twelve states established state-supported orphanages during and immediately after the war. Many state-run institutions remained open only through the mid- and late 1870s, when residents generally were old enough to make their own way in the world. But, despite the relatively short life span of many of them, public orphanages helped thousands of children to receive otherwise hard to obtain care. By contrast, state governments in the Confederacy lacked the financial resources to help children of deceased soldiers. Various Confederate veterans' organizations played a more significant role, attempting to provide at least some aid to needy children during the postwar era. The United Daughters of the Confederacy, the most important women's auxiliary organization in the postwar South, for example, sponsored academic scholarships for children of former Confederate soldiers.[36]

Wartime shortages of supplies also disrupted family life, especially in the Confederacy. Southern families often suffered from want of various household items, due to both the crumbling Confederate infrastructure and the tightening Union naval blockade. Many children remembered the lack of food in their households. One man who grew up in Civil War Arkansas recalled that "starvation is one of the sharpest memories of my childhood." Another Confederate youth described one of her greatest daily struggles as trying merely "to procure something to eat." Some children linked the lack of food to the lack of other common household items. "The war was continually rising in front of me," one disgruntled Virginian remembered later of his childhood, "to bar me from something I wanted, whether food, clothes, or playthings."[37]

## COMING OF AGE

Enduring the ordeal of the Civil War changed the world of American youth, but so did many other coming of age experiences. Even the very idea of adolescence was beginning to change during the 1860s and 1870s. Prior to the mid-nineteenth century, Americans generally referred to people in their late teens and early twenties when they talked about the passage from childhood to adulthood. But with the faster pace of American life and society following the conclusion of the Civil War, Americans turned their attention toward the maturation process among children in their pre- and early teens. But whatever their years, American youth faced many anxious and exhilarating experiences while coming of age during the late nineteenth century.[38]

Going to school represented a coming of age milestone that children experienced in increasing numbers during the postwar era. Americans had placed high value upon the educational basics of reading, writing, and arithmetic since the late colonial era, at least for white children. But formal education for young people became the norm only during the late 1870s, with the establishment of common schools in all states. Leading educational reformers believed that publicly supported schools would both foster social equality among students from diverse economic backgrounds and produce future workers and managers capable of sustaining economic growth. The push to extend educational opportunities to all white children caused common school enrollment rates to skyrocket during the postwar era. By 1870, 60 percent of white Americans between the ages of five and nineteen attended publicly supported schools, up from only 35 percent in 1830. Opportunities for higher education also increased with the passage of the Morrill Land Grant Act by Congress in 1862. The Morrill Act gave individual states land to support colleges that taught both practical and academic subjects. With the passage of the act, agricultural colleges and institutes of technology joined universities in growing numbers across the nation.[39] By 1870, the United States boasted 500 colleges and universities, more than all of western Europe combined.[40] These numbers must be read with some caution, however, because college students still formed a select breed in post–Civil War America. Only about 50,000 students attended college during the early 1870s, about 1 percent of the college-age population.[41]

Children who attended common schools during the late 1860s and early 1870s experienced an educational environment that their parents and grandparents would have found familiar in many ways. Most notably, educators continued to believe school an institution of moral uplift. William Holmes McGuffey, an Ohio college professor, authored a series of four elementary readers during 1836–37 that taught reading skills and moral precepts to equal degree. The books became the most widely used school texts during the mid- and late nineteenth century, selling more than 60 million copies by 1879.[42] Stories, poems, and essays in McGuffey's readers offered children proof that virtue and faith went with God; and that thrift and industry went with success.[43] McGuffey's *Second Reader*, for example, assured children in verse that:

> A little child who loves to pray,
>
> And reads his Bible, too,
>
> Shall rise above the sky one day,
>
> And sing as angels do.

A line from the *Fourth Reader* taught children that true happiness came from inside the person. "Wealth, rightly got and rightly used," McGuffey wrote,

" ... power, fame, these are all worthy objects of ambition, but they are not the highest objects, and you may acquire them all without achieving true success."[44]

Other elementary textbook authors followed McGuffey's lead, although never gaining the same level of distribution and sales. Salem Town, also the author of a reader, declared that his goal was "to improve the literary taste of the learner, to impress correct moral principles, and augment his fund of knowledge." S. Augustus Mitchell, the author of an elementary geography text, expressed a similar sentiment. "The introduction of moral and religious sentiments into books designed for the instruction of young persons," Mitchell promised his readers, "is calculated to improve the heart, and elevate and expand the youthful mind; accordingly, whenever the subject has admitted of it, such observations have been made as tend to illustrate the excellence of Christian religion, the advantages of correct moral principles, and the superiority of enlightened institutions."[45]

In other ways, much had changed in common schools from before and after the Civil War. Women increasingly replaced men as teachers, in part an attempt by educators to base classroom discipline and learning upon what they termed "moral suasion" rather than corporal punishment. Troublemakers, of course, still remained in the classroom. Boys in particular were into mischief, especially as they grew, according to one Illinois school official, "larger and lustier and more masculine."[46] School officials increasingly drew a hard disciplinary line, however, expelling young rowdies into the work world rather than submitting to their antics.[47] Women also became teachers in increasing numbers because, with few other employment alternatives, they were willing to work for lower wages than men. In Massachusetts, the state with among the most complete educational records, female teachers earned less than one-half the pay of male teachers.[48]

In addition to school officials hiring women teachers, they grouped students together by age. Prior to the mid-nineteenth century, educators made little distinction between learning needs among students of different ages. The result was that teachers instructed pupils who ranged in age and physical development from toddlers to young adults. George Moore, a school teacher in Massachusetts, recorded that the seventy students he taught in 1828 ranged in age from a four-year-old girl to a twenty-year-old young man. With children entering common schools in increasing numbers following the end of the Civil War, however, educators concentrated students by what they termed "age grading." School officials grouped young children between eight years of age and thirteen years of age into intermediate schools, and teenagers between fourteen years of age and nineteen years of age into high schools. The age range of high school students in small rural towns and villages often was younger (between eleven years of age and seventeen years of age), to enable students to begin sooner full time work on family farms. Age grading in intermediate schools and high schools also influenced the ages of students attending college. By the end of the nineteenth century, most college students ranged between eighteen years of age and twenty-two years of age, with much younger and older pupils a rarity.[49]

The increased emphasis upon public schooling in late-nineteenth-century America opened educational opportunities for both African American youth and young women. Blacks across the former Confederate states expressed an eagerness to learn, painfully aware that the denial of education had been a hallmark of the slave system. "If I never does do nothing more while I live," one Mississippi freedman and father promised, "I shall give my children the chance to go to school, for I considers education the next best thing to liberty."[50] Southern blacks worked with the federal government and various northern-backed benevolent societies to establish schools of their own. By the 1870s, about one-quarter of former slaves attended public school, while others received educational instruction at their church. Black schools often suffered from overcrowding and stingy state financial aid.[51] But to many African Americans, the advances in educational opportunities seemed miraculous. "It was a hard thing having to build that school for the white boys when I had no right to educate my son," Ambrose Headen recalled of building a private academy while a slave in Talladega, Alabama. "Then when the war was over and they bought that building for our children, I could hardly believe my eyes—looking at my own little ones carrying their books under their arms, coming from the same school the Lord really raised up for them. I rubbed my eyes and said, 'Ambrose, you must be dreaming.'"[52]

Young women also made striking gains in education during the postwar era. The first public high school for girls had opened in Massachusetts only during 1824. But by the early 1870s, girls constituted the majority of high school graduates. Many female students attended coeducational public schools, a far less costly alternative to single-sex academies. Between 1850 and 1870, the number of public high schools attended by both boys and girls in the United States had more than doubled, from 80 schools to 170 schools. The expansion of women into secondary education fostered greater access to higher education. By 1870, nearly one-quarter of college students were women. Many women attended newly created women's colleges, including Vassar, opened in 1865; and Wellesley and Smith, both opened ten years later. Other women attended previously all-male schools. Boston University and Cornell opened their doors to women during the postwar period, joining Oberlin, Antioch, and Swarthmore as coeducational institutions. Additionally, eight state universities opened under the Morrill Land Grant Act of 1862 admitted women. The number of coeducational colleges and universities continued to grow and, by 1900, over 100 such institutions were in existence.[53]

The mix of teenage boys and girls in high school and college facilitated the discovery of the opposite sex, although the process also certainly occurred almost anywhere and everywhere else. Adolescence, although always bringing at least some awkward moments, was an especially difficult life stage during the late nineteenth century in America. Many sexual and medical advice writers believed that teenagers going through puberty experienced what they termed the "convertibility of energy." Under the theory, advice writers argued that as teenagers gained in sexual capacity, they also gained in spiritual and physical energy. Conversely, anything that decreased one of these three energies also lowered the other two. The object for teenagers who hoped to emerge the better person from the adolescent experience was to maintain self-control over their thoughts and actions. Otherwise, physical and mental incapacitation might result, perhaps even leading to insanity and premature death.[54]

Unfortunately for adolescent teenagers, medical practitioners believed that almost any activity could drain one of their three primary energies. Masturbation was among the greatest self-abuses for young men and women to guard against. Many physicians believed that the spinal marrow directly connected a person's brain and his or her sexual organs. The spinal connection drained vital brain fluids whenever one experienced sexual climax. The rising sexual energy of young people made them especially at risk to self-harm.[55] One advice writer urged stringent self-control among teenage boys and girls because masturbation, if indulged too often, placed them "in imminent danger of becoming Insane, or at least of weak Intellect."[56] But other dangers to the health and well-being of teenagers seemingly lurked around every corner. Isaac Ray, a psychiatrist, warned that a host of actions could lead young people to disease and illness, from drinking coffee, which stimulated the urge to masturbate, to worrying over school, which diminished vital nervous fluids. Orson Fowler, a medical advice writer, shifted the blame for adolescent woes from teenagers to parents. Fowler argued that parents who urged their children toward perfectionism in their daily activities risked wearing them out. "If you would have [children] live to be a hundred," Fowler implored moms and dads, "give them the reins till they are twenty or upwards, and allow them to be boys and girls, instead of making them young ladies and gentlemen."[57]

Teenage girls received special attention from medical and sexual advice writers, who viewed them most at risk from falling into hysteria and insanity. Mid- and late-nineteenth-century medical authorities, as well as many other Americans, generally perceived girls as the weaker, emotional sex. Many Americans believed that girls by predisposition were more sensitive to their feelings than boys. Various nineteenth century writers described girls as "tremulous," "sentimental," and "susceptible to every gentle emotion of the soul."[58] Equally important, many other Americans believed that generations of supposed dependence upon men had left women and girls unused to the hustle and bustle of public life. When venturing outside the home for extended periods of time, women experienced psychological changes that, in the words of one contemporary, affected the "centers of sensation of the brain," and gave rise to "feelings of lassitude and tension."[59]

The surge of young women into previously all-male high schools and colleges during late 1860s and early 1870s gave advice writers pause. Although coeducational schools increased in numbers and popularity during the postwar era, many advice writers believed that they irreparably damaged the health of women students. E. H. Clark, author of *Sex in Education; or, A Fair Chance for the Girls,* published in 1873, was among the most vocal critics of coeducational schools. Clark argued that women needed more physical and mental rest from their menstruation cycles than attending school allowed them. The resulting strain from both overwork and overexertion pushed women into continuous decline of mind and body. The downfall began, Clark warned, with feelings of pain and misery and quickly deteriorated into bodily paralysis and mental hysteria.[60] Other advice writers believed that various social excitements experienced by young women while attending school overtaxed their otherwise fragile mental and physical health. Teenage girls who chose to spend their time focusing upon parties and fashions rather than studying risked various bodily ills, the worst being possibly delaying the onset of menstruation and thereby decreasing their chances to ever have children.[61]

Amid the many perils of teenage life, boys and girls turned their attention toward courting. Late-nineteenth-century couples displayed their affection in public more freely than earlier generations, strolling hand-in-hand and arm–in-arm to church services and to social functions. In all but the most wealthy families, couples also dated without the presence of a chaperon. The relative freedom of couples to do as they pleased in public prompted some critics to charge that dating had become too openly sexual. One magazine writer bemoaned in 1868 the "want of respectful reserve among young people of both sexes, their interchange of slang phrases, their audacious and dangerous flirtations." Another observer commented four years later that the "fast girl is now the girl of fashion."[62] Yet statistical evidence fails to support these claims. Premarital couples accounted for less than 10 percent of pregnancies recorded during the postwar era.[63] These numbers were less than one-half what they had been during the early nineteenth century, when about two out of every ten recorded pregnancies occurred among unmarried couples.[64]

Many young men and women eventually turned their thoughts toward marriage, as important a coming of age experience as any. The institution of marriage thrived during the mid- and late-nineteenth century, and the overwhelming majority of adult Americans married at some point during their lives.[65] The average age that couples took their vows had remained steady since the late eighteenth century, although evidence is somewhat limited. In general, however, men married during their mid-20s, and women married during their early 20s.[66] The wedding ceremony itself underwent more noticeable changes during the 1860s and 1870s, growing increasingly formal and public. Brides already commonly wore white dresses and veils by the Civil War and Reconstruction era, both symbols of inward purity. They also often crowned their heads with, in the words of one marriage etiquette writer, "a wreath of white flowers, usually artificial orange blossoms are preferred."[67] Many, although certainly not all, prospective husbands and wives began to send printed wedding invitations during the Civil War era. They moved well beyond immediate family members that characterized earlier generations of weddings, sometimes inviting hundreds of guests. Mid- and late-nineteenth-century couples also held wedding rehearsals, although not without occasional grumbling. One groom-to-be groused that at his wedding rehearsal, members of the wedding party "made so many blunders that we all felt sure of repeating them at the wedding. I am sure we ... were worse prepared than when we had begun."[68] Celebrations among newlyweds and their families and friends immediately following the wedding ceremony also became increasingly common, complete with dinner and wedding cake.[69]

Most marriages lasted permanently, although an increasing number ended in divorce. At the start of the war, the rate of divorce was extremely low across the nation, at only twenty-seven divorces for every 100,000 people. But during the postwar era, the numbers had increased, from 9,937 divorces in 1867 to 16,089 divorces in 1878.[70] Women initiated many of the divorces, seemingly more unhappy with their choice of husbands than with the institution of marriage. Most women who granted divorces during the mid-1870s cited their husbands for physical and mental cruelty, desertion, drunkenness, and neglect. But men also occasionally expressed unhappiness with their choice of spouse. Men receiving divorces most often claimed that their wife had "acted in a unwife-like manner." Husbands winning divorce on these grounds charged that their wives had failed to do everything from washing their clothes to bearing their children.[71] Husbands and wives having trouble obtaining divorces in their home state often moved to Indiana, which possessed the most liberal divorce laws in the nation. The Hoosier state permitted individuals seeking divorce only to inform their spouse of their decision if they chose to do so, a far less formal and public proceeding than throughout the rest of the nation.[72]

The decision whether to have a family soon occupied newlyweds. Some couples decided to attempt to avoid expanding their family. Their options were several, depending upon the year. It must be stated first, however, that many, if not most, Americans disapproved of contraception as interfering with God's plan for the world. Still, some couples wanted family matters more immediately in their hands. Women chose abortion more often than contraception through the late 1860s, at least according to reports from contemporary druggists.[73] Some women attempted to induce "accidental miscarriages" through the ingestion of abortive drugs, such as iodine, cotton root, and oil of tansy. Other women visited abortionists, although many of these practitioners reportedly had little more medical knowledge than their patients. By the early 1870s, women more often turned to contraceptive devices. They could choose from a wide range of methods, from approved medical devices, such as diaphragms and condoms, to popular superstitions, such as the belief that if a woman engaged in vigorous exercise (especially dancing and horseback riding) after intercourse, she would avoid conception. Married couples also mixed in long-standing practices such as coitus interruptus or the excuse of a woman's headache.[74]

Far more husbands and wives welcomed children than not, bringing full circle the coming of age experience. Most married couples became first-time parents about eighteen months after their wedding day. Public hospitals existed only to provide aid to the indigent, so women usually gave birth in the bedroom. But babies come when they come, and more than a few women gave birth in unplanned and unexpected locations. Americans viewed childbirth as a natural process so, wherever labor started, they often believed that no specific medical tools were needed. Physicians generally helped women through the birthing process in the city, if called to assist at all. Doctors were less numerous in the countryside, and neighbors and family members often helped mothers-to-be through their labor. The process of preparing for the arrival of help was not a task to be taken lightly. "A woman that was expecting had to take good care that she had plenty fixed to eat for her neighbors when they got there," one person described. "There was no telling how long they was in for. There wasn't no paying these friends so you had to treat them good."[75] But most mothers and mothers-to-be presumably welcomed the help, all the while bringing into the world a new generation of American youth.[76]

# PART TWO

# Popular Culture During the Civil War and Reconstruction

# 3
# Advertising

The promotion of goods for sale and distribution had a lengthy history in the United States by the outbreak of the Civil War in 1861. In Philadelphia, the then-young Benjamin Franklin advertised for "Super Fine Crown Soap" in the *Pennsylvania Gazette* in 1735. "It cleanses fine Linens, Muslins, Laces, Chinces, Cambricks, etc.," Franklin boasted, "with Ease and Expedition." Also in Philadelphia but nearly 100 years later, Samuel Chamberlain, a dentist, advertised "incorruptible porcelain teeth." To the interested, Chamberlain assured that the fake teeth "will retain their original color for any length of time, and are not decomposed by acids."[1] The marketing of Franklin and Chamberlain, although impressive at the time, paled by comparison to what was to come. Between 1860 and 1900, the amount of money spent by Americans on the promotion of goods for sale swelled from $50 million to $500 million.[2] The tenfold increase in advertising expenditures created a world of sales pitch and marketing unlike anything yet seen in North America.[3]

## NEWSPAPER ADVERTISING TAKES THE LEAD

Daily newspapers attracted the most attention from advertisers during the mid- and late nineteenth century, a result of their rapid increase in both numbers and circulation. The "dailies" had surged dramatically in number after the invention of the Hoe rotary press during the 1840s. Named after Richard Hoe, a manufacturer of printing equipment in New York, the Hoe rotary press utilized a revolving cylinder to print onto a continuous roll of paper. The result was a dramatic decrease in the time and cost to print newspaper sheets.[4] Publishers took full advantage of Hoe's invention and, between 1840 and 1860, the number of daily newspapers had increased from 138 to 372.[5] Despite the nearly threefold increase in publication, daily newspapers appeared unevenly across the nation. The North enjoyed three times as many papers as the South per person, reflecting the region's higher literacy rates.[6]

In addition to increased numbers, newspapers drew attention from advertisers because they had high circulation. By 1860, newspaper readership ran into the several million, the highest total to date.[7] Many of these readers lived in northern cities, where the penny press created high subscription levels. The penny press sold at one and two cents a copy (down from the generally set price at six cents a copy), an attempt by newspaper editors to capture the ever-growing urban market.[8] The low cost of the penny press scored record sales, especially with the quest for news among the reading public after the outbreak of the Civil War. In New York City, the *Tribune* and the *Times,* both among the most popular newspapers in the city, reached close to 190,000 daily subscribers by early 1862. In Philadelphia, the *Inquirer* sold to 70,000 people during the fighting.[9] By comparison, newspapers in the Confederacy sold far less briskly, battling against both small urban populations and scarcities of printing materials. In Richmond, for example, the *Dispatch,* the city's most well known paper, circulated only 18,000 copies per day during the Civil War.[10]

Beyond growing numbers and circulation lists, newspapers helped their own cause by implementing several advertising innovations. One change was the switch to daily advertisements in 1848. Previously, advertisements had run in up to one-year cycles, often becoming stale and outdated before their completion. Daily advertisements first appeared in the *New York Herald,* under the direction of James Gordon Bennett.[11] Bennett's hope was that continuously changing advertisements would add color to the local news already printed. "On this plan the advertisements form the most interesting and practical 'city news,'" Frederic Hudson, Bennett's managing editor, later explained. "They are the hopes, the thoughts, the joys, the plans, the shames, the losses, the mishaps, the fortunes, the pleasures, the miseries, the politics, and the religion of the people. Each advertiser is therefore a reporter—a sort of 'penny-a-liner,' he paying the penny."[12] The plan worked, if judged by the imitation of other newspapers. Within a few years, other publishers across the nation had followed suit, making daily advertisements the rule rather than the exception.[13]

Another newspaper innovation was the design and use of creative and eye-catching advertisements. Newspaper editors almost all had adhered to the so-called agate rule prior to the Civil War. They printed advertisements in five-and-one-half-point agate type, about the size of today's stock market quotations. "All advertisements were printed in the same style," Hudson of the *New York Herald* again proffered, "but neatly and systematically arranged.... There has been no typographic splurge for one to the injury of the other."[14] Although a perhaps noble objective, the decision to adhere to the agate rule resulted in a uniformity of appearance among advertisements that generated little public excitement.[15]

Robert Bonner of the *New York Ledger* was the pioneer in breaking the agate rule. A former newspaper printer and proofreader in Connecticut and New York, Bonner recognized the potential of innovative advertising to increase both profit and subscription. In 1856, Bonner created the advertising technique later known as iteration. He repeated six messages in separate vertical columns across an entire page. Each message began with a capital letter in 14-point type and mentioned the *Ledger*. The first column, for example, read, "Let the news go forth that the New York Ledger is out." The second column read, "Everybody is reading Cobb's new sensation story in the New York Ledger." When put together, the advertisement mentioned the *Ledger* 3,600 times. More eye-catching because of the large type, the first letters in each column spelled, "L-E-D-G-E-R." The result of Bonner's use of iteration was an advertisement striking in both its repetition and its visual presentation.[16]

In another break from the agate rule, Bonner ran four full pages of advertisement for the *New York Ledger* in a single issue of the *New York Herald*. The multiple-page spread was breathtaking in its originality, especially because other advertisements generally ran at most a few lines. Friends, however, worried over the financial cost of the stunt. In one instance, the local pastor immediately rushed to Bonner's office upon reading the four pages. In a tremble, he asked what the advertisement had run. Bonner replied with a smile, "Two thousand dollars." "Two thousand dollars! T-w-o t-h-o-u-s-a-n-d d-o-l-l-a-r-s!," the pastor gasped in disbelief. "Mr. Bonner, I have called upon you as a friend. This is a terrible waste of money. Would not an ordinary advertisement like that [pointing to a twenty-line advertisement] have answered your purpose?"

"If I had used the small space," Bonner queried, "would you have noticed my advertisement?"

"Why, no; possibly not."

"Of course not. And every other reader of the *Herald* is as astonished as you are and talking about it. That is the secret of advertising. I think you have confirmed my judgment. Those four pages are worth two thousand dollars."[17]

A third innovation in newspaper advertising was publishers' use of sensational gimmicks and stories to increase readership. Bonner was again in the lead. The New York City publisher paid well-known authors and public figures vast sums of money for their articles and stories. Bonner did not believe that these items were intrinsically worth much money. Rather, he enjoyed the flocks of new subscribers who wanted to read the pieces that the *Ledger* had purchased at such high financial cost. In two well-known examples, Bonner paid Charles Dickens, the famous British author, $5,000 for some of his writings in 1859. The same year, Bonner paid Henry Ward Beecher, a highly regarded New England minister, $30,000 for his *Norwood*, a novel published in several installments. Bonner's showmanship made the *Ledger* the talk of the town, the intended objective for its nearly priceless word-of-mouth advertising.[18]

James Gordon Bennett, Jr., who succeeded his father in publishing the *New York Herald,* one-upped Bonner and pulled the ultimate advertising and news gimmick of the Civil War and Reconstruction era. In 1870, Bennett sent Henry Stanley, one of his correspondents, to track down David Livingstone, a well-known Scottish doctor and missionary last seen alive while on exploration in central Africa. "Find Livingstone and bring news of his discoveries or proofs of his death," Bennett ordered Stanley, "regardless of expense." Stanley spent the next eight months describing his adventures to the fascinated readership of the *Herald.* The climax came when Stanley, after surviving disease, hunger, and battle, greeted Livingstone with, "Dr. Livingstone, I presume?" Stanley's salutation became famous throughout the United States, to the delight of Bennett and to the benefit of the *Herald*'s circulation numbers.[19]

A last innovation in newspaper advertising was the hiring of sales agencies. Prior to the mid-nineteenth century, rates for advertising had varied by paper. Prices ranged widely by geographic location, but they could cost upwards of $100 for space in a large-city newspaper. Advertising agencies, however, such as S. M. Pettengill and Company of New York and N. W. Ayer & Son of Philadelphia, purchased space in bulk from as many papers as possible. "They have arrangements with many Papers such as no other Agent can have," S. M. Pettengill boasted of its operations in 1859, "and they give customers this benefit."[20] The use of advertising agencies helped all involved. The newspaper sold space, usually in one-year allotments. The advertiser, who purchased as many lines as needed, received discounted rates. In turn, the advertising agency received a commission, generally between 12.5 and 25 percent of the sale price.[21]

George Rowell was the leading advertising agent of the day, a result of the publication of his *Rowell's American Newspaper Directory* in 1869.[22] The book was the first estimate of the number of subscribers to each of the newspapers published in the United States. The circulation data enabled advertisers to calculate the benefits of buying space in particular newspapers, rather than guessing at the outcome. Rowell utilized peer pressure to his benefit, estimating circulation figures for those publishers who refused to make known to him their subscriber lists. "Week by week, month by month and year by year he has pilloried the circulation liar relentlessly," one newspaper editor declared later of Rowell's accomplishment. " ... By this course a revolution has been wrought in the ethics of circulation statements."[23] Rowell died during the early twentieth century, during which time his book was still frequently updated.

Newspaper advertisements played an important role in the ability of both the Union and the Confederacy to wage war. The Lincoln and Davis administrations each advertised government bonds for sale.[24] The North achieved greater public support, because Secretary of the Treasury Salmon P. Chase promised payment after a specific number of years. One advertisement of July 1864 highlighted "The Government Loan of $200,000,000. This loan is authorized by Act of Congress of March 8, 1864, which provides for its redemption in Coin, at any period not less than ten or more than forty years from its date, at the pleasure of the Government." In the South, Secretary of the Treasury C. G. Memminger qualified payment upon Confederate victory. In a February 1864 advertisement, Memminger explained that payment of bonds only would occur "Two Years after the Ratification of a Treaty of Peace Between the Confederate States and the United States of America."[25]

The Union and the Confederacy also used newspaper advertisements to recruit soldiers and purchase war materials. Calls for volunteers stressed patriotism and duty, similar to those found on oft-printed recruiting flyers and billboards. "Volunteer Now or Never. The Last Chance," an advertisement in the *Columbus (Georgia) Enquirer* warned during late April 1862. "The Gallant sons of Georgia and Alabama are rushing to the rescue! They will not suffer to be dragged in by conscription but willingly and patriotically are rallying to their country's defense! All cannot get in, but those who come first will be received!"[26] The *Springfield (Massachusetts) Republican* sounded a similar call during April 1864. The advertisement thundered, "Patriots of Springfield. Arouse to the call of your country—fill up the ranks at once and finish up the work. 200 Able Bodied Men Wanted at the City Recruiting Office, Cabin in Court Square."[27]

Advertisements for war materials were more low key, although why is uncertain. Perhaps the men who wrote them found little excitement in the subject. More likely, the writers wanted to play down the lure of profit to avoid hucksters and fly-by-night operators. Whatever the reasons, calls for war materials lacked heavy doses of flare and fire. One Confederate advertisement during 1862 announced matter-of-factly, "Artillery Horses Wanted. The Quartermaster General of the Confederate States Army has authorized me to purchase the horses for my Battery. Mr. William Ingram, a member of my Company, has been appointed to buy them."[28] A Union advertisement on February 23, 1864, expressed a similar dryness. "Proposals will be received by the War Department until Tuesday, March 8, at 4 o'clock P.M.," the piece read, "for the delivery at the Springfield Armory, Mass., of 6,000 single sets of wrought iron work for United States Artillery Harness." The advertisement concluded with specifications for constructing the harness, omitting any reference regarding duty to country.[29]

Many advertisers skillfully exploited the war to sell their products. Some used headlines from the fighting to draw attention to their products. "Truth

Will Prevail," one northern ad trumpeted during late 1861. The truth in this case was that "Old African Coffee was the best." Another piece declared "The Union Must Be Saved!" Folks at home could do their part in preserving the nation by buying and using firecrackers supplied by the advertiser. Other advertisers played off sectional tensions. "War! War! War! Is Declared against Pains of Any Kind by Dr. A. W. Allen's Southern Liniment," ran one ad in Georgia after the secession of the Deep South during winter 1861, " … Caution to everybody—Don't use any more Northern Liniment until you have given the Southern Liniment a fair trial."[30]

New types and styles of advertisements appeared in newspapers during the postwar era. Large retail shops, soon known across the country as department stores, boomed during the late 1860s and early 1870s. To draw attention to their wide range of merchandise, big stores such as Marshall Field's in Chicago, Hudson's in Detroit, and Macy's and Wanamaker's in New York and Philadelphia advertised frequently in local newspapers.[31] A few stores designed their features in the old five-and-one-half-point type. Many, however, utilized display type, with large and varied fonts.[32] In one example, Macy's ran an advertisement in the *New York Daily Tribune* during late 1865 that alternated between large and small type. The store name at the top of the page was in thirty-point type, while the street address at the bottom was in five-and-one-half-point type. The promotion, and others like it, proved successful, making Macy's a mainstay in newspaper advertisement throughout the remainder of the nineteenth century.[33]

Entertainers also began to advertise their services during the postwar period. Local promoters announced various sporting events, especially baseball. But the most aggressive promoter of good times was Phineas Taylor (P. T.) Barnum.[34] Born in Connecticut in 1810, Barnum early turned to show business. By 1842, he had gained operational control of the American Museum, the soon-to-be-home of the greatest collection of oddities and wonders of the age. "Determined to spare no exertions in securing every attainable novelty," Barnum declared during August 1842 in one of his first newspaper announcements, "the manager is happy to announce that he has, at a most extraordinary expense, made arrangements with the proprietor of the greatest curiosity in the world, the REAL MERMAID!"[35] Barnum continued to use newspaper advertisements during the Civil War and Reconstruction era, with his customary flourish. "I AM HERE! At Lincoln Park! With My Greatest Show on Earth!" Barnum touted in the *Cincinnati Gazette* in 1879. He continued at rapid-fire pace, "Wonderful trained wild beasts! Grand Roman Hippodrome! Mammoth Museum! And the most refined, elegant, greatest, grandest, and most Magnificent Circus!"[36] Barnum remained a fixture in newspaper advertising until his death from old age in 1891.

Personal advertisements were a more ubiquitous form of self-promotion that appeared first in the *New York Herald* during the late 1860s. The messages were spicy, if not titillating, by the moral standards of the day. Three personals from an 1869 issue read:

MAUD—Will not be prudent for me to write. I want to see you so much. Little Friend.

Wanted—A situation as son-in-law in a respectable family. Blood and breeding no object, being already supplied; capital essential. No objection to going a short distance into the country.

Dear Charles—Should such a trifle as a handy hat-brush sever love? Come to your ruffled LU-LU.[37]

The openness of the personal advertisements received criticism from both the public and other newspapers. Still, the pieces were a lucrative source of revenue, often as high as $1 per line. Money talked, and the *Herald* continued to run personals into the early twentieth century.[38]

## MAGAZINES AND CATALOGUES AND THE RISE OF NATIONAL ADVERTISING

Magazines began to rival newspapers as the leading advertising medium in the United States following the end of the Civil War, for several reasons. The first reason for the success of magazines in attracting advertisers was their boom in numbers. Between 1865 and 1880, the number of magazines published weekly, monthly, and quarterly increased from 700 to 2,400. One American publisher, watching the surge of periodical publishing occurring around him during the late 1860s, declared that he and his fellow countrymen were seemingly possessed by a "mania of magazine-starting."[39] The nearly fourfold increase in magazine publishing during the postwar era occurred because Americans had the money to invest in such undertakings following the end of wartime financial constraints. Additionally, magazines benefited from the various changes in printing technology that had made newspapers easier and cheaper to publish during the 1850s and 1860s.[40]

The second reason magazines became one of the leading advertising forums during the late nineteenth century was because they reached a national audience. With both the reunification of the North and South and the westward push of various transportation networks, magazines circulated across the continent. *Peterson's National Ladies' Magazine*, a fashion and domestic advice periodical, was mailed to 150,000 women throughout the nation during the early 1870s. A few years later, *Frank Leslie's Popular Monthly* and *Harper's Monthly*, both illustrated news periodicals, mailed to over 100,000 subscribers each. To further increase national circulation, magazines often offered premiums for renewals and subscriptions. "We believe in chromos [varnish-finished lithographs]," the *Literary World* boasted in one sales pitch, "they do much to refine our homes, and to encourage a love for the beautiful.... "[41] The marketing of free gifts fell out of favor among magazine publishers by the late 1870s, as much as from overuse as from declining results.[42]

Magazines aggressively sought advertising money as a major source of operating revenue during the postwar era, another reason why the medium rivaled newspapers in the marketing and promoting of goods for sale. Prior to the end of the Civil War, magazine publishers often had refused outside advertisements as beneath the dignity of their notice. In a notable example as late as the early 1870s, *Harper's Monthly* refused to run advertisements for the Howe Sewing Machine Company, even at the princely sum of $18,000 a year. A financial crisis that swept the nation during the mid-1870s, however, forced many magazine publishers to court advertising money. Publishers generally based their advertising prices upon their circulation figures. The *Saturday Evening Post,* with 20,000 subscribers, asked only 25 cents a line during the early 1880s. *Leslie's Popular Monthly* charged advertisers $1 a line. Even *Harper's* bowed to the financial realities of the times, selling advertisement space for $2 a line.[43]

The final reason magazines excelled in filling their advertising space during the late 1860s and early 1870s was because they targeted specific national audiences, as exemplified by the *Youth's Companion.* A juvenile magazine that emphasized moral uplift, *Youth's Companion* sold 385,000 copies per issue by the mid-1880s, better than any other magazine.[44] The editors aimed their stories at adolescent-aged children, but advertisers geared their work toward the mothers. "Toasting—broiling baking—ironing," Standard Oil Company boasted in one ad, "anything that can be done with a wood or coal fire is done better, cheaper and quicker on a WICKLESS Blue Flame Oil Stove."[45] Advertisements for domestic products remained strong in *Youth's Companion* throughout the remainder of the nineteenth century. In a notable example, Mellin's Food payed a record-setting $14,000 for a back cover lithograph in 1893.[46]

Magazines used a variety of creative techniques to make effective their national advertisements. The most important technique was building consumer trust, because seller and buyer never saw one another. By the late 1860s, newspapers had fallen into the practice of *caveat emptor,* or "buyer beware." One newspaper editor, when told that many falsehoods appeared in his columns, huffed, "business is business, money is money." Sellers of patent medicines were the worst abusers, making outrageous claims for their products. The makers of Warner's Safe Kidney and Liver Cure touted that, through regular use of their medicine, "Bright's Disease, in its worst form, is curable." The makers of St. Jacob's Oil claimed that their product was the "most wonderful pain relieving and healing remedy ever discov-

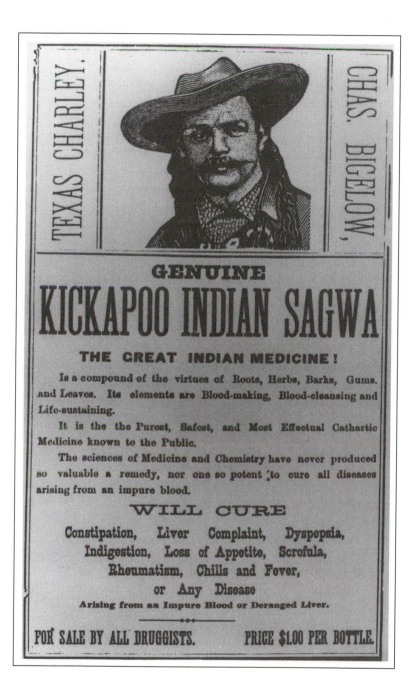

Typical cover of a magazine given away at a medicine show. Courtesy of the Billy Rose Theatre Collection, The New York Public Library for the Performing Arts, Astor, Lenox and Tilden Foundations.

*Frank Leslie's Illustrated Newspaper* satirizes both medicine
and medical practice.

ered." One bottle "cures rheumatism, cures neuralgia, cures pain, soreness and stiffness, heals cuts and sores."[47] With nearly unlimited freedom to make claims of better health and healing, patent medicine advertisements appeared liberally in many otherwise reputable newspapers.[48]

Magazine publishers recognized the exaggeration often found in newspaper advertisements, with mixed responses. Many editors decried the practice. "A model Advertisement-Writer in the [New York] *Herald* calls the Sewing Machine 'a swift-fingered sister of love and charity,'" one magazine writer scorned during the early 1860s. "Let us hereafter speak of the Cooking-Range as the warm-hearted minister to appetite and contentment; of the Daguerreotype Apparatus as the bright-faced reflector of beauty and worth; and, among other ingenious contrivances, of the Model Advertisement-Writer as the soft-headed distributor of mellifluous soap." Still, many magazines used similar advertising deceptions. "Every trick that can be resorted to for the purpose of inducing one to read an advertisement is practiced," Frank Leslie bemoaned in his *Illustrated Newspaper*, "and, it must be confessed, very often with complete success. How often have we been seduced into the reading of some witty or sentimental verse, that finally led us, by slow degrees, to a knowledge that somebody sold cure-all pills or incomparable trousers."[49]

John Powers led the fight to return honesty to magazine advertisements. An American by birth, Powers got his start in advertising by designing promotions for sewing machines in England in 1868. He returned to the United States where, during the early 1870s, he crusaded against exaggeration and falsehood in advertisement writing. "A good bargain in advertising, i.e., a low rate," Powers liked to caution his clients, "is always of less account than to say the right things to the right people in an acceptable way." Powers wrote advertisements for many products during the late nineteenth century. In each, he stressed crisp sentences that emphasized what the product was and what it did for the buyer. "The tidy house-keeper banishes flies; but one persistent buzzer sticks," Powers described in one piece. "The fly-fan keeps him off while you dine or doze in peace. It IS a luxury! Winds like a clock, goes an hour-and-a-half, and costs $3.00."[50] Powers had changed the world of marketing and sales through his methods, winning him encomiums as the "father of honest advertising."[51]

Catchy slogans were another creative technique used in magazine advertisements. Newspapers often had relied upon repetition to make their point, as demonstrated through Bonner's use of iteration to trumpet the *New York Ledger*. Magazines, however, attempted to explain through concisely worded messages why buyers needed certain products. In a well-known example, Proctor and Gamble advertised Ivory Soap in 1882 as "99 44/100ths pure." Although seemingly unnecessarily precise, the piece was effective because of its frankness. By contrast, other soaps had advertised themselves as "absolutely pure" and "110 percent pure." The use of slogans only was beginning by the late nineteenth century. But the pithy messages made superb use of words and space, and they remain popular today.[52]

Human interest advertisements that featured realistic-looking art work also captured magazine readers' interest. The pieces demanded considerable time and typesetting skill to produce, and they just were beginning to appear by the late 1860s and the mid-1870s.[53] Sapolio soap and powder were among the first products to utilize human interest advertising, appearing in *Frank Leslie's Illustrated Weekly* in 1869. The advertisement featured a man with a pleased expression studying his reflection in the bottom of a pan made clean and shiny with Sapolio. Below the picture, the text boasted that Sapolio "is the best thing known for polishing metal and brass signs."[54] Clothing companies also made use of human interest advertisements. Many began to feature a drawing of a model wearing their product, rather than a sketch only of the garment. The use of models made clothing advertisements more attractive to the eye, giving readers an idea of the look and fit of each piece, plus its various accessories.[55]

In addition to the work already done by magazines, mail order catalogues contributed to the rise of national advertising during the late nineteenth century through their wide geographic circulation. E. C. Allen was the pioneer of the mail-order catalogue, also known among Americans as a "price list." A local salesman in Augusta, Maine, Allen established the *People's Literary Companion* in 1869. The sixteen-page publication featured a handful of stories and poems and other literary pieces. The bulk of the work, however, listed engravings and lithographs for sale. Allen set *People's Literary Companion* at 50 cents a copy, a nominal price for the day, although he often gave away issues for free. By 1870, the mail-order catalogue reached a circulation of 500,000 copies across the nation, earning Allen the title of "mail-order king" among his contemporaries.[56]

Montgomery Ward built upon Allen's creativity and carried the mail order catalogue to the height of its advertising successes during the 1870s and 1880s. Ward worked as a traveling salesman for a wholesale dealer in Missouri following the Civil War, where he witnessed the high prices that farmers paid for many of their daily goods in local stores. Determined to eliminate the middleman between seller and buyer and thereby reduce prices, Ward printed and mailed multi-paged catalogues to rural households. Ward guaranteed savings of 40 percent to buyers on household and farm items that ranged from needles to writing paper; and from trunks to harnesses. He also included woodcut illustrations of nearly all advertised items, giving the reader an accurate idea of the look of each piece. National prominence quickly followed Ward's first efforts and, by 1884, his catalogue numbered 240 pages and advertised nearly 10,000 items for sale.[57]

Ward pioneered several methods to build consumer trust for his products, an action as critical for the financial survival of mail-order catalogues as for magazines. In part, Ward assuaged consumer fears by identifying his

A typical partial page of *Frank Leslie's Illustrated Newspaper*.

catalogue with the Patrons of Husbandry. A national farmers' organization popularly known as the "Grange," the Patrons of Husbandry had campaigned against the high cost of store-sold goods in rural communities. Ward adeptly capitalized upon their discontent, proclaiming his catalogue as "The Original Grange Supply House." Ward also published testimonials from Grange officials regarding the durability and high quality of his goods and allowed members a ten-day grace period to pay their bills (rather than either in advance or upon delivery). Equally important to building consumer trust, Ward guaranteed that all goods shipped were "subject to examination." The buyer could return any item found unsatisfactory, with Ward either replacing the good or refunding the money, as well as paying for the shipping. How many customers returned defective items is uncertain, but Ward's willingness to offer the guarantee earned the loyalty of many buyers.[58]

Ward occasionally became victim to his own success, with potential customers asking for items not even advertised. Lonely farmers were the worst transgressors, many seeking to buy a wife through the mail. "As you advertise everything for sale that a person wants," one bachelor hoped, "I thought I would write you, as I am in need of a wife, and see what you could do for me." Another farmer was more specific. "Please send me a good wife," he detailed. "She must be a good housekeeper and able to do all household duty. She must be 5 feet 6 inches in height. Weight 150 lbs. Black hair and brown eyes, either dark or fair." Ward, the consummate salesman, seized such openings. He informed prospective husbands that selecting a wife through the mail was not a service offered by his business. Ward added, however, that "after you get the wife and you find that she needs some wearing apparel or households goods, we feel sure we could serve both you and her to good advantage."[59]

In addition to Allen and Ward, publishers of other mail-order catalogues advertised a variety of consumer goods. A sampling from one column of national advertising from one such catalogue indicates the range of items. The Florence Manufacturing Company of Massachusetts touted its dental plate brush as "absolutely indispensable if you wear Artificial Teeth." H. H. Tammen, a mineralogist in Colorado, advertised "Glittering Gold Quartz, just as taken from the Mines in the Rocky Mountains." Those wishing more shopping options should send a "stamp for large illst. Catalogue of Minerals, Agate Novelties, Indian Relics, etc." The Marchal and Smith Piano Company of New York also made an appearance. "We sell direct to families," the piece explained, "(avoid Agents and Dealers whose profits and expenses double the cost of every piano they sell) and send this ... Rosewood Piano, Warrented [sic] for 6 years, for $196!" Marchal and Smith had the answer for customers uncertain about making the purchase. "We send it," the advertisement guaranteed, "with beautiful Cover and Stool, for trial in your own Home before you buy."[60]

Many mail-order publishers advertised labor- and time-saving machines. Some catalogues displayed typewriters, sewing machines, and other household gadgets. "It is the size of a sewing-machine, and is an ornament to any office, study, or sitting-room," writers for Remington "type writers" described in an 1875 advertisement. "It is worked by keys, similar to a piano, and writes from thirty to sixty words per minute—more than twice as fast as the pen—in plain type, just like print." Because the typewriter helped users to learn letters and punctuation, the advertisement promised that there is "no more acceptable, instructive, or beautiful CHRISTMAS PRESENT."[61] Other catalogues advertised for buggies, wagons, and surreys. "The Best on Wheels," Bradley and Company of New York and Boston advertised of its various vehicle styles. "Light, strong, convenient and low priced. Handy to get into and out of. Handy for single horse or pair. Handy for one person or more. Handy to load or unload." For those worried about how to get a surrey or buggy from Bradley to their homes, the company promised to send a free circular, "How to purchase direct from the manufacturer."[62]

Magazine and mail-order catalogue advertisements were far from perfect in reaching all potential buyers during the Civil War and Reconstruction. In a notable example, *Ladies' Home Journal,* one of the most long-lasting and financially successful publications to cater specifically to female readers, appeared only late in the nineteenth century. Still, magazines and catalogues made impressive strides in advertising content and technique between 1861 and 1877. Their resourcefulness was a source of both admiration and bewilderment to many observers. George Wakeman, a writer for *Galaxy* magazine, expressed such mixed sentiments after the Civil War. "The names of successful advertisers have become household words," Wakeman observed in 1867, "where great poets, politicians, philosophers and warriors of the land are as yet unheard of; there is instant recognition of Higg's saleratus and Wigg's soap even where the title of Tennyson's last work is thought to be 'In a Garden' and Longfellow understood to be the nickname of a tall man."[63] Whatever the opinion of contemporary Americans, the world of advertising, with all its accompanying good and bad, had come to stay.

# 4

# Architecture

Architecture has always been important to individuals and society because it shapes the environment and, in so doing, acts as both a skin and an extension of individuals. Generally it is conservative, changing only slowly. The 1860s and 1870s, however, witnessed dramatic developments in American architecture, construction techniques, and building materials. Until the early nineteenth century, American architecture was largely vernacular, based on traditional forms. The specialized architect did not yet exist. Building plans were carried in the culture's collective conscious, and construction was undertaken either by the final consumer, or by tradesmen not far removed from the final consumer.[1]

The coming of the Industrial Revolution brought a major change in popular architecture. Mass production of building materials, and even of entire structures, made possible infinite variations in design. Building design was handled increasingly by professionals who might be far removed from the final consumer.[2]

Early American builders and architects came from widely varying backgrounds and held dissimilar philosophies and aims in building. Many were self-taught; the advent of the highly trained professional architect was largely a late-nineteenth-century phenomenon. In the absence of trained architects, the design of public buildings often fell to civil engineers. In 1870, there were 4,000 engineers, of which only 175 had engineering degrees. But architects were being recognized and encouraged to specialize. Their early experience was working directly with local craftsmen, builders, and interested community members. Most had not yet reached the level of professionalism that would allow them to execute complex designs to be followed by engineers and workers. Several times during the nineteenth century, architects tried to organize into groups to protect and further their professional interests. In 1837, the American Institution of Architects drew up its constitution, but the organization never prospered. It was followed in 1857 by the American Institute of Architects, dedicated to discussing all "branches of the Arts and Sciences" related to architecture. The first American professional architectural magazine, *The American Architect and Building News,* did not appear until 1876.

American architecture of the 1860s and 1870s took traditional designs and techniques as its point of departure but modified them in response to changing public tastes and the introduction of new building materials and techniques. Educated critics of architecture saw little of lasting beauty or quality in the new styles, especially as applied to mass-produced, middle-class housing. In such housing, some observers detected a lack of individuality in the American character.[3] To Ada Louise Huxtable, a conservative architectural critic, such popular architecture represented "the tastelessness of a new middle class society that accepted substitute gimcrackery for materials and ideas."

## PRIVATE HOMES

The early American house, like most other aspects of American life, was strongly influenced by the environments from which the settlers had come. The English influence was obvious in many early homes, while German, Dutch, and other influences were evident to a lesser extent in some areas. Even the log house—long a symbol of the American pioneer and a political icon—was of Scandinavian origin. Early American houses east of the Appalachians tended to be two stories tall and one room deep, with a central hallway and stairs separating the one or two rooms on each wing of the house. Kitchens and other rooms were added as the need for extra space grew.

In cities and towns, houses were often built directly on the street, with no front yard, and row houses—residences built with connecting side walls—were favored to conserve land. By the beginning of the Civil War, housing design was undergoing changes. In the more spacious new suburban communities that began to spring up around the cities, individual family houses were sited farther back from the street, providing more privacy and a front yard that allowed an open vista and a greensward. Large front porches became prominent architectural features.

Building plans for houses of all styles were readily available in the popular literature of the day. Magazines like *Harper's Monthly, Harper's Bazaar,* and *Scribner's Monthly* published guides for building, furnishing, and maintaining houses. *Godey's Lady's Book,* between 1846 and 1892, published 450 house designs. Several magazines founded in the 1860s, including *The*

*American Builder and Architectural Review* and *American Builder's Journal,* were directed at the builder and carpenter.

House pattern books, featuring plans ranging from simple cottages to elaborate villas, were available by the score by the late 1860s. "There never was a time when so many books written for the purpose of bringing the subject of architecture—its history, its theory, its practice—down to the level of popular understanding were produced as in this time of ours," wrote a prominent art critic in the 1870s, reflecting the outpouring of comments on housing and architecture during the Reconstruction. The postwar suburban ideal, the most popular of these books were Andrew Jackson Downing's *Cottage Residences* and *The Architecture of Country Homes* and Gervase Wheeler's *Rural Homes.* Although the authors of some of these books were trained engineers or architects, others were builders or carpenters of mediocre ability, who simply grafted whatever decorative elements were currently in vogue onto stock structures. Many of these books served as little more than suggestions for local builders to adapt and copy to the best of their ability, but the Palliser Company, publisher of *New Cottage Homes and Details,* sold complete sets of architectural plans for a nominal fee.

The widespread adoption of balloon-frame construction helped to reduce housing prices. The so-called balloon frame had originated in Chicago in the 1830s and quickly gained popularity in the Midwest, but it became popular nationally only after the war. It substituted inexpensive, lightweight nailed wooden frames and panels for the more substantial, handpegged timber, brick, or masonry construction used in higher-quality houses. The plans and precut materials for balloon-fame houses were often packaged and sold by mail-order houses and lumberyards and delivered unassembled to the owner's lot for substantially less than the cost of a finished home. Once the foundation was laid, construction of these homes required little more than basic carpentry skills and the ability to read a printed plan. One Chicago-based mail-order company offered plans and materials for a three-bedroom house for $350.

Though there are no reliable figures available as to the percentage of people who owned their own homes before the 1880s, we can estimate that during the 1860s and 1870s the figure may well have been as high as 50 percent. Private dwellings varied widely in style of architecture and number of rooms, from a modest five-room cottage that could be bought (excluding the land) for $250 to large two-story houses for the affluent for $10,000. The average white-collar house cost no more than $5,000. Families earning $2,500 to $8,000 per year were willing to commit themselves to $4,000 for the house of their dreams.

Houses reflected the hopes and accomplishments of their inhabitants. "There is no country in the world where there are so many large and fine houses, in proportion to the number of inhabitants, as in these United States," said a native booster in 1865, adding "We build our houses mainly for the purpose of being looked on." But everybody wanted and needed a house. During the nineteenth century, some 70 percent of the population boarded at some time in their lives. Many others lived in row houses and dingy apartments. In the boardinghouses, most singles lived in one room with scant furnishings and ate at a common table, with monthly room and board costing $50 to $100. Such existence was looked upon as merely tolerable at best and everybody looked forward to the time when he or she could live in a private residence.

Domestic American Victorian architecture was a hodgepodge of styles borrowed from ancient civilizations and exotic locales. Its derivative nature is reflected by the names of the popular architectural styles of the day, including Gothic Revival, Romanesque, Renaissance, and Second Empire, among many others. One distinctly American element was the addition of "gingerbread," the fancy wooden scrollwork that adorned the exteriors of many Victorian homes. Exterior colors tended to be dark, often with brightly contrasting trim.

The average private residence of the 1860s and 1870s consisted of from three to eight rooms. Larger homes boasted two parlors, one for show (kept nicely furnished but unused except for formal occasions) and the other to be used as a living-dining room. Bedrooms and bathrooms were thought to be private and usually were situated on the second floor.

Farmhouses generally were built of readily available local materials and were often more conservatively and traditionally designed than their urban counterparts. Brick and sawn lumber were the favored building materials, although native rock was more commonly used in the hilly regions, where it was plentiful. Farmhouses varied tremendously in size and quality. Many were commodious, six-to-eight-room structures, but others were much more modest. In the South especially, rural homes were often little more than one- or two-room cabins. In the most isolated regions, particularly the Appalachians, homes were still crudely built of logs, chinked with mud and sometimes covered with bark shingles. On the treeless prairies, many early settlers constructed their houses of sod, the only readily available building material. The sod house had many variations and levels of ingenuity, ranging from simple roofed pits hollowed out of embankments to ambitious attempts at replicating traditional, free-standing farmhouses. These residences could be comfortable or miserable, depending on the nature of the material used in construction and the degree of protection offered against inclement weather. The floors were usually packed bare earth, and the walls and roof were living sod. The average sod house required an acre of sod for construction, weighing some ninety tons. Sod houses were at the mercy of the weather, leaky in wet weather, dusty in dry. Because the sod continued to grow and provided some warmth in the winter, the walls very often became home for prairie animals and insects. Although most sod structures were intended as temporary residences, photographs of the period show that at least some owners made improvements to their earthen homes with the addition of glass windows, whitewashed interior walls, stoves, and other amenities. As more settlers moved westward, the sod house gave way to wooden-framed structures adapted to the often harsh climate of the Great Plains. Two stories were lowered to one, and the central-hall plan was modified and expanded to two rooms deep. With ample land available, these houses tended to be more spacious than those in the cramped Eastern cities.

Carpeting was the favored floor covering for those who could afford it. Mass-produced floor covering took a leap forward with the development of linoleum in England by Frederick Walton. Walton experimented with a mixture of oxidized linseed oil, ground cork dust, rosin, gum, and pigments. The gummy mixture was pressed between heavy rollers and then further processed by grinding and mixing with other ingredients. The result was a durable, hard-surface flooring material that could be embossed or given other decorative treatments. In 1872, Walton emigrated to New York and, with Joseph Wild, established the American Linoleum Manufacturing Company. He named his company town on Staten Island "Linoleumville."

Wallpaper had been in use since the sixteenth century, but it remained an expensive luxury until the coming of the Industrial Revolution in the early nineteenth century. With the introduction of mass production and high-speed printing, the price of decorative wallpaper fell to the point that the middle class could easily afford it. Frederick Walton invented another popular wall covering, which he called Lincrusta-Walton. It was essentially linoleum to be hung on the wall, and it was said to be suitable for virtually every use, including friezes, wainscoting, borders, splash screens, and decorative panels. Like Walton's linoleum floor covering, it could be manufactured in any color, although dark tones were the favorite, and it could be patterned to imitate marble and other surfaces. Not surprisingly, such products were severely criticized by the art world.

## PUBLIC BUILDINGS

In its public structures, the United States wanted to be first to build in a democratic motif. By 1800, two distinct styles of architecture dominated public buildings in the United States. One was the modified British style favored in the New England and Middle Atlantic states. The other, more widely disseminated and enduringly popular, was heavily influenced by Thomas Jefferson's classical ideals. The modified British style was promoted by Charles Bulfinch, a Harvard graduate who spent two years touring Great Britain and Europe. There, he was influenced by the brothers John

Adams and John Wood Adams, two leading architects of the period. The influence of Jefferson's more popular neoclassical architectural philosophy is readily apparent in many federal buildings constructed after 1790, especially in public structures throughout the South. Reflecting Jefferson's political philosophy, these buildings were designed in the style of ancient Greece and Rome. Jefferson thought of those periods as providing models most appropriate for a nation that had shaken off its close relationship with Europe and wanted a style more fitting for the promise of a great new nation. His philosophy was carried on by Benjamin Latrobe (1764–1820), who was, in his own words, a "bigoted Greek" in his architectural preferences.

By the end of the Civil War, much of the public had become dissatisfied with both of these traditions. In trying to achieve a distinct American style of architecture after the war, architects designed buildings to reflect geographic uniqueness, freedom of expression, an expanding society, and individual freedom and strength. Architects and building owners spoke of buildings that embodied character, truth, and reality, which they perceived as the basic tenets of American society.

John Ruskin's books *The Seven Lamps of Architecture* (1849) and *The Stones of Venice* (1851–1853) served as important guides for postwar American architects. American architecture of the 1860s and 1870s is generally classified as High Victorian, of which there were many variations, including Gothic, Italianate, and Second Empire. These styles might be called a spiritual up-reach and flexing of muscle. Buildings in these styles tended to be tall. Exterior walls were heavily textured and sometimes integrated unusual color schemes or mixed stone of several colors to achieve the overall desired shades, an important concept for Ruskin.

High Victorian Gothic reached back in history to what were considered strengths in spirituality and subsequently incorporated features of English and Continental medievalism, some of Ruskin's fundamental principles. The massiveness and strength of the stone in these buildings was emphasized by tall, narrow windows set back from the plane of the wall. Doors, windows, and other openings were outlined by overriding arches. A typical characteristic was the soaring tower or turret.

Coexisting with High Victorian Gothic, High Victorian Italianate was characterized by three distinct features: (1) the straight-sided arch, with the arch itself originating from a point some distance above the capital or other important feature; (2) the flat-topped arch, which reverses the relative positions of the straight lines and curves; and (3) the rectangular arch, produced by bending an arched molding around the upper third of a rectangular opening. The resulting buildings tended to be squarer than those in the Gothic style and were sometimes flat-roofed, with a less pronounced thrust toward the sky. According to one English critic, the Italianate style "distorted convention, crashed through the rules of taste, was 'self-made'; it gave an impression of structural frankness, assigning to the ornamental attributes of architecture a subsidiary, merely pretty role." It was, in short, what art historian Marcus Whiffen calls "thoroughly democratic (in the special American sense)."

The Second Empire style could best be described as cluttered and over-done. High mansard roofs reached for the sky, dormer windows punctu-ated the roofline, and bracketed eves dipped at crazy angles. Chimneys became elaborate architectural statements, and pillars and columns ap-peared in every conceivable form and location, whether to actually sup-port something or simply to be decorative. The Second Empire monuments that remain today are highly prized as marvels of eclectic taste. One is the Corcoran Gallery (now renamed the Renwick Building) in Washington, D.C. , designed by James Renwick in 1859. Another is the Executive Office Building (originally the State, War, and Navy Building), standing just be-hind the White House, presumably designed by Alfred B. Mullett during Ulysses S. Grant's administration. Also notable is the Philadelphia City Hall (1874–1881), in its time the largest building in the United States and still an architectural marvel.

"Stick" style buildings show a Swiss influence, but the style is thought to be one of the two truly American styles of the nineteenth century. Being a "natural" form of construction with its vertical use of wood, it adhered closely to the ideal of "truthfulness" that recurred in American architecture of this period. The stick style was not suited to large buildings and so is seen most often in churches and private homes.

## COMMERCIAL BUILDINGS

In the 1860s, commercial buildings of all sorts, especially offices and re-tail stores, began to feel the squeeze of cramped quarters. Department stores had grown out of smaller, specialized retail shops in response to customers' demand for one-stop shopping. Retailers like A. T. Stewart, Lord & Taylor, Arnold Constable, and R. H. Macy in New York City; John Wanamaker in Philadelphia; and Jordan Marsh in Boston responded by constructing sprawling stores to meet all of the customers' needs under one roof.

One of the pioneers in this concentrated expansion was Alexander Turney Stewart, who in 1846, following a successful career selling Irish laces, ex-panded his business to a series of shops called the Marble Dry-Goods Palace that covered an entire block on Broadway in New York City. When his busi-ness outgrew those premises in 1859, Stewart commissioned a new five-story structure on a twenty-acre site. Completed in 1862, Stewart's Cast Iron Palace utilized a newly developed building system. The structural skeletons of these new buildings were load-bearing iron beams, the great strength of which al-lowed wider areas to be spanned than had been possible with wood-beam construction. All weight was carried by the iron skeleton, and facades were covered with relatively light-weight sheets of decorative cast iron rather than the heavy brick or masonry used in earlier structures. Because the cast iron facades were not load-bearing, designers were free to utilize larger window openings, opening up the exterior walls and allowing interiors to be flooded with natural light. So promising was the strength of this new construction method that James Bogardus, one of its greatest exponents, claimed he could build an edifice extending ten miles into the sky.

While iron was revolutionizing building design, stamped sheet metal was being adapted for decorative interior use. Metal beaten into sheets and employed for architectural and ornamental purposes is a craft known from ancient times, but only after the war did changing public taste and advances in automation allow the decorative sheet metal industry to grow by leaps and bounds. At the 1876 Centennial Exposition in Philadelphia, the sheet metal pavilion raised by the Kittredge Cornice and Ornament Company of Salem, Ohio, proved to be a major attraction. It was touted as a "practical illustration of the adaptability of sheet metals to architectural and general building purposes."[4] Although criticized for their lack of "naturalness" and artistry, pressed-metal ceilings, which were largely fireproof, came to grace many public and commercial buildings, although their use in private residences was limited. They remained popular through the end of the nineteenth century.

The greater height possible in iron buildings made the elevator a necessity. The elevator was not new; a power-operated lift had been used as early as 1835, but it was hoisted by ropes that sometimes broke. In 1851, Elisha Graves Otis invented the safety brake, a ratchet device that would engage lugs on the wall of the elevator shaft in the event of a fall. Realizing that the elevator should operate on an independent source of power, Otis invented a steam-engine drive system in 1855. The Otis elevator, with its many subsequent improvements, provided the lift that would make high-rise buildings a practicality.

With the development of new construction techniques, commercial buildings began to reach ever higher. By the end of the war, many companies, especially in New York City, were feeling squeezed for office space. The obvious answer, given the new technology, was to go up. The first corporation to construct a high-rise office was the Equitable Life Assurance Society of the U.S. In 1864, its directors began to expand the offices, but not until 1867 did they settle on a consolidated location in New York City. When completed, the new Equitable Life Building stood seven or eight stories tall (depending on how one counted the floors) and was served by two elevators. The elevator shafts, rising 130 feet, were the highest in the world. Constructed by Otis Tufts, who had played a major role in the development of the elevator, these lifts were spacious enough to contain seats and were said to be the "largest, most complete and comfortable ever constructed ... in constant but noiseless motion. Rendering the grand stairway of the building almost an ornamental superfluity." From this promising beginning, high rises began to appear all over New York City and other metropolitan areas.

## FAMILY HOUSING

Essentially American house styles east of the mountains tended to be two-story, I-design, that is one room deep, with a hallway separating the one or two rooms on each wing of the house. As need for more space grew, a kitchen and other needed rooms began to lengthen one side of the house. The resulting rise upwards into a two-story frame building was useful both as an economy measure—to conserve heat—and to cut down on the use of building materials.

As settlers moved west, these house plans were kept in mind though they had to be modified. Two stories were lowered to one, with the I-frame modified to be two rooms deep with kitchens running down one side. Outhouses were supplied where needed, especially the small building housing the toilet facilities. Throughout these country and small-town houses, residents generally had sufficient living space, either inside the house or on the outside.

In the cities, increasingly, residents were cramped by lack of space. The individual house itself could be of vastly varying proportions and appearances. The majority of people still lived in residences ranging from modest to hovels. In cities, most working people and those newly arrived lived in single rooms in boarding houses. Sometimes they ate their meals with the person running the boarding house. Otherwise they had to provide for themselves in their rooms or in the various other eating establishments available, serving greasy, unsanitary, and tasteless food for modest charges. These boarding houses, and low-rise apartment buildings, usually up to four stories in height, had no elevators, low visibility because of the nearness of other low-rises, small and dirty windows, and poor heating and insufficient ventilation. People froze in winter and burned in summer. The poor had been living in cheap tenements for at least a decade. Most were two-story, with the family, typically consisting of five members, living in four rooms, lacking water and gas, with no means of ridding themselves of garbage other than piling it in the streets. Stretched out in working-class slum neighborhoods, these buildings extended for blocks. The newly developing apartment houses were becoming an eyesore to the well-off, as well as to those who had to live in them. Usually occupied by up to a hundred people, they were shoddily constructed and uncomfortable. These postwar houses were looked upon as the breeding ground for crime, sexual promiscuity, and general ugliness.

The poor who were fortunate enough to have individual dwellings usually lived in wooden frame houses built by the local carpenter in the tradition of those around him, in the traditional I-frame with a central hall running between the two sides and rooms on either side.

Houses of the more affluent citizens were of mainly wooden or brick construction, often having the plans drawn up by skilled folk architects who based their plans on the experience they had from building other houses.

In the absence of trained architects many other buildings were designed by civil engineers. In 1870, there were 4,000 engineers but only 175 had engineering degrees. But architects were being recognized and encouraged to specialize. Their early experience was working with craftsmen and local workers.

## THE BUILDING WALLS

For the walls of houses, cement had been used since the Greeks and Romans and was considered a splendid building material. Throughout the eighteenth century and the first half of the nineteenth, cement as a building material was the favorite of the British. In 1871, David O. Saylor, in Lehigh, Pennsylvania, opened the first Portland cement company in the United States. This Portland cement, fired at a very high temperature and therefore a hardy building material, eventually developed into the concrete block, which is still used today. At first cast in varying sizes, eventually the concrete block was standardized in the eight-by-eight-by-sixteen-inch size.

Though the standard block color was light gray, it could be shaded to practically any color desired. Originally designed with a flat surface, it soon developed into various surfaces and came to serve the Reconstruction period well as an economical building material.

Several times during the nineteenth century, architects had tried to organize into groups to further their profession and to protect their interests. In 1837, the American Institution of Architects, among several, drew up its constitution. But the organization never prospered. In 1857, it was followed by the American Institute of Architects, dedicated to discussing all "branches of the Arts and Sciences" related to architecture. This humanistic approach, though seemingly all-inclusive, was narrow and sufficiently focused to insure success.

Just as one is known by the clothes he or she wears, one is also known by the residence with which he or she is identified. This was especially true of the Reconstruction period, which Mark Twain (and C. D. Warner) in their book *The Gilded Age* (1873) properly saw as being an age of glitz and pretense. In many ways, for the rich and powerful, or the strong and lucky, it was a time for people to distinguish themselves, even if at the same time they despised the life style they aspired to. Mark Twain is a good example. He grew up in Hannibal, Missouri, a witness to the poverty of people resembling his fictional characters Huckleberry Finn and the slave Jim. Twain traipsed around the world desperate for success but never sure that he had achieved it and not comfortable in his accomplishments. Little wonder then, like most successes of his day, as soon as he could raise the cash to show off his personality he built a nineteen-room house at Nook Farm, near Hartford, Connecticut, with all the rooms cluttered with every gewgaw imaginable. The mansion was shaped roughly like a Mississippi steamboat, and Twain's favorite room was the pilot's house. The Reconstruction period could tolerate and support such outward displays of gild, and where possible people felt compelled to spread it on.

# 5

# Clothing and Fashion

Because clothes of any people generally are an extension of them and their customs, the wardrobe worn by Americans has always reflected their culture. In antebellum America, clothing had been fashioned for individuals, was hand-sewn and expensive to produce, and clearly identified the classes. The poor sometimes wore clothes handed down from the wealthy, however, blurring class lines. In 1840, for example, the British Consul in Boston complained of what he perceived as America's equality in clothing, especially the fact that servant girls were "scarcely to be distinguished from their employers."

With the invention of the sewing machine, clothing and fashion became more democratized. Efforts to build mechanical stitching machines to replace women's fingers had long been under way. In 1830, a French tailor, Barthelemy Thimmonier, had invented a rudimentary sewing machine. Several years later, Walter Hunt developed another a sewing machine, although it apparently was neither workable nor salable. The first practical sewing machine, using dual threads and an under-thread shuttle, was finally developed by Elias Howe in 1845 and patented the following year. Howe's invention sparked a great sewing machine war. Isaac Singer, an inventor of some repute who also had a flair for showmanship, added a few improvements to Howe's basic machine and consequently declared himself the inventor of the improved sewing machine. He refused to pay Howe royalties, and Howe and Singer struggled in the courts for three years. Howe was finally declared the exclusive owner of the sewing machine patent, and Singer was ordered to pay royalties. Howe was awarded $15,000 from Singer and received a royalty for every machine made in the United States. Other manufacturers of sewing machines soon joined the competition, precipitating further legal wrangling. To settle the disputes, the Great Sewing Machine Combination, which merged the two, was formed in 1856. Though Howe prospered, Singer by 1879 could boast that three-quarters of the sewing machines made in the United States—and there were well over 700,000 by that time—were his.

The proliferation of improved machines had effects throughout society. Advertised as being ten times as fast as the human hand, the sewing machine was hailed by many as a great labor-saving device for women. *Godey's Lady's Book* heaped praise upon the sewing machine in 1860: "What philanthropy failed to accomplish, what religion, poetry, eloquence, and reason sought in vain, has been produced by—The Sewing Machine." The sewing machine did not necessarily reduce women's workloads, however. Two years later, the *Atlantic Monthly* asked the penetrating question, "Where is the woman who can say that her sewing is less a tax upon her time and strength than it was before the sewing machine came in?" The author claimed that the machine, instead of satisfying a basic need, had in fact created a growing demand for more complicated clothing. "As soon as lovely woman discovers that her sewing machine can set ten stitches in the time that one used to require, a fury seizes her to put ten times as many stitches in every garment as she used to." The widespread acceptance of the sewing machine allowed the fashion industry to expand quickly. The sewing machine led the way in revolutionizing American clothing—all kinds of new undergarments were developed, for example, and the home seamstress could now copy the creations of the best London and Paris fashion houses. Hemmers, binders, tuckers, rufflers, puffers, braiders, and others machine attachments were invented to satisfy the desire for new styles.

Further contributing to the revolution in American clothing was the emergence of the paper-pattern industry. By the 1850s, patterns for stylish and up-to-date clothing were printed as tissue-paper inserts in *Godey's Lady's Book* and other popular women's magazines. Quick to spot an emerging trend, Ebenezer Butterick, James McCall, and others expanded the paper pattern industry, copying the latest fashions from Europe. By the early 1860s, a thriving market had developed for the paper patterns, which were printed in graduated sizes and included explicit sewing instructions.

Together, the sewing machine and the paper pattern industry made fashionable dress accessible to households of only modest means and gave rise to the first fashion publications. In 1860, the husband-and-wife team of Madame Ellen Louise Demorest and William Jennings Demorest began publishing *Madame Demorest's Quarterly Mirror of Fashions*, and they later inserted specially printed fashion sections in the *New York Illustrated News*. Ebenezer Butterick followed in 1867 with his *Ladies Report of New York Fashions*. By the end of Reconstruction, the paper pattern industry was so well established that the 1876 Centennial Exposition in Philadelphia boasted two pavilions of dress patterns, one by Butterick and one by the Demorests.

Following the war, an emerging middle class demanded more ready-made clothing, and manufacturers developed the machinery and factories to provide it. With the coming of mass clothing production, and the resumption of cotton shipments from the South, inexpensive clothes could be produced that, except for differences in the quality of material and workmanship, were difficult to distinguish from more expensive garments. By the 1870s, all but the poorest or most isolated families purchased at least some commercially mass-produced clothing, the popularity of which was hastened by development of chain and department stores. Mail-order catalogs brought ready-made clothing and an awareness of fashion to even remote corners of the nation. The result was a surprising degree of standardization in American dress during the 1870s. "The uniformity of dress is characteristic of the people of the United States," *Harper's Bazaar* reported. "The man of leisure and the laborer, the mistress and the maid, wear clothes of the same material and cut."[1]

## MEN'S CLOTHING

Men's business dress, usually of wool, tended to be loosely cut, with detachable starched cuffs and collars lending a more formal look. The plain white shirt, the business uniform of the 1860s, gave way in the 1870s to colors and stripes, and neckwear became increasingly garish as the nineteenth century progressed. Top hats of silk, beaver, or other exotic materials remained popular with the professional classes, but new styles such as bowlers and derbies also met with increasing favor. Straw hats were popular in summer. Facial hair, particularly moustaches and mutton-chop sideburns, was considered stylish, and in some quarters the clean-shaven face was considered effeminate. For the professional, a trip to the barbershop was a weekly ritual.

Laborers wore plain, rugged work clothes of canvas, denim, and other coarse fabrics. Levi Strauss's copper-riveted denim trousers were the choice of Western miners and laborers. Originally offered only in brown, by 1870 they were dyed a deep indigo, the beginning of the uniquely American blue jean. On ranches in the American West, work clothing was heavily influenced by the functional attire of the *vaquero*, or Mexican cowboy.

The urban footwear of choice was the leather-soled high-top shoe, fastened with either the traditional button or the newly introduced shoelace. Sport shoes with rubber soles and fabric tops were considered fashionable for lawn games such as croquet or tennis. Laborers and farmers wore heavy-soled boots, sometimes studding the smooth soles with hobnails for better traction.

## WOMEN'S FASHIONS AND ACCESSORIES

Women's fashion in mid-nineteenth-century America reflected society's attitude toward the place of women in society and the male attitude toward sex. It was a picture of restraint of the female form, reflecting the ambivalent attitude of men and women toward sex. The small waist emphasized the female bosom and invited sexual titillation, while at the same time the full-length skirt discouraged physical closeness and intimacy. Rural women in their daily wear were less concerned with fashion. They favored unadorned floor-length skirts of gingham, calico, or other durable cloth, and few owned extensive wardrobes.

To the fashion-conscious of the era, the ideal female body silhouette was the hourglass. Tales of dubious origin circulated of women having lower ribs removed and toes amputated to better squeeze into tight bodices and shoes. Skirts ballooned outward—sometimes dangerously so—supported by hoops, bustles, and heavy crinoline petticoats of linen and horsehair. Newspapers reported tragic fires caused when the cumbersome wide dresses brushed against stoves and fireplaces, and the public complained that the wide dresses obstructed traffic in crowded places. By the late 1860s, the crinoline petticoat fad was subsiding in favor of the bustle, a wired petticoat that swept the dress outward only in the rear, emphasizing the bustline and buttocks and allowing more passing room on the sides. Women's undergarments were often quite elaborate. Brightly colored and patterned chemises, petticoats, and long drawers were in vogue, leading one fashion magazine in 1876 to declare, "Underclothing has reached a luxury unknown in any age."

The voluminous skirt was always the subject of jokes because of its impracticality. *Frank Leslie's Illustrated Newspaper* (May 21, 1864), for example, ran a cartoon titled "Cause and Effect" in which a housemaid is upsetting all the furniture around her with her flaring skirt. The caption reads: "Drat the bothering China cups and things. They be always a-knocking up against one's Crinoline." The cartoon is a cut at female fashions as well as at Irish domestics aping the fashions of their betters.

Women's headgear was no less fancy. Well-dressed women were expected to wear large, heavy hats. Head covers of all kinds were constantly lampooned for their pretentiousness and impracticality. *Frank Leslie's Illustrated Newspaper* (February 4, 1865), for example, in a cartoon titled "Scene at a Fashionable Perfumer's Store on Broadway," shows a well-dressed young lady in a store letting a medical doctor examine something she is going to buy: "Lady—'Now, I appeal to you, Doctor, is it not pretty?' Doctor—'Ah, yes—dumb bells, very good—especially for the chest.' Lady (indignantly)—'Dumb bells! No 'tis a pretty hair ornament.'" Other cartoons pointed out how large hats blocked all forward vision, especially at the theater, and therefore should be outlawed at least in such places of entertainment.

*Harper's New Monthly Magazine* ran a fashion page in each issue. *Frank Leslie's Illustrated Newspaper,* in one of its many cartoons, is criticizing both the female fashion of the day (left) and the Irish housemaid (right). The caption reads: Housemaid—"Drat the bothering China cups and things. They be always a-knocking up against one's Crinoline."

Women's hair was worn long, and ways to manage it had to be devised. One such device was the waterfall, popular as early as 1845, which consisted of a mass of internal material called a "rat" that was covered with hair and worn at the back of the neck. It looked vaguely like a small waterfall, and the longer and fuller it hung down the neck, the more beautiful it was thought to be. The waterfall hairdo spawned so much derision that *Harper's Weekly* on a single day (July 1, 1865) carried two waterfall cartoons on the same page. In one a chic young lady with a hairdo bulging on her shoulders like a heavy pack reassures another woman that all is safe: "Heavens, Jemima! What makes you look so frightened?" "Oh, don't be alarmed, Ophelia. It's only my Waterfall. It has to be so large now to be in fashion that it is actually pulling my eyebrows over to the back of my head." In the other cartoon, one man rushes up and accosts a young lady. He has a large bag of hair in his hand and says to the girl: "Excuse me, Miss; but you have dropped your Waterfall." This hairdo was scorned in numerous popular songs as well. One minstrel show song asserts that when the singer got rich, he aims to buy his girlfriend a waterfall so that she can be respectable. However, the waterfall was often associated with women of questionable character. "The Girl with the Waterfall" tells of a naive young man who is ogled by a pretty woman wearing a waterfall. When he follows her into her house, apparently at her invitation, he is beaten up and robbed by a bruiser, apparently her companion. Having learned his lesson, he declares he will "never hence go near a girl that wears a waterfall."

Crafty entrepreneurs devised numerous other devices used by women to beautify and restrain their hair. By the 1870s, the waterfall was considered old-fashioned and had given way to coiffures that piled the hair high on the head. Dyed hair came into vogue, the most popular tones being Titian red and Venetian blond. Makeup also began to gain limited acceptance among the general populace, although its excessive use was still associated with "loose" women and prostitutes.

The general public offered surprisingly little resistance to the fashion excesses of the day, even when those excesses endangered safety or health. Doctors for years had advised against the heavy clothing, insisting that the great weight of hoops, bustles, petticoats, and heavy skirts hanging from the waist deformed the human body, while tight corsets and bodices presented a real health hazard by restricting breathing capacity and cramping the internal organs. Yet even women designers of underwear aided and abetted these fashions. Madame Caplin, a prolific designer of women's clothes, created twenty-three corsets to accommodate girls from the early teens on. The dangers such garments presented didn't go unnoticed in the press. In July 1861, Helen C. Lewis published an article titled "Crooked Spines in Girls" in *Arthur's Home Magazine* that blamed the tight lacing of corset for scoliosis in teenage girls.

The Dress Reform Movement of the 1850s had attempted, with little success, to address the problem of such unhealthy and impractical clothing. Focusing on health rather than esthetics, a small but vocal group of American reformers protested the tight corsets and bodices, unwieldy bustles and petticoats, and dragging trains of long dresses that collected debris from filthy streets. One such protester, Amelia Bloomer, publisher of the temperance magazine *The Lily*, introduced a women's outfit consisting of a knee-length skirt worn over baggy, Turkish-style trousers. Despite their comfort and practicality, "Bloomers" were widely condemned and ridiculed. The editor of the prestigious *New York Times* railed against the new outfit, "There is an obvious tendency to encroach upon masculine manners manifested ever in trifles, which cannot be too severely rebuked or too speedily repressed." Songs like "The Bloomer Gallopade" pointed out the perceived absurdity of such attire, while "The Bloomer Costume" (1851) lambasted women who took on masculine mannerisms, in so doing abandoning their proper role:

The women then would strut about,

Nor once consult our wishes;

While we at home would have to stay

And wash the greasy dishes!

Or darn the stocking, patch and cook,

Else in canal they'd souse us—

Oh! Devil take the one, who, first

Invented Turkish trousers.[2]

Faced with such stiff resistance, Bloomers failed to gain much acceptance until the end of the nineteenth century, when they enjoyed a brief vogue as a bicycling and gymnastics outfit.

Fashions to a certain extent began to be influenced by new discoveries in medical science after the war. The public gradually became aware of body fat. Women giving up the corset found they had to resort to diet and exercise to attain a naturally slim waist. But the 1860s and 1870s were generally a period when rotundity for men and women alike was considered acceptable and, in some circles, a mark of prosperity and good health. The Fat Man's Club, an exclusive club that heartily approved of the obese, was founded in 1866. Harriet Beecher Stowe liked the full figure, and Elizabeth Cady Stanton was praised for her plumpness because it supposedly showed matronly qualities. Actresses were supposed to be voluptuous; the great actress Lillie Langtry, although considered beautiful, was sometimes criticized for being lanky. But awareness of the heath problems of obesity began to appear. The first doctor's scale was developed in 1865, and weight records began to be kept in 1874. The caloric content of food was understood by the late 1860s, and medical manuals of the 1870s began to discuss the nutrition.

## MILITARY CLOTHING

The Civil War created demand for large amounts of clothing for the troops. The standard uniform of the U.S. Army before the war had been a dark blue wool jacket that extended to the mid-thigh and a pair of sky blue wool pants with a colored stripe alongside the outside of each leg. When the Civil War began, however, the supply of uniforms could not keep up with the sudden demand, so both Union and Confederate forces were uniformed in a wide variety of styles, colors, and fashions. Volunteer and militia regiments often adopted their own distinctive, even eccentric, uniforms. Especially popular among Union volunteer units was the Zouave uniform of the French army in North Africa, consisting of a dark blue jacket, baggy Turkish-style pants held up with a red sash, white leggings, and a red fez. Ethic origins were reflected in some units' uniforms. The 39th New York Infantry Regiment (Garibaldi Guard) wore a uniform that was modeled on the sharpshooters of the Italian Bersaglieri Light Infantry, while the 79th New York Infantry Regiment (Highlanders) wore Scottish kilts for a time. Such uniforms soon proved to be highly impractical in combat conditions and often made it difficult to distinguish friend from foe on the battlefield. By 1862 some standardization was evident in Union uniforms, and by 1863 a standard Union uniform, almost identical to the prewar uniform, was mandated throughout the Union army. The exception was headgear, which remained largely a regimental decision.

Distinctive uniforms were also popular with the Confederate troops. The Confederate army attempted to establish a standard uniform, modeled closely on the standard Union uniform. Confederate uniforms were to be gray rather than blue, but because of material shortages, uniforms were also produced in a range of colors. The so-called butternut uniform was sewn from homespun cloth dyed a brownish hue with oil from butternut or walnut trees. As shortages worsened in the South, Confederate soldiers were forced to piece together nonstandard uniforms from any available source, including clothing taken from the Union and Confederate dead.

In fashion, as in so many other aspects of life, the Reconstruction had changed people's tastes and habits. Gone were the restrictions of the earlier period and come were the pleasures of the freedom the new clothes permitted. Fashions, always dictated by French styles, were now reflecting more sharply the differences between the several social and financial levels. In so doing, they were generating certain animosities in the social strata and, as a kind of unintended backlash among the several levels of society, they were promoting democracy in the new United States. Recognizing that one is recreated by his/her fashions, many people reached out and brought back to their attire the new fashions and the new personalities.

# 6
# Food

The large size of the land and the scarcity of people seemed to drive most Americans at the middle of the nineteenth century into being hospitable. Separated by considerable distances and lacking in human contact, they generally welcomed people, known and strangers, into their homes. By and large their hospitality was not abused, although treatment of strangers and uninvited guests varied from North to South. In the more isolated areas of the northern states, travelers and strangers were usually taken in at nightfall and provided with food and a bed for the night, or even for longer periods, at no cost. The feeling was that visitors needed lodging and should receive it freely. Visitors were prized for establishing contact with the outside world.

An excellent case in point is John Chapman (1774–1845), one of the frontier's most famous and lasting heroes. Folklore is the creation of society's needs and wishes. Such was Chapman, lovingly called "Johnny Appleseed" during his life, the War and Reconstruction years, and even to our day. Johnny, a Swendenborgian mystic, took upon himself the task of spreading religious mysticism, apple seedlings, and literacy throughout the frontier. He established apple nurseries in Pennsylvania and Fort Wayne, Indiana, and spent his time walking from one farm house to another, leaving apple plants and reading material, which he would later pick up and move on to the next reader. Johnny's visits were always eagerly anticipated and he was always welcome.

In the rural South, where towns were few and far between, some Southerners saw no lack of hospitality in charging uninvited guests a dollar for supper, bed, breakfast, and care of the guest's horse. The more aristocratic plantation owners often provided these services free of charge, especially to obvious gentlemen and ladies. But they also welcomed everyday strangers, peddlers, and others and milked them dry of gossip and news. The examples provided by Mark Twain in *The Adventures of Tom Sawyer* and *The Adventures of Huckleberry Finn* reveal how rural Southerners were eager to see and host strangers, and the strangers were eager to fleece them. The same was not true in the mountains and backwoods, where settlers were more cautious, and sometimes even hostile, in dealing with people they did not know. Sometimes they greeted the uninvited and unwelcome stranger with a pointed gun.

The situation in the rural areas was in marked contrast to that of the major metropolitan areas, where the traveler was confronted with an overwhelming array of choices in food and lodging. For the affluent traveler, luxurious hotels offered all the comforts of home. Boarding houses and rented rooms sufficed for the average person. In New York, the Delmonico family's chain of restaurants set the standard for fine dining, hosting such famous personages as Mark Twain. Delmonico's set a ground-breaking precedent in 1868, when they gave their stamp of approval to women dining unaccompanied by men. On the other side of the continent, the proliferation of fine hotels and restaurants in San Francisco led one visitor to remark, "What ever other ingredients may enter into merry-making, it is obvious that love and gluttony come first."[1]

Stomachs of those who had the means to pay benefited from the war. During the 1830s and 1840s, the American and European diet was mainly meat and cereal. It was generally agreed that vegetables were harmful to one's health. Meat and bread and fruits were healthful and satisfactory. But forces promoting the eating of vegetables were developing. Just before the war, farmers, who knew fruits and vegetables were not dangerous, began delivering them into towns and cities and selling them on the streets and in chain stores and markets. Development of the refrigerated railroad car in the 1840s opened new sources and markets, and people began to observe the nutritive effect of fresh vegetables.

At first the new menu went to the well-to-do, who made something of a fetish of it, with the growth of refrigerated cars. As more foods became available it became fashionable to eat hearty and to serve conspicuously. Two or more soups, the same number of meats, several vegetables, various desserts, and numerous wines were standard. The results, of course, were obesity.

The poor had to get by on far less. For those without the time or the means to indulge in fine dining, the big cities offered oyster bars, saloons, and free lunch counters that specialized in an early form of fast food. Patrons were encouraged to gulp their meals (which sometimes came free with the purchase of a nickel mug of beer) and to depart as quickly as possible. At home, families had to get by on meat and potatoes, often without the meat, and whatever fruits and vegetables they could grow. At any time they were, of course, half starved.

## DAILY MEALS AND FOOD PREPARATION

Patterns of food consumption varied widely across America, reflecting conditions in various regions, especially those stressed by war. In the poorest households, cooking was still done in an open fireplace, but most could afford at least a basic wood-burning stove, which became common after the 1840s. Gas-fired kitchen stoves were also manufactured, but they were said to pose such dangers from explosion or asphyxiation that they gained little acceptance. Modern kitchens instead boasted wood- or coal-fired cast-iron ranges, some of them quite elaborate. In the relatively few homes that had indoor plumbing, kitchen ranges were sometimes connected to hot water tanks, supplying heated water for bathing and household chores.

One great inconvenience of daily domestic life was the need to obtain fresh water. Outside of the major metropolitan areas, households had to rely on wells and pumps, and water quality varied tremendously. Streams and groundwater were often contaminated, especially downstream from towns and factories, and waterborne diseases were common. Urban households generally had fewer problems obtaining water. In the larger cities, development of public water supplies had begun long before the outbreak of the Civil War. The first public water system, the Baltimore Water Company, was chartered in 1792, and Nashville and other smaller cities had working public water systems in place by the 1830s. In 1837, New York undertook the most ambitious public water supply project of the antebellum era. Employing almost 4,000 immigrant laborers in its construction, the system carried water from the Croton River into New York City through an elaborately engineered series of dams and aqueducts.

In food consumption, as in many other aspects of life during the 1860s and 1870s, Americans tended to overindulge. Obesity was not recognized as a health hazard, and in some circles it was even considered to be fashionable and a mark of prosperity. There was little understanding of nutrition. Many cookbooks were available, but Eliza Leslie's *Miss Leslie's New Cook Book* (1857) was among the most popular.

## REGIONAL MENUS

In both the North and the South, meat and potatoes were the staple foodstuffs, although modified by regional and ethnic preferences. Cheese was a particular favorite, as were raw fruits, breads, and other baked goods. Vegetables were generally held in lower esteem and when prepared at all were often simply boiled until limp. Frying in butter, lard, or bacon grease was the favored means of cooking.

In the South before the War, great variations in patterns of food consumption were obvious on different financial and social levels. In general. cattle were scarce in the southern states, so milk products were not in great supply, though each plantation usually kept enough cows for milk and oc-casional slaughter. Pork, on the other hand, was a southern staple. Pigs were more numerous than cattle in the South because they required less care and feeding. They were often turned loose to forage in wooded area until round-up time in the fall. As ranchers were to do later in the West, farmers in some parts of the country drove pigs in vast herds. In the French Broad area of North Carolina, an estimated 150,000–175,000 hogs a year were herded to market. One observer viewed the "parade of hogs as they gathered from far and near" and it seemed that "all the world were hogs and all the hogs of the world had been gathered there, destined for the Carolina slaughter pens and the cotton growers' smokehouses." During slaughter time in the fall, pork was enjoyed fresh. At other times it was preserved as salt pork or as smoke-cured bacon and hams. In the poorer homes, pork was scarcer and was often used sparingly, mainly for seasoning.

In the South, vegetables of all kinds, especially home-grown ones, were eaten widely. Some were dried. Green corn was dried on the cob by being hung in the sun or in a warm room. Beets, cabbage, carrots, cauliflower, onions, parsnips, potatoes, radishes, rutabagas, sweet potatoes, turnips, and squash were stored in warm earth cellars. Meats were pickled, salted, and smoked. Smoking not only preserved bacon and ham but improved the taste.

Throughout the war, food was plentiful in the wealthier northern house-holds. One recorded breakfast, for example, was described as consisting of cornbread, buckwheat cakes, boiled chicken, bacon, eggs, hominy, fish, and beefsteak. Dinner, served at 3:00 P.M., was just as overwhelming, consisting of soup, mutton, ham, beef, turkey, duck, eggs, greens, potatoes, beets, and hominy, all of which was served with champagne and a dessert of plum pudding and tarts, ice cream, preserves, and peaches preserved in brandy. Supper, served at 8:00 P.M., offered essentially the same menu but was sim-ply taken in lesser quantities.

The situation was different in the southern states, however, especially after the Union blockade made food scarce in some areas. One traveler, Captain Fitzgerald Ross, returning to Richmond, Virginia, in December 1863, reported that food was plentiful in the hotels and boarding houses, where "not hundreds, but thousands upon thousands of people take their meals, and one may fairly conclude that what is set before them is what they are accustomed to expect at their own homes." He then gave the menu at the well-known Oriental Saloon in Richmond for January 8, 1864:

SOUPS ($1.50): beef, chicken, macaroni, vegetable, clam, oyster, terrapin, turtle, mock turtle. FOWLS ($3.50): turkey, goose, ducks, chickens, FISH ($5.00): rock, chub, shad, perch, herrings, crabs and lobsters. MEATS ($3.00): beef, mutton, pork, lamb, veal. STEAKS ($3.50): beef, pork, mutton, veal, venison. SUNDRIES ($2.50–$3.50): ham and eggs, boiled eggs, poached eggs, scrambled eggs, fried eggs, omelette. OYSTERS $3.00 and $5.00: fried, scalloped, roasted, raw. BIRDS ($3.50): partridge, Sora, robin, snipe, plover, woodcock. VEGETABLES ($1.00): cabbage, tomato, green peas, black-eyed peas, cucumbers, onions, lettuce, squashes, snaps, Lima beans, Irish potatoes, sweet potatoes, salad, asparagus, celery. DRINKS: pure coffee (often "Confederate coffee," $3.00), tea and milk ($2.00). WINES: Champagne and Madeira ($50.00), Port, Claret ($20.00) Cherry (sic) ($35.00). LIQUORS: French brandy ($3.00), apple, peach, Holland gin and rye whiskey ($2.00). MALT LIQUORS: Porter, ale ($12.00). CIGARS: Fine Havana ($1.00) and other fine brands. BREAD, $.50, butter, $1.50, hot rolls, $1.50. Game of all kinds in season. Terrapins served up in every style.[2]

Elsewhere, the effort to starve the Confederacy into submission was more effective. After Vicksburg, Mississippi, fell to the Union in May 1863, reporter Alexander St. Clair Abrams recorded the supply of provisions available to even the most affluent in that city:

Many families of wealth had eaten the last mouthful of food in their possession, and the poor class of non-combatants were on the verge of starvation.... Starvation, its worst forms, now confronted the inhabitants, and, had the siege lasted two weeks longer, the consequences would have been terrible. All the beef in the city was exhausted by this time, and mules were soon brought in by requisition, and their meat sold readily at one dollar per pound, the citizens being as anxious to get it as they were before the investment to purchase the delicacies of the season. It was also distributed among the soldiers, to those who desired it, although it was not given out under the name of rations. A great many of them, however, accepted it in preference to doing without any meat, and the flesh of the mules was found equal to the best venison. The author of this work partook of mule meat for three or four days, and found the flesh tender and nutritious, and, under the *peculiar circumstances*, a most desirable description of food.[3]

Accompanying Abrams's evaluation just quoted was another account of the food inventory just before the fall of Vicksburg. One restaurant owner is supposed to have served rabbit-and-mule stew, in which the ingredients were equal: one rabbit for one mule. There were numerous tales of rats being eaten. One Louisiana Creole wrote home that the rats at Vicksburg were almost as good to eat as those in Louisiana.

A satirical bill of fare was published in the *Chicago Tribune* and reprinted in the *Southern Punch* for the Hotel de Vicksburg for July, 1863. The soup is mule tail, the roast is mule sirloin or rump, the entrees, mule head, mule beef, mule ears, mule spare ribs or liver; side dishes are mule salad, mule hoof hosed, mule brains a-la-omelette, and so on; the jellies are mule foot; dessert is white-oak acorns, beach beechnuts, blackberry leaf tea, "Genuine Confederate Coffee"; liquors are Mississippi water, limestone water, "spring water 'Vicksburg brand' $1.50." The menu is signed "Jeff. Davis & Co., Proprietors." The menu is followed by a "card" with the following

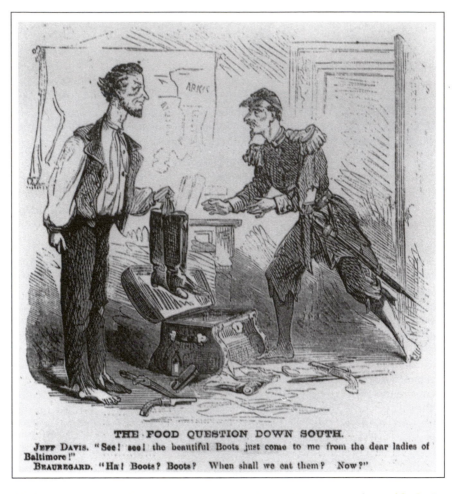

THE FOOD QUESTION DOWN SOUTH.

JEFF DAVIS. "See! see! the beautiful Boots just come to me from the dear ladies of Baltimore!"

BEAUREGARD. "Ha! Boots? Boots? When shall we eat them? Now?"

Yankees never missed an opportunity to emphasize the success of their blockade of the South. (From *Frank Leslie's Illustrated Weekly*)

guarantee: "The proprietors of the justly celebrated Hotel are now prepared to accommodate all who may favor them with a call. Parties arriving by the river or Grant's inland route, will find Grape, Canister, & Co's. carriages at the landing, or any depot on the line of intrenchments. Buck, Balk & Co., take charge of all baggage. No effort will be spared to make the visit of all as interesting as possible." The fact that this bit of irony was reprinted in a southern publication demonstrates the grim sense of humor and willingness to suffer that drove the Confederates.

The eating habits of slaves varied from that of middle- and upper-class whites, although evidence suggests it was similar to the fare of many poor whites, especially those living in the mountains and backwoods. To save time, slaves on large plantations were served from a central kitchen. On small land holdings, they ate in their individual cabins, cooking their own foods. Generally slaves were given their rations weekly, usually on Saturdays, and could therefore consume it as they pleased, provided they could in some way feed themselves if their rations ran out. On some plantations they were fed some of the same foods that whites ate, but also much food that upper-class whites would not eat. Many were allowed certain types of wild game—fish, squirrels, raccoons, groundhogs, opossums, rabbits, and certain wild fowl—but not choice game like deer or pheasant. They were also fed the less desirable parts of chickens (necks, gizzards, and feet) and hogs (especially the feet and the small intestines, or chitlins). Sometimes they enjoyed much better food, like ham and gravy, fried chicken, ash cake and hoe cake, cornmeal, grits, hominy, molasses, and bacon fat. They ate a variety of root crops, grains, and vegetables, including okra, peas, collards, turnips, black-eyed peas, cornmeal, fresh and dried corn, potatoes, yams, peanuts, and forest nuts. No milk or milk products were furnished them. The diet was poorly balanced, although the inclusion of vegetables seems to have prevented rampant malnutrition.

In the West, Americans discovered an abundance of native foods, ranging from buffalo and elk to wild berries. Delicacies such as elk and bear were processed and shipped east to fine restaurants. Miners and cowboys scavenged whatever wild game they could, supplementing the local food supplies with a diet of beans, salt pork, sourdough biscuits, and coffee. Tortillas, tamales, enchiladas, chili, and other Mexican fare was common in the Southwest and was soon assimilated into American menus.

## SOLDIERS' RATIONS

Soldiers' rations were spartan. Rations in camp included hardtack (hard biscuits, often infested with weevils), sugar, soft bread, flour, rice, cornmeal, dried potatoes, salt pork, dried peas, beans, fruits, bacon or ham, pickled beef (called salt horse), onions, molasses, salt, pepper, and vinegar. Fresh meat was a rare treat. Officers received better rations, but both officers and enlisted men had to endure reduced rations when on active duty. Hungry troops often resorted to foraging, and a group of soldiers could quickly lay waste a garden or orchard. When they could afford it, they supplemented their rations with purchases from the sutler, who with his wagon of outrageously priced foodstuffs and other necessaries was always close at hand, even in battle.

Coffee played an important part in the diet of soldiers on both sides of the conflict. It became popular during the Civil War because of its stimulant qualities and was one of the most important items in a soldier's ration. Prices ranged from 14 cents to 42 cents a pound, and soldiers would pay almost any price to the sutler who might supply extra rations. All companies carried a coffee mill as part of their kitchen equipment, but soldiers on both sides of the conflict carried their beans in their pockets and often chewed them when there was not time to brew a pot. Yankee soldiers were reputed to drink a half-gallon or more of coffee a day when it was available. Confederate soldiers, after the port of New Orleans through which the Confederacy imported its coffee was closed by the war, had to substitute caffeine-free concoctions brewed from roasted acorns, chicory, dandelion roots, sugar-cane, parched rice, cotton seed, peanuts, wheat, beans, sweet potatoes, corn, okra, and probably other available foodstuffs. The importance of coffee in the lives of soldiers is well demonstrated in the reminiscences of a former Massachusetts artillery man, John Billings, recounted in his book *Hardtack and Coffee* (1887):

Little campfires, rapidly increasing to hundreds in number, would shoot up along the hills and plains and, as if by magic, acres of territory would be made luminous with them. Soon they would be surrounded by the soldiers, who made it an almost invariable rule to cook their coffee first, after which a large number, tired out with the toils of the day, would make their supper of hardtack and coffee, and roll up in their blankets for the night. If a march was ordered at midnight, unless a surprise was intended it must be preceded by a pot of coffee.... It was coffee *at* meals and *between* meals; and men going on guard or coming off guard drank it at all hours of the night."

## FOOD PRESERVATION

Across the nation, and particularly in the South, preservation of food was problematic. Root crops and hardier vegetables—like beets, cabbage, carrots, cauliflower, onions, parsnips, potatoes, rutabagas, sweet potatoes, and turnips—were stored in spring houses or cool earth cellars. In colder climates they were nestled under straw or stored in barrels. Some fruits and vegetables—particularly apples, peas, beans, and corn—were preserved by sun-drying. Meat, fish, and seafood was dried, pickled, salted, or smoked. Smoking not only preserved bacon and hams but improved the taste.

During hot weather, foods were kept cool in running water or in icehouses. In 1850, *Godey's Lady's Book* called the icehouse a "necessity of life." Icehouses were filled with ice harvested when it was thickest, providing natural refrigeration that usually lasted through most of the summer. Northern entrepreneurs developed a lucrative business in ice exports, and even Henry David Thoreau's beloved Walden Pond was harvested for its ice. The amount of ice shipped to the South was staggering. In the 1830s, New Orleans alone used 8,000 tons. In the early 1860s, this amount rose to a staggering 28,000 tons. Vapor-compression refrigeration, although

**TINGLEY'S PATENT**
HORIZONTAL
# ICE-CREAM FREEZER

Is recommended for FAMILIES, HOTELS,
SALOONS, and WHOLESALE MANUF.-
TURERS

As the best Ice-Cream Freezer in the market.

**It saves ICE,**
**Saves TIME,**
**Saves LABOR.**

And produces the finest quality of Cream
known to the Art.

Send for Descriptive Catalogue.

**CHAS. G. BLATCHLEY, Manufacturer,**
**505 COMMERCE STREET,**

F. L. HEDENBERG & SONS,
No. 7 Bond Street.
Dear Friend:

## Revolving Refrigerators.

PARLOR, HALL, AND OFFICE
STOVES, COOKING RANGES,
HEDENBERG'S PORTABLE HEAT-
ERS AND FURNACES,
HOT-AIR FURNACES FOR COAL
AND WOOD,
REGISTERS, VENTILATORS,
ETC.

This Refrigerator is made in an octagon form, and is
very ornamental as well as useful. The ice-chamber is
situated at the top, occupying one half the area of the
box, and about half its depth. The other half of the top
of the box, to half the depth of the ice-chamber, is the
milk and butter closet. It has a zinc bottom, and is en-
tirely separate from other parts of the Refrigerator. Access is gained to this as well as the ice-chamber, by rais-
ing the top. Under the milk and butter is a wine-closet
of the same size. The balance of the Refrigerator is in
one general apartment, where all kinds of meat, poultry,
fish, fruit, &c., &c., can be kept in a pure, healthy state.
The shelves consist of wheels, which turn on an axis,
bringing any article that may be desired in front of its
respective door. They are well ventilated, use very little ice, and have three times as much shelf-room as any
other refrigerator which takes the same space on the
floor. Please call and see them, or send for circular
giving full description. They can be shipped to any part
of the country with safety.
  *N. B.*—Prompt attention paid to heating, ventilating,
repairing, &c., &c., in city or country.

F.L. Hedengerg & Sons
Revolving Refrigerators
Harper's Weekly, April 14, 1860, Page 238

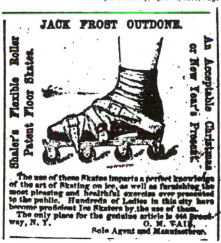

**JACK FROST OUTDONE.**

Shaler's Flexible Roller
Patent Floor Skates.

An Acceptable Christmas
or New Year's Present.

The use of these Skates imparts a perfect knowledge
of the art of Skating on ice, as well as furnishing the
most pleasing and healthful exercise ever presented
to the public. Hundreds of Ladies in this city have
become proficient Ice Skaters by the use of them.
  The only place for the genuine article is 444 Broadway, N. Y.

O. M. VAIL,
Sole Agent and Manufacturer.

Advertisements of newly developed objects available. The freezer and
refrigerator are from *Harper's Weekly*, April 14, 1860. The four-wheel
in-line ice skates, forerunner of today's in-line skates, were advertised
in *Frank Leslie's Illustrated Weekly*.

patented in 1834 by Jacob Perkins, did not become practical until after the war. Dr. John Gorrie patented a successful ice-making machine in 1851. Unfortunately, Gorrie was never able to develop a market for his machine because of resistance from the Northern ice merchants.

Primitive iceboxes were constructed with a metal-lined wooden box inside another wooden box, with the space between filled with charcoal or ashes as insulation. The icebox had seen limited use since early in the nineteenth century, and by 1860 various kinds of ice boxes were in use. One of the fancier models was an octagonal "revolving refrigerator," with shelves that turned to bring the desired food to the door space. The fixture was more efficient than ordinary models because every item on the revolving shelves at one time or another touched the ice. Any thickness of ice from six inches up was suitable for refrigeration, although snow was not.

A major breakthrough in food preservation came in 1810, when the Englishman Peter Durance patented the tin-coated steel can as a method of food preservation. By the next year, others had opened canning factories, and "embalmed meat," as some took to calling it, was soon a staple in England. Another Englishman, William Underwood, went to Boston in 1821, where he established a food canning plant overlooking Boston Harbor. Underwood canned all kinds of products, ranging from simple fruits and vegetables to catsup, jams, jellies, and mustard. In 1828, he shipped canned milk to South America. Underwood's operation was the beginning of the canning industry in the United States and is America's oldest canning company. Metal canning was not possible at home, but the glass Mason jar, introduced in 1858, soon became popular as a practical and inexpensive means of preserving foods at home.

By the 1860s, canned foods were commonplace. Just before the outbreak of the Civil War, a Baltimore canner named Isaac Solomon discovered that the addition of calcium chloride (a salt) to the water in which the cans were cooked raised the water temperature, substantially reducing processing time from several hours to thirty minutes. During the Civil War canned foods were relied upon by soldiers and sailors as a dependable ration. One of the biggest suppliers was Gilbert C. Van Camp, who was awarded an army supply contract in 1861. At the end of the fighting, the troops returned home with high praise for safe, portable canned food. The postwar canning business prospered, growing from a prewar annual output of five million cans to an output of thirty million cans after the war.

## MARKETS

American shoppers before the Civil War were usually limited to the fresh produce, canned goods, and processed foods stocked by local farmers' markets, grocers, or general stores. This means that local foods were seasonal and depended on the weather. Adverse conditions, such as cold spells, droughts, and wet spells, could severely limit or eliminate locally grown foods and cause hardships. The development of the chain grocery store after the war made a much wider choice of materials available to the American cook. The chain grocery store was born in 1859, when George F. Gilman and George Huntington opened the doors of their small shop in New York City called the Great American Tea Company. By 1869, they had become so successful that they took on the name of the Great Atlantic & Pacific Tea Company and began to expand westward.

Grocery stores grew in popularity after the war. By 1880, Gilman and Huntington had opened 100 stores.[4] America's second chain grocery store, Jones Brothers Tea Company of Brooklyn, opened in 1872 and eventually became the Grand Union Company, still in business today. With the obvious success of these enterprises, numerous others began and grew throughout the remainder of the century.

## SNACKS

Snacks, or fast foods, have always been necessary in all cultures. Popcorn has played a minor though significant role in American cultures from the first days. Like apple pie, it has been a symbol of America through the ages. Its origins are shrouded in mystery. Indians reportedly were eating popcorn when the Europeans arrived. In 1785, Ben Franklin and others reported that native Americans popped corn by filling an iron pot with sand, placing it over heat, and retrieving the grains as they popped.[5] Popcorn was adapted eagerly by European settlers, and by the mid-1820s, seed merchants were growing and selling it. The term *pop corn* was first listed in John Bartlett's *Dictionary of Americanisms* in 1848. Two years later, Susan Fenimore Cooper, daughter of the author James Fenimore Cooper, reported that acres of popcorn were being raised around the large towns in upstate New York.

During the Civil War, soldiers popped and ate corn when they could. By the end of the war, its popularity had spread from one end of the nation to the other. By 1875, it had become a staple in grocery stores and at concession stands at circuses, carnivals, and street fairs. Several methods of popping were tried in the early days, with varying degrees of success. Grains were popped in a kettle with fat or lard or were placed in a heavy frying pan with butter and shaken back and forth and round and round to make sure that they heated uniformly. The first patent for a corn popper was issued in 1866. The paper bag was introduced in the early 1860s as a container for popcorn, peanuts, and cracker-jacks, syrup-covered popcorn or popcorn-and-peanut balls.

Peanuts have been grown and eaten around the world under many names, including monkey nuts, groundnuts, goober peas, ground peas, pindas, and pinders. Apparently the first peanuts grown in America for market were sold in Nashville in 1850. Although now generally consumed in the United States as a snack food, the peanut was of far greater nutritional importance during the Civil War. Roasted and ground, peanuts were used by Southerners as a coffee substitute. Peanuts served as snacks for Union troops and as a food staple among hungry Confederate citizens. They were introduced into New York City as a snack food around 1870 and soon found their way into peanut brittle and other confections.

A snack that was new to America at the time of the Civil War was the pretzel, made from a simple dough of wheat flour, water, and yeast that is first boiled, then baked and salted. The pretzel was introduced by German immigrants but initially didn't obtain widespread popularity. With the opening of the first commercial pretzel bakery in Lititz, Pennsylvania, in 1861, the pretzel soon became a favorite (and relatively healthy) American snack food.

Candy has always been popular in America, and simple candies like taffies, brittles, fudge, and candied fruits were often made in the home. The perfection of the revolving steam pan in 1851 made the mass production of inexpensive candy possible. In 1861, Daniel Peter of Switzerland developed a way to mix cocoa, milk, and chocolate and thus make milk-chocolate candy, and in 1866, Daniel G. Chase invented a machine for printing endearing messages on candies. By the end of the nineteenth century, most American towns and villages had candy stores or drug stores that sold sweets.

Ice cream has long been America's favorite dessert. Its origin is the stuff of mythology, with various exotic beginnings claimed, most of them impossible to verify. Whatever its origin, ice cream was being made in home freezers by the early nineteenth century. Early ice cream freezers differed only slightly from the type still used in homes today. A metal cylinder, surrounded by a tub of salted, crushed ice, was cranked to stir the milk, sugar, and other ingredients. A major breakthrough in freezer design came in 1843, when the U.S. Patent Office issued a patent to Nancy M. Johnson for a cylinder with a close-fitting lid and a dasher with a removable crank. Johnson sold her invention for $200, and the company that bought it became the first in an ever-expanding group of businesses that began to manufacture ice cream commercially. Ice cream freezers came in numerous shapes and designs. One 1860 model consisted of a horizontal barrel mounted on a four-legged stand and apparently was quite versatile, being recommended for families, hotels, saloons, and wholesale manufacturers.

Wholesalers entered the ice cream business in the winter of 1851–52, when Jacob Fussell, a dairy farmer in Seven Valleys, Pennsylvania, first delivered ice cream to nearby Baltimore. In 1856, Fussell opened an ice cream plant in Washington, D.C., but during the war he refused to sell to the Union army, although the sutlers wanted to buy his entire stock. During the 1860s, the ice cream business expanded dramatically, first along the East

Coast and then, by 1868, as far west as Lawrence, Kansas, where A. M. Field opened an ice cream plant.

With improvements in freezer design and cooling technology, ice cream became a common treat no longer reserved for the wealthier classes. At a dollar per gallon, ice cream prices generally remained in the reach of most people. Vanilla, then as now, was the most popular flavor, with the more expensive chocolate running second. In the drive to be inventive and to attract customers, no flavor was considered too bizarre. Exotic flavors like tutti-frutti, chestnut, asparagus, cinnamon, and truffle were tried. One of the most exotic was Irish moss, the recipe for which advised that the moss must be "rinsed well to cleanse it of sand and a certain foreign taste."

Ice cream was easily transportable in ice packing. The forerunners of our Good Humor Man were working the streets of New York and other cities in the early nineteenth century, selling from wheelbarrows, wagons, or containers strung on his back. The sellers sang and chanted their come-ons to attract children, their main sales target.

After the war, ice cream cakes and molds of all shapes became popular. A whole zoo of animals served as models for ice cream molds, and it was only a short step to covering these treats with nuts and chocolate. The first scoop to serve ice cream was patented in 1878.

## BEVERAGES

Consumption of mineral water reached fad proportions during the mid-nineteenth century. The Astors, Vanderbilts, and other American aristocrats initiated the mineral water craze, and all sorts of extravagant claims were made for the supposed health benefits of various waters' mineral content, sometimes rivaling the wildest claims of the patent-medicine vendors. Gettysburg Katalysine Spring Water became a best-seller when stories spread that soldiers wounded at the battle of Gettysburg had made miraculous recoveries after drinking the local mineral water. The bottling of mineral water was a major industry, reaching its peak around 1860 and remaining strong until the 1890s.

A less healthy counterpart of mineral water was soda pop, which supposedly originated in 1807 when Philadelphia druggist Townsend Speakman mixed carbonated water, widely believed to be of medicinal value, with some berry juice and sugar to improve its flavor. The basic idea soon caught on, and soda pop was first commercially bottled in Philadelphia in 1835. Ginger ale, introduced from Ireland in 1852, was one of the most popular soda pops, but American manufacturers soon developed all kinds of ingenious flavors. In 1863, James W. Tufts built and patented the first soda-fountain machine for use in his Boston drugstore.

Black and green tea were favorite beverages, and where they were not available, native herbal substitutes sometimes sufficed. Henry David

Thoreau wrote that on a trip down the Allegash River, his Indian guide pointed out dozens of different herbs useful for making teas. Medicinal teas were commonly brewed from catnip, greenbrier roots, maple sap, sassafras leaf and root, black birch, black spruce, cedar, molasses, wintergreen, juniper berries, hops, ginger, and many other plants.

Coffee, already mentioned as a favorite of the troops, was also a staple among the civilian population. In 1859, the per capita consumption was eight pounds per year. The ground coffee was usually boiled directly in the water, then topped off with an egg to settle the grounds. One of the early recipes called for "two spoonfuls to each pint of water; mix it with white yolk and shell of an egg, pour on hot but not boiling water, and boil it not over ten minutes." Several of the coffee companies we know today began their operation during the Civil War period. In 1864, Caleb Chase began his independent company, and in 1878 he joined with James Sanborn to form the Chase & Sanborn Company. On the West Coast, 14-year-old Jim Folger went into the coffee business in 1850. After several false starts and a bankruptcy, Folger by 1875 had repaid half his debts and was thriving.

Beer was an American staple throughout the nineteenth century. Regarded more as a food than as an alcoholic beverage by many Americans, it tended to be low in alcohol content and was often consumed in some quantity throughout the day. Easily brewed from inexpensive ingredients, it was made in the home, in taverns, or in small breweries. Beer was not bottled until the 1850s, but was consumed on the spot in taverns or hauled home in buckets. The pottery beer bottle was introduced in the decade before the Civil War, but by the mid-1860s, the glass beer bottle had became standard. Milwaukee and St. Louis were established as major brewing centers during the war, and beer making was taken over during the 1860s and 1870s by large commercial brewers like Pabst, Miller, Schlitz, Anheuser, and Busch, names still famous today. Pale lager, first brought to America by German immigrants in the 1840s, became the overwhelming favorite. Consumption of lager outstripped that of hard liquor after the end of the Civil War.[6]

Alcoholic beverages were a central feature of proper Victorian entertaining, with a different wine, liquor, or cordial often served at each course of a fine meal. The finest wines, imported from Europe, were reserved for the wealthy, while the working class had to content itself with the often uneven products of a nascent American wine industry. By 1840, fifteen states were producing a considerable amount of wine, with Ohio, Missouri, and New York as the leaders. On the West Coast, several wineries began operation in the 1860s and 1870s. Homemade wine, fermented from whatever fruits might be available, was popular in the more remote regions. Whiskey was the favorite hard liquor, followed by brandy and rum, and flavored cordials were a popular dessert. Every major city had its distilleries, but in the remote mountains, moonshining—the illegal production of liquor—

was considered an honorable tradition with roots extending back to colonial times. Home distilling was legal until 1862, when the first federal liquor excise tax was passed. The tax simply drove home distillers into hiding, where they continued to produce their corn whiskey and fruit brandies.

Foodstuffs as the staff of life have always existed on two levels—the necessities and, where possible, the extras. During the war the Union, while enjoying plentiful food, tried to help defeat the Confederacy through deprivation by blockade and other means. Though they made severe inroads in many places, the Unionists could not use lack of food alone to bring the Confederacy to its knees. After the War, the Confederacy remained somewhere between the desperately poor and starving and the wealthy and vulgarly wasteful. The gild, or lack of it, that Mark Twain witnessed everywhere prompted him to name this period the "gilded age."

# 7

# Leisure Activities

In sports, as in most other aspects of life, Americans during the Civil War and Reconstruction period took their games seriously. Sport was a great builder of character. "Sport was not to be frivolous, or simply fun," writes sport historian Robert Crego, "but rather had to serve a purpose—great or small."[1]

Because of cultural differences, sports in the Old South took a somewhat different course, with less emphasis on moral and spiritual uplift and more allowance for physicality. "Lower-class whites in the South had their own low-brow versions of [the gentry sports such as horse racing, fencing, wrestling, and boxing]," writes Robert Crego, "(e.g., brawling instead of wrestling, racing nonthoroughbred horses, cockfighting, and forms of boxing that also entailed sword fighting). Sport was a mark of masculinity in the Old South, and gambling (e.g., on cockfights and horse racing) provided a common ground for the two segments of society to meet."[2]

Americans stood on the verge of a dramatic expansion in their opportunities for leisure activity. Outdoor sport and games and other forms of organized play boomed in popularity during the Civil War and Reconstruction, enabling Americans to enjoy themselves as never before.[3]

## PARTICIPATING IN SPORTS AND OTHER OUTDOOR GAMES AND ACTIVITIES

Americans' interest in sports and other outdoor activities increased dramatically during the mid- and late 1860s, part of a nationwide campaign to encourage the health benefits of exercise. Many Americans began to push for greater physical activity among their countrymen, fearful that too many had fallen into sedentary lifestyles. City dwellers drew the most derision for their cushy lifestyles.[4] Edward Everett, a nationally known Unitarian minister, bemoaned the fact that the "Americans as a people, at least the professional and mercantile classes, have too little considered the importance of healthful, generous recreation."[5] Oliver Wendell Holmes, an equally well-known author, was even more dismissive of the want of exercise among urban residents. In an article published in *Harper's Monthly*, Holmes railed that "such a set of black-coated, stiff-jointed, soft-muscled, paste-complexioned youth as we can boast in our Atlantic cities never before sprang from the loins of Anglo-Saxon lineage."[6] Everett's and Holmes's efforts, among others, caught fire. Americans became sports-crazed during the postwar era, leading to the publication of the first national magazines devoted exclusively to sports, including *Sporting Times* and *Sports and Games*.[7]

Baseball became the leading pioneer in America's newfound sports craze. Once thought of as a "gentlemen's game," the sport had gained widespread popularity among Union and Confederate soldiers during the Civil War because of its ease of play. Players only needed a ball and a bat to get started although, in a pinch, a sturdy tree branch and a walnut wrapped in string made do.[8] Scores generally ran high because the pitcher had to hit each base-runner with the otherwise bouncy and oversized ball to record an out. In one contest, a team from the 13th Massachusetts defeated a team from the 104th New York, by a score of 66 to 20. In another nail-biter, two teams from New York regiments battled to a 58 to 19 final score.[9] Despite lopsided scores, players enjoyed the exercise and the outdoors. Captain James Hall of the 24th Alabama described that members of his regiments played baseball throughout the early spring of 1864 "just like school boys."[10] A Union soldier in Tennessee also declared that he filled the days during April 1864 playing baseball. The man's enthusiasm for describing the sport may have outpaced his playing skills; he admitted after one defeat that he and his teammates got "lamed badly."[11]

Civil War soldiers brought home their passion for playing baseball, and the sport boomed in popularity. The National Association of Base Ball Players, founded in 1858, was the first national baseball organization established in the United States. An amateur league in which players received no money for their participation, the National Association expanded rapidly. Between 1860 and 1867, the number of teams joining the league jumped from 50 clubs to 202. Teams in the National Association came from seventeen states across the newly reunited Union, as well as from the District of Columbia.[12] The fourfold increase in team membership and the geographic range of the National Association convinced many Americans that baseball was the nation's sport of choice. "Since the war," one observer commented during the late 1860s, baseball "has run like wildfire." Another man agreed, declaring that baseball was the "leading feature in the outdoor sports of the United States." Even more emphatic, a writer for *Sports and Games* hailed baseball as the "national game of the United States."[13] The exuberance of these three comments requires some qualification because the National Association excluded African American players from membership in 1867, like many other sports organizations at the time.[14]

Amateur baseball clubs gave way to professional baseball teams during the late 1860s and early 1870s, a result of corrupt practices increasingly entering the game. Some of the violations were relatively minor, such as communities offering especially talented players high-paying jobs to live in their town. In one instance, the Excelsior Club in Chicago offered Albert Spalding, the future sporting goods manufacturer, $40 a week to work as a wholesale grocery clerk. Spalding may have made a fine grocery clerk, but he made a better pitcher, the true reason for his receiving the otherwise unusually generous job offer.[15] Other rules violations were more egregious, gambling chief among them. Some observers accused individual players of accepting bribes to influence their play on the field. Worse, some observers accused entire teams of taking money to throw the outcome of a game. Members of the National Association vigorously protested the illicit payment of both players and teams. But, in the words of one prominent sports historian, "their organization was losing its control" over the supposedly amateur game of baseball.[16]

The creation of the National League of Professional Baseball Clubs in 1876 helped to reverse the tide of corruption in the sport. Professional teams from New York, Philadelphia, Hartford, Boston, Chicago, Cincinnati, Louisville, and St. Louis initially constituted the league. The Cincinnati Red Stockings were the senior team, its players receiving salaries that ranged between $800 and $1,400 to tour the country as early as 1869.[17] The organization of the National League gave rise to many of the characteristics of modern-day professional baseball, with the creation of franchises, major and minor leagues, and player contracts. The National League also introduced new types of player equipment, including mitts for all infielders and outfielders and a glove and a mask for the catcher.[18] Some old-time players scoffed at the equipment changes. "We used no mattress on our hands, No cage upon our face;" ran one chant popular among former players, "We stood right up and caught the ball with courage and with grace." Yet, for better or for worse, the days of bruised faces and swollen hands as commonplace among baseball players were forever gone.[19]

Croquet was the only other outdoor game to rival baseball for playing time among Americans. Introduced from England at the end of the Civil War, croquet boomed in popularity across the United States because it allowed men and women to play together.[20] "Of all the epidemics that have swept over our land," one magazine editorial declared during the late summer of 1866, "the swiftest and most infectious is croquet."[21] Couples who were courting took quick advantage to turn croquet from athletic game to social occasion. Young men and women flirted and socialized with one another under the watchful eyes of their parents and friends. The authors of an early croquet rules book suggested the varied physical and social benefits that couples gained from playing the sport. "Grace in holding and using the mallet," the writers extolled, "easy and pleasing attitudes in playing, promptness in taking your turn, and gentlemanly and ladylike manners generally throughout the game, are points which it is unnecessary for us to enlarge on."[22] By contrast, popular songs often poked fun at the dual reasons why young men, at least, took up croquet. One popular song ran,

> I saw the scamp—it was light as day—
>
> Put his arm around her waist in a loving way,
>
> And he squeezed her hard. Was that croquet?[23]

Disputes based upon gender occasionally entered into the otherwise idyllic world of croquet. The writers of the croquet rule book feared that some women played games all their own. They warned prospective players that "Young ladies are proverbially fond of cheating at this game; but they only do so because they think that men like it."[24] The problem of "spooning" was more controversial. "Spooning" occurred when croquet players swung their mallets in arcing, pendulum-like strokes to generate more power in hitting the ball. Women in hoopskirts lacked the range of motion to "spoon" the ball, thus placing them at competitive disadvantage.[25] "We agree that spooning is perfectly fair in a match of gentlemen," one magazine editorial argued, "but it is decidedly ungenerous when played with ladies, unless those ladies are bloomers."[26] Still, the occasional controversy over the breaking and bending of the rules of croquet failed to diminish enthusiasm for the game. Croquet sets sold exceptionally well throughout the Reconstruction years, some even including wickets equipped with candle sockets so that players could continue their game well into the night.[27]

Spectator sports gained popularity between 1861 and 1877, college football chief among them. American college students had long played various forms of football, but the first recorded intercollegiate game occurred between Rutgers and Princeton in 1869. By the mid-1870s, Princeton, Harvard, and Yale dominated the sport, earning them "The Big Three" as nickname. The games played by The Big Three became the highlights of the fall social season, especially when against one another. The contest between Princeton and Yale on Thanksgiving Day, 1878, drew 4,000 fans. Although small by modern-day standards, the fan attendance at the Princeton-Yale game was extremely large for the day, and rising. By the late 1880s, the game was drawing 40,000 spectators, all hoping to cheer their team to victory.[28]

Although football was popular among spectators, the game began to achieve standardized rules only during 1876. Representatives from Harvard, Yale, Princeton, and Columbia met to standardize rules drawn from English rugby. Among the most notable changes involved reducing the number of players on the field for each team from fifteen to eleven; assigning each player a specific position; and changing rules for running, passing, and kicking the ball. Additionally, the football line of "scrimmage" replaced the rugby line of "scrummage." The last mentioned rule change enabled players to put the ball into play by passing it back from a clearly defined line of scrimmage, rather than kicking out the ball from a jumbled huddle on the line of scrummage. The newly formed Intercollegiate Football Association sanctioned the same rule changes in 1881, applying them to college football teams across the nation.[29]

College-aged men took to playing football because those who physically excelled at the game arguably earned more respect from their peers than participants in any other sport. The game was undeniably violent, with its emphasis on blocking and tackling. Additionally, little protective gear cushioned the blows, with shoulder pads and helmets yet to become standard equipment.[30] Despite the potential for injury, men continued to attempt to impress their teammates and opponents. In a notable example, a young man from North Carolina attended college in upstate New York in 1873. The boy silently endured taunts from his classmates for his "Southern pride" and his "conceited" manner. Football, however, allowed him physical release for his otherwise closely held frustrations. "Ah! But I like to show these Yankees what a 'Reb' can do on the foot-ball field," he recorded in satisfaction at the end of one fall afternoon. "I, made desperate by their ways, made frequent alarming charges, and their cries of 'Good enough' kind of soothe my feelings."[31]

In addition to football, horse racing and prize fighting were popular spectator sports between 1861 and 1877. Horse racing appealed to nearly all Americans for its speed and color, as it had since the colonial era. Mid- and late-nineteenth-century Americans indulged their passion for fast horses at sites that varied in quality by where they lived. Large cities like New York, Baltimore, Cincinnati, Nashville, Louisville, and New Orleans boasted fashionable racetracks.[32] The racetrack at Jerome Park in New York hosted among the most spectators, with seating for 8,000 people. Leonard Jerome, August Belmont, and the other owners of Jerome Park prohibited the sale of liquor in order to give the racetrack, in the words of one newspaper reporter, "an air of gentility fit for ladies."[33] Small communities had racetracks that lacked many of the same amenities. Few had grandstands, with spectators instead standing behind rail fences.[34] Yet racetracks in small towns and villages lacked nothing in excitement. "The event every Saturday afternoon in Wichita is a horse race," one resident of the Kansas town declared. "The track is just north of, and in plain view of the town. Last Saturday, the race was between a Texas horse and a Wichita mare. The mare won the race, and it is said over a thousand dollars changed hands."[35]

Many Americans lacked the patience to wait for scheduled horse races. During the Civil War, cavalry soldiers, who constituted between 15 and 20 percent of the manpower of Union and Confederate armies, needed little prompting to see who had the fastest mount.[36] "I have bin Horse racesing since I left home," one southern volunteer happily declared during the winter of 1862. "I have lost one hundred dollars an have got a race to be run on Saturday next I have got [a horse] bet on the race and if I loose him I will loose a heap more on the day of the race. I am going to win or loose something."[37] The same man, if he survived the war, likely expressed derision for laws passed in many cities and towns during the 1870s that prohibited reckless driving. The laws aimed to curb racing among delivery boys in horse and wagon as much as to attempt to prevent unsafe driving among other people on the roads.[38]

Prize fighting was another spectator sport enjoyed by many Americans, although more often than not on the sly. Boxing was a brutal sport during the postwar era, with the two combatants fighting with bare knuckles and few rules. Many communities outlawed the sport, considering it barbaric and unchristian. The legal restrictions placed against boxing added to its allure among young men, whom one contemporary dismissively described as a "brutal gang." Boxing matches became sought-after entertainment, although they occurred in remote locations and with little forewarning. During one championship fight between John Morrissey and John Heenan held on the Canadian border during the 1850s, 2,000 spectators sailed across Lake Erie from Buffalo, New York, to watch the event.[39] Only with the adoption of the Marquess of Queensberry rules during the 1880s did boxing lose much of its public stigma. By the late nineteenth century, fans flocked to see bouts featuring nationally known boxers such as John Sullivan, popularly known as the "Boston Strong Boy," and Jim Corbett, popularly known as "Gentleman Jim."[40]

In addition to participatory and spectator sports, several outdoor "fads" swept across the nation during and after the Civil War. Gander-pulling was the fad with the earliest history, dating to the colonial South. In the sport, riders mounted on horseback galloped full-speed toward a well-greased and still-living gander hung by its feet from a tree branch. The horseman rode underneath the tree branch and attempted to grab and pull off the bird's head, hanging barely within their reach.[41] One North Carolinian living during the antebellum era declared that the bloody spectacle of gander-pulling was "anticipated with rapture by all bruisers either at fist or grog, all heavy bottomed well balanced riders, all women who wanted a holiday and had the curiosity to see the weight and prowess of their sweethearts tried in open field."[42] Gander-pulling remained popular among Confederate soldiers, although securing an uneaten goose long enough to dangle from a tree likely remained problematic. The stunt proved especially popular at dress parades, when gathered soldiers and civilians cheered successful attempts.[43]

Bicycle riding was another sports fad that gained popularity. Bicycles became common sights during the late 1860s, before dropping from view for many years. Early bicycles had wood frames with a high front wheel and a low rear wheel. The seat was perched over pedals fitted on the front wheel, making for an exciting but unsteady ride.[44] Schools designed to teach bicycle riding opened in cities across the nation. According to one New York journalist, every evening one could see "upward of a hundred and fifty gentlemen, doctors, bankers, merchants, and representatives from almost every profession, engaged preparatory to making their appearance upon the public streets."[45] Whether the reporter meant his description as encouragement for bicycle riding is unclear, given the bone-jarring collisions that occasionally occurred between bicyclist and pedestrian. High front wheel bicycles disappeared almost as rapidly as they appeared. Various design improvements led to the reemergence of bicycles during the late 1870s, most notably the creation of a drop frame for women riders. The fad became sport and, by 1887, nearly 100,000 Americans were riding bicycles.[46]

Lawn tennis was a third sports fad to sweep the nation during the postwar years, particularly among women. Introduced from England during the mid-1870s, lawn tennis gained a popular following because it emphasized grace and poise. Players softly patted the ball back and forth with their racquet over a net stretched across any level piece of ground. Players appeared on either side of the net well groomed and dressed, because they were not expected to run for the ball. Instead, players allowed balls to pass by them if hit too far to either side. The emphasis upon fashion style as much as athletic talent appealed to women, because physical strength mattered little in playing the game. Additionally, men and women played tennis together, making the game one of the few outdoor sports that couples shared with one another, beside croquet. The creation of the United States National Lawn Tennis Association in 1883 began to change the play of tennis. The Lawn Tennis Association instituted rules that encouraged physical play, such as serves and smashes. The new methods of play quickly transformed tennis from leisurely game to competitive sport, culminating in the organization of national tournaments during the late nineteenth century.[47]

The final sports fad to capture the fancy of the nation during the Civil War and Reconstruction era was roller skating. First taken up by Americans during the mid-1860s, roller skating quickly caught fire. Cities from New York to San Francisco built massive skating rinks, and towns and villages in between had smaller versions. The Casino in Chicago was among the largest skating rinks in the United States, with room for 3,000 spectators and 1,000 skaters. The Casino also was among the trendiest rinks in the nation. Skaters whirled around on hard maple floors while listening to band music. They also created new dances, among the most notable the Richmond Roll, the Picket Fence, the Philadelphia Twist (described as the skater "rolling his limbs far apart and laying his head sideways on one of them"), and the Dude on Wheels. Admission to skating rinks was relatively inexpensive, ranging from 25 to 50 cents, depending upon location and amenities.[48]

## A NATION OF JOINERS

Foreign observers described Americans during the early nineteenth century as a nation of joiners, but the observation holds equally true for those living during the Civil War and Reconstruction era. Americans spent their leisure time between 1861 and 1877 joining almost every conceivable type of religious and secular organization and activity. Even mining towns on the Comstock Range in Nevada boasted a staggering range of entertainment options for those who wished to participate. "The Comstock is an improving place to live on," one local newspaper boasted during late 1876.

Both Gold Hill and Virginia [City] are well supplied with schools, and there is no lack of churches. We have more saloons than any place in the country. Every Sunday when there is a show in town we have a matinee and an evening performance.... Every Saturday night small boys parade up and down the principal street of Virginia [City], carrying transparencies which inform our sport-loving people where cockfighting might be enjoyed. Faro, keno, chuck-a-luck and roulette may be found in every second saloon, and a special policeman, wearing his star, frequently conducts the game. Taking everything into consideration, there are few pleasanter places to live than on the Comstock.[49]

For the more serious-minded residents of Gold Hill and Virginia City, one could join a variety of fraternal organizations including, among others, the Sons and Daughters of Temperance and the Fenian Brotherhood.[50]

Americans spent much, if not most, of their leisure time participating in church-related activities. Many parents considered church attendance a family affair, with good reason. Ministers increasingly turned their sermons toward examining Christian values and ideals rather than expounding upon various interpretations of Scripture. "The modern preacher," one churchgoer argued, "preaches more and argues less."[51] Henry Ward Beecher and Phillips Brooks were among the most well-known ministers of the day, and their sermons and lectures drew large crowds. Other ministers with large popular followings included Henry Bellows in New York, James Freeman Clarke in Boston, and William Furness in Philadelphia.[52] But church was not all talk, and music enhanced the experience. Many churches featured organ music, accompanied by parishioners who sang from memory and hymnals. The musical effort at American worship services impressed the occasional foreign visitor. "There is more frequent and more melodious singing," one English visitor wrote of American religious customs by comparison to those in his home country. "It is not thought sinful to comply with the exhortations of the Psalmist: 'Rejoice in the Lord, O ye righteous.'"[53]

African Americans displayed even greater religious enthusiasm at church services than whites, at least according to contemporary observers. Blacks spent much of their leisure time at church during the postwar era, for the first time allowed to worship free from white oversight. In a notable display of religious devotion, black church services generally lasted two hours, twice as long as white church services. Church members actively participated throughout much of the worship service, as the spirit moved them. Churchgoers clapped, shouted, and waved, all to demonstrate love for and devotion to God. Additionally, spirituals filled the air. Among the most frequently sung titles included "Were You There When They Crucified My Lord?," "Wade in the Water," and "I Can't Stay Behind." White observers often expressed dismay at the boisterousness and exuberance displayed by black congregations. Black churchgoers returned the sentiment, believing whites too staid and too quiet in their devotion.[54] "I goes ter some churches an' I sees all de foks settin' quiet an' still," commented one black woman, explaining the difference in religious attitudes, "like dey dunno know what de Holy Sperit am. But I fin's in my Bible, that when a man or a 'ooman gets full ob de Holy Sperit, ef dey should hol' der peace, de stones cry out."[55] Blacks and whites increasingly withdrew into their own churches during the postwar years, each worshipping the same God but in different manner.[56]

Americans enjoyed themselves at religious activities outside worshipping at church, including attending camp meetings and joining various Christian organizations and charities. Camp meetings long had characterized American religious life, both to reinvigorate the faithful and to save the wayward. Religious revivals continued during the postwar era, each meeting generally lasting from a few days to a few weeks. Attendance ranged into the hundreds and the thousands of people, with many participants traveling long distances to reach the meeting site. Preachers spoke during the morning, afternoon, and evening, exhorting listeners to reform and repent to save themselves. The effect often was electric. "During the exercises," one participant in a Kansas revival meeting exclaimed, "the power of God came down among the people, Sinners cried for mercy, Saints rejoiced and shouted aloud the high praises of the Lord of Hosts." Despite concerted efforts, only the rare preacher possessed the rhetorical flair to move an entire audience. "Lots of people went to the meetings who were not members of any Church," one eyewitness to a camp meeting admitted, "and the whole thing partook very much of the nature of a week's picnic.

There was plenty to eat and drink, and considerable amusement was to be found by the not too serious part of the community."[57]

In addition to attending camp meetings, Americans expressed their religious enthusiasm by joining various Christian organizations and charities. The Young Men's Christian Association (YMCA) and the Young Women's Christian Association (YWCA) were among the most nationally known religious organizations, then as now. The YMCA came to the United States from England during the 1850s, while the YWCA came during the mid-1860s. The YMCA was the more successful of the two branches in establishing its presence in the United States, if nothing else because of its longer organizational existence. By the mid-1870s, the YMCA counted 1,000 branches across the nation with 100,000 members. The YMCA and the YWCA both emphasized Christian faith and devotion, especially Bible readings and lectures. But both groups also highlighted expanding the mind and the body in other ways, with study classes, music concerts, and athletic games.[58]

The Woman's Christian Temperance Union (WCTU) was another national religious organization. Founded during 1874, the WCTU crusaded for the national prohibition of alcohol. The WCTU began small, receiving its start from efforts by local women to ban the liquor trade in several small towns and villages in southern Ohio. The women used aggressive public tactics to attempt to achieve their goals. Outside saloon doors, they marched and sang religious hymns. Once inside, they held prayer sessions at the bar. A few of the more militant women wielded axes, threatening to smash all liquor bottles within their reach. The anti-alcohol campaign recorded several successes. In Hillsboro, Washington Court House, and Zanesville, city councils banned the sale of alcohol. The road was not all smooth, however, and, in Dayton, onlookers heckled women prohibitionists. From southern Ohio, the temperance campaign spread across much of the rest of the nation. Members of the WCTU made themselves easily recognizable in public, wearing a white ribbon on their clothing to symbolize purity from alcohol. The WCTU had become a national force by the late nineteenth century, numbering 10,000 branches and 500,000 members. Much of the growth of the WCTU occurred while under the leadership of Frances Willard, who became president of the group in 1879 and remained a tireless campaigner for women's rights.[59]

Fraternal organizations and other secular groups provided Americans with the opportunity to seek public entertainment beyond participating in church-related activities. Fraternal and secular organizations just were beginning to flourish during the late 1860s and early 1870s, providing members a sense of order and stability amid the many social, economic, and political changes that characterized the postwar era. Exact membership figures in these groups are unknown, because membership often was secret.[60] One prominent social historian recently argues, however, that hundreds of thousands of Americans belonged to at least one lodge, club, fraternity, or society, by the mid-1870s.[61] These numbers were relatively small by comparison to the larger population, but they cleared the way for the most intense period of fraternization in American history yet to come. Fraternities flourished as never before during the late nineteenth century and, by the late 1890s, one out of every five American males was a member.[62]

The National Grange of the Patrons of Husbandry, popularly known among Americans as the Granger movement, was among the largest fraternal orders during the postwar years. Established by farmers during the late 1860s, the Granger movement protested the perceived victimization of agriculture by railroads, banks, and other moneyed interests. Hard economic times suffered by farmers during the 1870s caused the Granger movement to gain rapidly in membership. The organization recorded its highest membership numbers to date during 1875, at 850,000 members. Popular backing made the Granger movement the driving force in agricultural life. The Grangers established cooperatives and banks and pushed through legislation regarding railroads and grain elevators, among other notable economic and political accomplishments. Improving agricultural conditions caused the Granger movement to go into decline during the 1880s. The organization lost much of its membership base and political clout by the end of the nineteenth century, although continuing to remain in existence in various forms.[63]

Members of the Granger movement worked toward achieving serious economic and political goals, but they also took time to have fun. Local granges sponsored for their members a plethora of picnics, dances, and other social festivities. The highlights of the social season, however, occurred during separate celebrations for Harvest Day, celebrating the end of the crop-growing season; Children's Day, praising the contribution made by youth to farming and agricultural life; Anniversary Day, commemorating the establishment of the Granger movement on December 4 of each year; and Independence Day, celebrating the nation's birthday. Food, games, singing, and the occasional parade characterized each of the four celebrations.[64] One participant later recalled the material abundance present at Granger picnics and celebrations. "There were nice boiled hams, turkeys, chickens," he described, "and a variety of meats, cakes of all kinds, and a general supply of 'knick-knacks' and everything that [the] heart could wish." Another member recalled the good cheer and comradeship that characterized Granger social occasions. He declared that participants would long remember one gathering "as a day pleasantly and profitably spent."[65]

Amid the growing inclination among Americans to join fraternal organizations, few Union and Confederate soldiers came together to form national veterans' groups. Their reluctance to relive their days of military service with their former comrades is surprising to modern-day readers, given the spectacle that the war has become. But many Civil War veterans wanted no part of remembering the trials and hardships that marked their periods of military service. One Union veteran admitted that he and his fellow comrades were too near the war "to see anything but the raw facts. The glitter of gun barrel and sword, the red carnage of the field, the terrible echoes of ... artillery, were yet close realities."[66] Other former Union and Confederate soldiers showed little desire to remember the war because they were too busy attempting to make up for lost time. "In those days," one veteran explained, "the great interest lay rather in what was before than in what was behind us."[67] Whether through memories too vivid or schedules too busy, few former Civil War soldiers joined veterans' organizations. In a notable example, the Grand Army of the Republic, the most important Union veterans' group, numbered only 30,000 members in 1878.[68] Veterans' groups only began to flourish during the late nineteenth century, when soldiers feared that the rest of American society was on the verge of forgetting their wartime sacrifices and accomplishments.[69]

Whether church member or fraternal brother; Civil War veteran or civilian; nearly all Americans joined in public celebration of various religious and national holidays. Christmas remained a largely private and family-oriented celebration, but several other holidays were on the rise in public popularity during the 1860s and 1870s. St. Patrick's Day parades drew large crowds among the Irish American population of New York City; while Mardi Gras festivities gained in participation among residents of New Orleans. Additionally, Americans observed Memorial Day, first commemorated to honor the memory of Civil War dead, with flowers, speeches, and parades. Many white southerners also celebrated Confederate Memorial Day (or, perhaps more accurately, only celebrated Confederate Memorial Day) to remember their fallen. Other holidays were on the decline during the mid- and late-nineteenth century. Most notably, George Washington's birthday, a day traditionally marked by festivities and relaxations, fell increasingly from public attention. In San Francisco, city officials moved public ceremonies commemorating the first president's birthday from the center of the city to the outskirts of the city. Across the country, in New York City, members of the Seventh Regiment (militia) stopped holding a parade to mark Washington's birthday during the late 1870s.[70]

Public celebrations of the Fourth of July rose above that of other holidays. The Fourth of July long had been the nation's premier public holiday, but the day took special meaning during the postwar era. Many northern communities publicly welcomed home returning Union soldiers for the first time on July 4, 1865. In Eau Claire, Wisconsin, for example, a small town north of Madison, citizens hosted an elaborate dinner for local veterans, as well as delivering a speech on "Union."[71] Even some southern communities hoped that common celebration of the nation's birthday might heal sectional divisions still lingering from the Civil War. "May the day mark a new era of true peace," one New Orleans newspaper declared on Independence Day, 1865, "of reconstructing in heart as well as in form, of people of all parts of the common country bound together on principles of justice and acknowledging one future and one destiny."[72] Still, some Southerners remained less than gracious in defeat. "Being good Christians," one die-hard Confederate sniffed, "we did not join in the celebration of the 4th."[73]

The Fourth of July also took special meaning during the postwar era because the nation celebrated its centennial birthday during 1876. Patriotic celebrations occurred across the nation, with parades, speeches, and other public festivities. The most spectacular commemoration, however, occurred with the opening of the Philadelphia Centennial Exposition on May 10, for a six-month run. Designed to tout American unity and progress, the exposition featured 30,000 exhibits on nearly every aspect of American life. The objective of the almost overwhelming number of exhibits was, in the words of one director, to demonstrate that the "mass of the people whilst engaged in their daily and necessary pursuits, enjoy a larger measure of personal comfort and dignity than those of any other nation."[74] After paying a 50-cent admission fee, visitors walked through exhibitions on manufacturing and science, agriculture, machinery, and horticulture. Those individuals still with energy remaining strolled through exhibits that included, among many others, the United States Government Building, the Woman's Building, the Nevada Quartz Mine, the Bible Pavilion, and the Butter and Cheese Factory. Those seeking refreshments went to various ethnic restaurants, popcorn stands, and beer gardens, the last named option a rarity at festivals that promoted family entertainment and one that opened only after considerable debate. Other visitors smoked cigars purchased from cigar booths, before making their way to see the Torch of Liberty from the still-to-be-finished Statue of Liberty.[75]

The Centennial Exposition drew both record crowd numbers and rave visitor comments. The first day of the exposition alone drew more than 200,000 visitors, including President Ulysses S. Grant. By the close of the exposition during the late fall of 1876, ten million people had toured the grounds. These were record numbers for any visitor attraction in the United States and meant that about one of every four Americans had made his or her way inside the entrance gates.[76] Seemingly all went home impressed by what they had seen. "One thinks only of the glorious triumphs of skill and invention," one visitor admitted after witnessing various machinery exhibits, "and wherever else the national bird is mute in one's breast, here he cannot fail to utter his pride and content." Another visitor declared, "How the American heart thrills with pride and love of his land as he contemplates the vast exhibition of art and prowess here."[77]

Not all Fourth of July celebrations were as elaborate as those staged in 1865 and 1876. During the decade in between, Americans enjoyed more quiet observances of the holiday. For some, family picnics marked the occasion. Their actions were in contrast to many earlier generations of Americans, when drunk and rowdy behavior often characterized Independence Day celebrations. "The time seems to be coming," the *New York Tribune* approvingly noted during 1871, "when the Fourth of July shall be a holiday plain and simple, devoted to rest and recreation and some sort of civic observance which will recall for ever the beginnings of the republic."[78] For other Americans, fireworks displays were the highlight of any Fourth of July celebration. Residents of New York City observed the nation's birthday during 1870 by watching what were among the grandest pyrotechnic displays of the postwar era. Emblems of George Washington, Liberty, and Justice all blossomed against the nighttime sky. The finale of the show featured fireworks that formed a "grand union battery of red, white, and blue stars and stripes." The 1870 Fourth of July celebration became the talk of the town. Boasted one local newspaper, the display covered "over thirty thousand square feet of fire" and featured the "most brilliant and beautiful colors known in art."[79]

Americans were a people who knew how to enjoy their leisure time during the Civil War and Reconstruction era. Visiting Europeans still occasionally complained that Americans were too busy making their way in the world to fully appreciate their pastimes. One American writer conceded the point, quipping that the average citizen "works, eats, and haw-haws on a canter."[80] But Americans had come far in seeking their fun. By the start of the late nineteenth century, Americans had established the passion for playing outdoor sports and games and joining fraternal and social organizations that continues to characterize the nation today.

# 8
# Literature

The Civil War sparked an outpouring of popular literature, ranging from poetry and sentimental novels to anecdotes and parodies. War literature appeared widely in books, newspapers, magazines, story papers, broadsides, pamphlets, and dime novels. At its best, it articulated new attitudes toward race, gender, and violence. While mainstream authors like Nathaniel Hawthorne and Herman Melville largely ignored the issues of race and gender, the popular press of the time, in both the North and the South, was awash in literary works that revealed a national preoccupation with those subjects.[1]

The growth of interest in reading from the earliest days of the republic was phenomenal. By 1825, libraries in the five largest American cities had twenty times more books to lend than the entire country owned in Washington's time,[2] and bookstores were everywhere. At the outbreak of war, the North dominated all aspects of publishing and largely dictated the nation's literary tastes, although a few southern writers like Paul Hamilton Hayne and Henry Timrod could boast a small national following. The Bible was widely read, as were Shakespeare's works, and the most popular poets included Byron and Tennyson. European novels popular with American readers included M. E. Braddon's *Eleanor's Victory*, Charles Dickens's *Great Expectations*, and Victor Hugo's *Les Misérables*.

Among the most widely read and influential novelists of the early nineteenth century was Sir Walter Scott (1771–1832), whose stirring tales of nationalism and patriotism continued to galvanize American readers, especially in the South, for years after his death. Numerous American authors, like James Kirk Paulding, John Pendleton Kennedy, William Gilmore Simms, and others, followed in Scott's literary footsteps, though not with his success. The most successful American follower of Scott, and perhaps the father of the American novel, was James Fenimore Cooper (1789–1851). Cooper had lived on the New York frontier and drew on local legends of the previous century's American Indian Wars to create his Leatherstocking Tales—a series of five novels about frontier life, including *The Pioneers* (1823), *The Last of the Mohicans* (1826), and *The Deerslayer* (1841), which ended the series and captured the romance of that era. Cooper inspired many imitators, including Lydia Maria Child's *Hobomak* and *The Rebels*, Mrs. Catherine Sedgwich's *Hope Leslie*, John Kennedy's *Rob of the Bowl*, and Robert Montgomery Bird's *Nick of the Woods*. The most prolific and popular was Joseph Holt Ingraham, whose *The Pirate of the Gulf*, about Jean Lafitte, was the first of a hundred novels he wrote. Longfellow, feeling the sting of having *The Pirate* dedicated to him by its admiring author, called Ingraham the worst novelist who ever lived. Ingraham could write on literally any subject, and his *Prince of the House of David* (1855) sold hundreds of thousands of copies. Another widely read author of the antebellum period was Herman Melville (1819–1891), whose 1851 *Moby Dick* is an excellent example of the whaling novel, a popular genre of the period.

Books were augmented by a flood of magazines and newspapers—575 magazines and 2,931 newspapers in 1860. Magazines and newspapers of the mid-nineteenth century published much of the literary output of American authors and also provided the raw material from which authors took their subjects. *Harper's Weekly*, with a claimed monthly circulation of 500,000 copies, and *Atlantic Monthly* were the two most prestigious literary and political magazines of the Civil War era. The popular press during the war filled their sheets with war stories of all sorts, ranging from the eyewitness reports of military correspondents to sentimental or sensationalized fiction.

The distinction between "high" and "low" literature was not so clear in the public's mind as it would become in the later nineteenth century, and the popular magazines of the 1860s were neither self-consciously high nor low in their content or audience, tending to hold the middle ground.[3] Certain authors, like Louisa May Alcott, published under their own names when writing for the more prestigious magazines but took pseudonyms when writing for the cheap story papers.

## UNCLE TOM'S CABIN

One of the most influential novels of the prewar years was *Uncle Tom's Cabin; or, Life among the Lowly* (1852), by Harriet Beecher Stowe (1811–96). Stowe, daughter of the fiery evangelist Lyman Beecher and brother of Henry Ward Beecher, was introspective and restrained in her attitudes. Deeply affected by the slavery question, she somewhat diffidently and leisurely began writing about slavery and the South, although she knew little of the region and the society there. Her novel initially was published as a serial in *The National Era* over the course of 1851 and 1852. Republished in book form in the latter year, it became a best-seller and was widely adapted for the stage.

Uncle Tom, the main character, is a noble, high-minded Christian slave in the Shelby family. Financially insolvent, the Shelbys are forced to sell their slaves. Tom's wife and daughter flee across the icy Ohio River, but Tom refuses to go out of affection for his owner. He is subsequently sold down the Mississippi and on the trip downriver saves the life of a white child, Eva St. Clare. Her mischievous companion is Topsy, whose father purchases Tom and takes him to New Orleans. Tom is then sold to Simon Legree, a brutal planter. Because he will not reveal the whereabouts of two runaway female slaves, Tom is beaten to death by Legree.

Deeply sentimental and melodramatic, *Uncle Tom's Cabin* has given society three unforgettable characters—Little Topsy who "never was born, never had no father, nor mother, nor nothin'"; Simon Legree, the personification of the evils of slavery; and Uncle Tom, the epitome of the potential good in people, although in modern times the character has been seen by some blacks as a symbol of simple-minded submission to whites. The novel became one of many voices raised in opposition to slavery, but it was also intensely criticized on the grounds that Stowe did not have firsthand knowledge of what she was writing about. Such criticism did not prevent her from following up in 1853 with *A Key to Uncle Tom's Cabin* and *Dred, A Tale of the Great Dismal Swamp*. Abraham Lincoln supposedly praised *Uncle Tom's Cabin* as the "little book that caused the big war," and the importance of the work grew in Stowe's mind until it became to her a kind of biblical statement.

By the early 1860s, respected publications like *Frank Leslie's Illustrated Newspaper* and *Harper's Weekly* had begun to explore all aspects of African American life more fully than had Stowe and other prewar authors. The racial stereotypes popularized by Stowe and others persisted at first in even the best publications, but the discussions took a decidedly serious turn following emancipation in 1863, and there were at least tentative attempts to portray authentic black heroism in the popular press. The heroic performance of black Union troops at Fort Wagner on July 18, 1862, did much to further shift the tone to celebration of black courage and freedom. Louisa May Alcott's short story "The Brothers," based on that event and published in the *Atlantic Monthly* in November 1863, was indicative of the shift.

## DIME NOVELS AND STORY PAPERS

A literate public was a reading public when they had access to literature at a low price, and the dime novels, story papers, and other cheap publications served that need. Introduced in the 1850s, the so-called dime novels were cheap paperbacks that enjoyed tremendous popularity for more than four decades. They provided the reading public with countless mass-produced novels, mostly of dubious quality. Dime novels were sold at every newsstand and were advertised far and wide in all the popular magazines. They were usually printed in press runs of 60,000 to 70,000 copies, a large run by period standards, and the most popular went through numerous reprintings. Ten cents was the usual price, although some series sold for a nickel or a quarter. The American West was a popular subject, as were war stories. Among the best-selling of the early dime novels was *Malaeska, The Indian Wife of the White Hunter* (1860) by Ann Sophia Stephens, which reportedly sold 65,000 copies in a few months. On the basis of that success, Erasmus and Irwin Beadle hired Edward S. Ellis to write the novel *Seth Jones: Or the Captives of the Frontier.*

The Beadles soon developed a formula for the dime novel and stuck with it. They constantly reworked the same basic plots, hiring writers to flesh out the booklets to 30,000 to 50,000 words. Authors were paid from $50 to $250, depending on length and sales expectations. Beadles' Dime Novels were bound in thin salmon-colored paper covers graced with often lurid illustrations, and millions of copies were reportedly sold to soldiers during the war. The Beadles aimed for the highest moral standards. Their directions to their authors prohibited "all things offensive to good taste ... subjects or characters that carry an immoral taint ... and what cannot be read with satisfaction by every right-minded person, young and old alike." In addition to their dime novels, the Beadles published the Dime Library, which offered instruction on everything from etiquette and health to popular sports.

Beadle's success spawned many imitators. George Munro established his firm in 1863 and published his Ten-Cent Novels for the next thirty years. Robert De Well began a dime-novel series in 1867 and over the next ten years published 1,118 titles. Munro's brother Norman started publishing dime novels in 1870. Sinclair Tousey, a founder of the American News Company, announced a series of "first-class novelettes" in 1863 devoted to war stories and aimed specifically at soldiers. T. R. Dawley followed with a similar series in 1864, Dawley's Camp and Fireside Library. No matter how poor the plot or the writing, the dime novels found an eager audience among enlisted men. John Billings recalled of the war period, "There was no novel so dull, so trashy, or sensational as not to find someone so bored with nothing to do that he would wade through it."[4]

The popularity of the dime novel outlived Reconstruction, and it is a testimony to the enduring popularity of the genre that one of its last and most successful such publishers, Street & Smith, was not founded until 1889. At first grinding out adventures based on real-life characters like William F. ("Buffalo Bill") Cody, Daniel Boone, and Kit Carson, the authors soon found they had to invent new characters, which they did, with such wonderfully suggestive names as Deadwood Dick, Deadshot Dave, and Rattlesnake Ned. Plots and outcomes were in the realm of sheer fantasy, with tremendous dif-

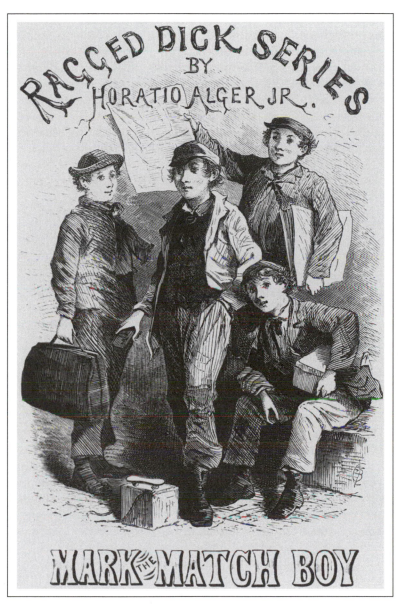

"Rags to riches" stories by Horatio Alger, Jr., comforted and may have inspired many youths. (Courtesy of the Popular Culture Library, Bowling Green State University.)

ficulties always overcome and evil always vanquished. Some authors' output was prodigious. Colonel Prentice Ingraham, son of the novelist Joseph Holt Ingraham, wrote 700 dime novels, 200 of them about his friend Buffalo Bill. Edward Zane Carroll Judson, who wrote under a dozen or more pen names, wrote between 300 and 400 dime novels. Such staggering production was later characteristic of the pulp magazine authors who supplanted the dime novelists. Authors' names were secondary to titles in importance.

Beadle's Dime Series published 631 titles, its Pocket Novels series, 272; its Dime Library published 1,103 titles, the Half-Dime Library 1,168, Tousey's Five-Foot-Wide Library listed 1,353 titles, his Wild West series 1,294. The following advertisement, from *Frank Leslie's Illustrated Weekly* (May 9, 1864), is indicative of the content of the dime novel:

**Munro's 10 Cent Novels!**

They are No. 1. The Hunters.—2. The Trapper's Retreat.—3. The Patriot Highwayman.—4. The Hunted Unionist.—5. The Track of Fire.—6. The Man-Eaters.—7. Charlotte Temple.—8. The Death Face.—9. The Indian Slayer.—10. The Tiger of the Ocean.—11. The Hunter's Triumph—12. The Ocean Rover.—13. The Tory Outwitted.—14. Zeke Sternum, the Lion-Hearted Scout.—15. The Scourge of the Seas.—16. The Captive Maiden.—17. Long-Legged Joe.—These books are for sale by all News Agents, and sent postpaid on receipt of price—ten cents each. George Munro, 137 William St., N.Y.

More respectable than the dime novels, though less popular, were the story papers. Some dime novel publishers issued weekly story papers as well, including *Beadle's Banner* (1872–1897), Elverson's *Saturday Night* (1865–1902), George Munro's *Fireside Companion* (1866–1907), and Norman Munro's *Family Story Paper* (1873–1921). The most popular story paper of the Civil War era, however, was the *New York Ledger*, edited by Robert Bonner. In contrast to the sensational dime novels, the *Ledger* was intended for family readership and was nonsectarian and apolitical. *Flag of Our Union*, a Boston story paper, also abjured politics, preferring instead to offer "only such agreeable entertainment as shall minister to the better feelings of our nature, such as shall be welcome in the domestic circle." However, both papers eventually published some war fiction and poetry as the conflict progressed. In the South, material shortages forced the *Southern Illustrated News*, which included works by Paul Hamilton Hayne and other respected Southern poets and authors, to publish in the cheap story-paper format.

## THE DOMESTIC NOVEL

Some of the most prolific American authors of the mid-nineteenth century were women, many of whom specialized in short stories and often published them anonymously or pseudonymously. Short stories were featured in the leading magazines of the time, most notably *Harper's Weekly, Atlantic Monthly,* and *Godey's Lady's Book. Harper's* preferred a sentimental formula of separated lovers, of which the most successful practitioners were Louise Chandler Moulton, Elizabeth B. Stoddard, Mary Abigail Dodge, Helen W. Pierson, and Nora Perry. The authors featured in *Godey's Lady's Book* tended to be even more sentimental. The *Atlantic* preferred more realistic works, including those by Rebecca Harding Davis and Louisa May Alcott.

The outpouring of literary works by women during the Civil War was in part a response to new challenges and opportunities presented by the conflict. Louise Chandler Moulton, in "One of Many" (1863), claimed that homebound women suffered more than men in wartime due to their passivity. With much of the male populace away at the fighting or otherwise engaged in support roles, however, women inched into expanded roles that society had to have filled if it was to survive. Women authors had things to say, and some depended on their income from writing for support of themselves and their families. Just as World War II brought greater liberation to women in America, the Civil War and Reconstruction opened new doors to women, especially in the North, where women tended to be more assertive than their southern counterparts. Many women recognized and applauded the change. "I shall not confine myself to my sphere," wrote Gail Hamilton (pseudonym for Mary Abigail Dodge) in *Skirmishes and Sketches* (1865). "I hate my sphere. I like everything that is outside of it— or, better still, my sphere rounds out into undefined space. I was born into the whole world. I am monarch of all I survey."[5]

At first expressing themselves largely in sentimental poetry and domestic novels and short stories, women authors increasingly became more observant of the real world, their place in it, and their determination to expand and fill that place fully. The popularity of the domestic novel, popularized by Louisa May Alcott and others, revealed a long-hidden rift in American culture. The plot of the domestic novel was simple and was often used to criticize mistreatment of women. Invoking sexual innuendo, sentiment, and religion, these novels illustrated that waywardness was costly. They sentimentalized and sensationalized such basic problems of the day as drinking, gambling, abuse, prostitution, breakup of the family, and poverty. For these novels Nye lists four basic plots: (1) the decline and rise plot, tracing the rise of the wife from misfortune; (2) "the pursuit plot, in the tradition of Richardson's *Pamela;* (3) the renunciation plot," in which the heroine renounces her independence for the security of the home, a near obsession in the culture of the time; and (4) "the domestic tragedy plot," exposing the causes and consequences of the broken home.[6]

Domestic novels dominated mass-market fiction through the middle decades of the nineteenth century. Sara Willis Payson (1811–1872), writing under the pseudonym Fanny Fern, was an especially prolific contributor to magazines like the *New York Ledger.* Her father, Nathaniel Willis, was the founder and editor of the sternly moralistic children's magazine, *The Youth's Companion*. Escaping a bad second marriage, and with two children to support, Payson turned to writing. Her first essay appeared in *The Olive Branch*. It was quickly reprinted, and Payson soon became one of the highest-paid authors in nineteenth-century America. Often blatantly sentimental, but not without touches of humor and satire, her pieces addressed a range of nineteenth-century domestic and social issues, from the subterfuge of a widow eager to remarry to the death of loved ones. Her first book, a collection called *Fern Leaves from Fanny Fern's Portfolio* (1850) became a national best-seller, and she followed with numerous other popular works.

Other financially successful women authors included Maria Susan Cummins (*The Lamplighter*, 1854) and Mrs. Marion Harland (*Alone*, 1864). *Macaria; or, Altars of Sacrifice* (1864) by the southern author Augusta Jane Evans, was one of the few best-sellers published in the Confederate States, and Evans followed that success with *St. Elmo* in 1866. But the most successful was E. D. E. N. (Emma Dorothy Eliza Nevite) Southworth, who published 62 domestic novels. These novels in one way or another included angelic heroines who successfully defended their virtue and profited from it; poor families; and staunch servers of Christianity. They found a ready market in the sentimentality of the war years.

Domestic novels were turned out by men as well. Sylvanus T. Cobb produced 22 novels, 937 pieces of shorter fiction, and 2,143 essays and sketches. To the *New York Ledger* he contributed 2,305 items. Timothy Shaw Arthur's *Ten Nights in a Barroom; and What I Saw There* (1854), written in the heat of the temperance crusade, reportedly was second only to *Uncle Tom's Cabin* (1852) in popularity for a time. Arthur's novel was published in paperback with the picture of a pleading young girl obviously dispatched by her mother to bring the drunken man home from the saloon with the cry, "Father, come home!" The novel is awash in examples of men ruined by alcohol. Joe Morgan, the honest father, is ruined by drink; Frank Slade is murdered by his father in a drunken rage; and Judge Hammond drinks his way from bench to gutter. Even more prolific was E. Z. C. Judson, who wrote under the pseudonym Ned Buntline. His most successful expose was *The Mysteries and Miseries of New York* (1848), a collection of frightening stories about New York City's prostitutes, thieves, gambling halls, and brothels that he claimed were "drawn from *life, too-real life*, written with the pen of truth." These exposés spawned many others, among them Edward Cropsey's *The Nether Side of New York* (1872).

The widespread popularity of the sentimental and often formulaic domestic novel caused Nathaniel Hawthorne to complain that "America is now wholly given over to a damned mob of scribbling women." Mark Twain became livid at the mere thought of their appeal, especially such novels as Elizabeth Stuart Phelps's *Gates Ajar* (1868), with its feminized theology and promise of a heaven in which the family and the domestic household would be re-created in spiritual form. Appealing to the sentimental and self-righteous side of society, with some tangential appeal to prurient interest, domestic novels lost much of their popularity after the war, but the genre did not die out. They are with us today in the mass-market romance novel.

## OTHER GENRES

Two earlier genres of popular fiction, the mystery tale and the historical romance, reemerged after the war. The historical romance was an old form that had been popular since the birth of story telling. It abandoned reality for fantasy and told its stories in the realm of imagination where any kind of characters and action could be presented. Women became very adept at the historical romance, and even with the contemporary romance, because they were often led to believe that they had no sense of the deeper aspects of reality and therefore had to engage in fantasy.

The historical romance branched off into various forms, such as the love story, the western, detective, and gothic. Edgar Allan Poe (1809–1849) was especially good at both the gothic and detective. He first Americanized the detective story in the 1840s with his tales of "ratiocination and detection," including "The Murders in the Rue Morgue" (1841), "The Mystery of Marie Roget" (1842–1843, based on the actual murder in New York City of Mary Cecilia Rogers), and "The Purloined Letter" (1845). French and English stories of crime and detection developed a following in the United States during the 1860s and 1870s. Emile Gaboriaux's *L'Affaire Rouge* (1866) was published in the United States as *The Crimson Crime*. British author Wilkie Collins attracted a large American following with *The Woman in White* (1860) and *The Moonstone* (1868). One American who set out to challenge Collins's reputation was Anna Katherine Green, the daughter of a well-known lawyer. In *The Leavenworth Case* (1878), by she introduced the fat, amiable lawyer, Ebenezer Gryce, whose fatherly appearance and demeanor belied his shrewd and unrelenting detective work.

There was also a revival of interest in the historical romance following the war. Francis Marion Crawford wrote some forty-five historical novels with Europe, and especially Italy, as the setting. Lew Wallace, a Civil War general who became governor of the New Mexico Territory, published a best-selling historical novel, *The Fair God*, in 1873. His most popular novel, *Ben Hur* (1880), was not published until several years after the end of Reconstruction.

## POETRY

During the Civil War and Reconstruction, Americans knew the traditional poets like Shakespeare and Milton, but there was also another form of poetry that was widely appreciated: the instructive and everyday poetry by and for the people. In his *Library of Poetry and Song* (1872), William Cullen Bryant pointed out the values of both kinds of poetry. Some poems were "acknowledged to be great." Others, though less perfect in form, "have, by some power of touching the heart, gained and maintained a sure place in the popular esteem." Following the philosophy of the time, Bryant believed both forms were worthy art. Other poets and commentators on poetry preferred popular poetry. Henry M. Coates's *Fireside Encyclopedia of Poetry* (1879) included only poems that "have touched the human heart."

Henry Wadsworth Longfellow (1807–1882) wrote musically cadenced poems that were everywhere admired. His "Psalm of Life," with its uplifting and inspiring sentiment, was widely read and appreciated. The public took it to their heart and gave it the ultimate compliment, setting it to song and parodying it in dozens of ways. Walt Whitman (1819–1892) is difficult to place in the popular poetry of the Civil War and Reconstruction eras. Though he lived during the period, his work transcended it. During the war, he was a nurse in Washington, D.C., and once got to shake the hand of his hero, Abraham Lincoln. His *Democratic Vistas* outlined his vision of democracy.

The heat of war generated much popular poetry. Much took a predictably sentimental view of the tragedy of war and people's feelings in reaction to it. Many popular poems were set to music and sung straight or parodied. Perhaps the most sensationally popular poem of the war was John Greenleaf Whittier's "Barbara Frietchie," published in the *Atlantic Monthly* in 1863. The poem was based on an apocryphal incident in Frederick, Maryland, that had been relayed to Whittier by novelist Emma Southworth. It told of an aged woman's defiance of Confederate General Stonewall Jackson in flying the Union flag from her window, in which Whittier had his heroine utter the immortal line, "Shoot if you must this old gray head, but spare your country's flag." The incident was almost certainly a fabrication, but Whittier's poem captured the imagination of a nation hungry for heroes. It was widely reprinted throughout the North and even made into a popular song.

In the North, the Reverend Theodore Tilton wrote the hymn-like "God Save the Nation," Harvard philosophy professor F. H. Hedge penned "Our Country Is Calling," and George H. Boker, a prominent playwright, wrote "March Along!" For the South, Albert Pike, a lawyer, editor, and poet-turned-Confederate-general, wrote "Southrons, Hear Your Country's Call." James Randall's "My Maryland" was sung straight as well as being parodied and twisted into dozens of different versions. In both parts of the nation, hundreds of poems with titles like "Following the Drum," "The Soldier's Mother," and "The Volunteer to His Wife," were written in reaction to the horrible sadness of parting, loneliness, and death.

The northern longing for reconciliation predominated in the works of such poets as Edmund Clarence Stedman, Thomas Bailey Aldrich, Edward

Roland Sill, Cincinnatus Heine, and Thomas Buchanan Read. Some of the poems were so passionate in their appeal to patriotism or reconciliation, or to human dignity and universal love of mankind and country, that they appealed equally to both sides. Stedman's "Wanted—A Man" was such a poem. The poem so impressed President Lincoln that he reportedly read it to his cabinet in 1862, when it was clear that the president needed above all else a general of the army who could do his duty.

In southern poetry, nostalgia and defiance were common themes. The southern poet Henry Timrod, called upon to produce a Confederate anthem, initially refused, then in March 1862 penned "A Call to Arms," just one of many such calls to battle that would be produced by Southern writers during the course of the war. Paul Hamilton Hayne, known in his lifetime as the "poet laureate of the South," began writing verse while in law school, which he left to take over the *Literary Gazette.* Too frail for military service, he tuned to writing patriotic and martial poems. Hayne's sentimental poems exalted the glories of antebellum life and were blamed for contributing to sectional divisiveness, although Hayne personally was said to be nonpartisan. After the war his works were published widely in the *Atlantic Monthly, Scribner's Monthly,* and other respected magazines.

## MARK TWAIN

A slowing of momentum following the war allowed the growth of more leisurely and mature thought, as seen in the work of Mark Twain (pseudonym for Samuel Langhorne Clemens, 1835–1910). Twain's work reflects the birth, growth, and accomplishments of American literature and democracy. Although some of Twain's prolific output is of embarrassingly poor quality, his best work—including *The Adventures of Tom Sawyer, The Adventures of Huckleberry Finn,* and *Life on the Mississippi*—is unexcelled. In Twain we see the occasionally erratic evolution of democratic literature as American writers began to move beyond simple imitation of European styles and domination by Eastern intellectuals.

Mark Twain was raised on the banks of the Mississippi River, on which floated the colorful commerce and citizenry of a developing nation. "It was a heavenly place for a boy," Twain recalled of his boyhood home of Hannibal, Missouri. For two years, Twain served as pilot on the riverboats on the Mississippi under the watchful eye of Captain Horace Bixby, who said of his younger cub pilot, "He knew the river like a book, but he lacked confidence." Throughout Twain's life he sought to gain that confidence. Influenced by his father's agnosticism and blind hope for material success, and his mother's strong Presbyterian positivism, Twain recognized early in life the pretensions and contradictions inherent in American society, as well as in his own personality.

Twain's writing career seems to have begun with publication of a humorous piece called "The Dandy Frightening the Squatter," published in the Boston *Carpet Bag* on May 1, 1852. He followed this with travel pieces sent to hometown papers after he left Hannibal in 1853. During the Civil War, Twain served very briefly with a pro-Confederate citizens' militia, an experience he later recalled without pretense or sentiment in "The Private History of a Campaign That Failed." In July 1861, he set out with his pro-Union brother, Orion, for Carson City, Nevada, where Orion had been appointed secretary of the territory of Nevada.

Twain got more training with a job on the Virginia City *Enterprise,* as a journalist in San Francisco, and on a newspaper-sponsored trip to the Sandwich Islands. He had his first major success with the publication, in the November 18, 1865, issue of the *New York Saturday Press*, of "The Celebrated Jumping Frog of Calaveras County." Widely republished, the story brought Twain the fame that he sought, and in October 1866, he went on the lecture circuit. Following publication of his first book in 1867, Twain further strengthened his public appeal in a series of letters written while on a European tour, which were later published as *The Innocents Abroad* (1869).

Twain had a difficult time growing into his profession. "When I began to lecture, and in my earlier writing, my sole idea was to make comic capital out of everything I saw or heard," he confessed to Archibald Henderson, his biographer. He sometimes failed to recognize when his Western brand of humor would not be appreciated in the more restrained East. At John Greenleaf Whittier's birthday dinner on December 17, 1877, for example, he made an embarrassing gaffe with a joke about encountering three drunks in the High Sierras impersonating Emerson, Longfellow, and Holmes. The attendees were not amused, leaving Twain, as William Dean Howells said, "with his joke dead on his hands." Nevertheless, Twain continued in his ways, pleasing the masses while being largely shunned by the Eastern intellectual establishment. In 1873, he and Charles Dudley Warner published *The Gilded Age,* set in Washington and revealing the corruption he had witnessed in 1867 to 1869, when he had served as private secretary to Senator William Stewart of Nevada. Observing, "We have no distinctly native American criminal class except Congress," he declared.

But Twain did try to see the brighter side and to write about America as a land of hope and promise. He never outgrew his youth on the glorious Mississippi River and often drew on his childhood adventures in his work. But more than most other literary people, he suffered the agony of a nation split by the conflict over slavery and growing wider apart culturally because of economics.

In *The Adventures of Tom Sawyer* and *The Adventures of Huckleberry Finn,* Twain pictured childhood on the river as basically idyllic, but with an ominous undercurrent. *The Adventures of Huckleberry Finn* (1885), begun in 1876 though not published until after the Reconstruction, is Twain's memory of his ordeal of growing up in the land and time of slavery.

The story begins with the poor and unschooled Huck Finn being abused by his drunken father. After having been locked up in a cabin by his father, Huck escapes and goes to Jackson's Island where he meets Jim, Miss Watson's runaway slave. To escape the townsfolk who are looking for Huck's drowned body and the runaway slave, the two float off down the river on a raft. On the trip south, they encounter many adventures with the citizens on the bank which serve to cement their democratic bond all the more tightly. They become two against the world.

The real test of their bond comes at the end of the book. After many adventures in the evil and power of the citizenry off the security of the river, Huck and Jim, along with the phony royalty, the "Duke of Bridgewater" and the "Dauphin," "Louis XVII of France," Huck discovers that the "King" has sold Jim to Mrs. Phelps, Tom's Aunt Sally. Knowing the horror of slavery, Huck is nevertheless overcome with the guilt of having been instrumental in the abduction of Jim from Miss Watson. Here Twain reflects most powerfully in twin concluding statements the mental conflicts of the citizens of the slavery problem and the Reconstruction adjustment.

Agonizing over the realization that aiding Jim's escape is contrary to religious precepts, Huck realizes that he must avoid hell by returning Jim, so he writes the letter telling Miss Watson that Jim is downriver on the Phelps farm. Then Huck, at peace with himself for the moment, thinks "how good it was all this happened so, and how near I come to being lost and going to hell." Then he continues to think of the good times he and Jim have had and what a fine human being Jim is and how undeserving of slavery. As he continues to brood, the evil of his decision wracks his conscience more and more and he faces the choices: "It was a close place," he says. "I took it up, and held it in my hand. I was a trembling, because I'd got to decide, forever, betwixt two things, and I knowed it. I studied a minute, sort of holding my breath, and then says to myself: 'All right, then, I'll go to hell'— and tore it up."

The second reflection of Reconstruction society is more personal. After the war, many people, ex-Confederates and winning Unionists alike, became uncomfortable with the crowding of the cities in the East. They looked upon society as lacking in opportunity and saw the open West still as the land of opportunity. Twain, like many others, longed for the good old days that he was going to picture in *Life on the Mississippi* (1883). The second powerful statement in *Huckleberry Finn* is the development of that urge.

Life has settled down for Huck. Jim has been freed and the three companions of old—Tom, Huck, and Jim—are planning a new adventure "amongst the Injuns, over in the Territory," but Huck, like many of his fellow countrymen, yearns for individual freedom and opportunity they expect to find in the west, so he determines to shake off civilization and go it alone: "I reckon I got to light out for the Territory ahead of the rest, because Aunt Sally she's going to adopt me and sivilize and I can't stand it. I been there before."

## AMERICAN REALISM

American literary realism, as developed by Twain's friend William Dean Howells (1837–1920), strove for a photographic presentation of externalities. American Western humor in the early tales of Mark Twain, Bret Harte, and others used regional characteristics to set characters and locales apart from those of other regions or nations. Realism also pointed out these differences but reduced their significance by showing that human nature—what Howells called "poor real life" with "thy foolish and insipid face"—was the same everywhere, and infinitely interesting.

Other American realists included Elizabeth Drew Barstod Stoddard (1823–1902) and Rebecca Harding Davis (1831–1910). Both employed realistic settings, though at times they indulged in romantic exaggeration and sentiment. Stoddard mixed almost photographic pictures and literal transcriptions of life with analyses of emotion and psychological drives. *The Morgensons* (1862) captured the difficulties of growing up, while in *Two Men* (1865) and *Temple House* (1867), Stoddard captured the tensions in middle-aged women. Davis consciously sought her material in "this commonplace, this vulgar American life," as she said. In "Life in the Iron Mills," published in the *Atlantic Monthly* in 1861, Davis drew two pictures of human existence: a consumptive iron puddler and his hunchbacked sister versus the rich, dilettantish mill owner and his friends. *Margaret Hawth* (1862) is a story of slum life, while *Waiting for the Verdict* (1868) is a novel about race. *John Andross* (1874), generally thought to be her most effective work, traces the victims of Lana Maddox.

John William DeForest (1826–1906) was perhaps the first bona fide realist, treating war, slavery, and other contemporary issues objectively. His *Miss Ravenal's Conversion from Secession to Loyalty* (1867), considered the best of the early Civil War novels, pictures not the romance of war, but the reality—the fear, filth, stupidity, red tape, and human vultures who feed on conflict. *Playing the Mischief* (1876) exposes the same political corruption that so infuriated Twain. *Overland* (1871), descriptive of life in the West, was popular even though DeForest's West did not come from firsthand observation. His post-Reconstruction works, such as *A Daughter of Toil* (1886, published serially) and *A Lover's Revolt* (1898), were more romantic than realistic. But he read the world through clear and realistic glasses and had directed his vision to recording life as it was, not as he wished it might be.

The development of various forms of literature during and after the war and Reconstruction was natural and inevitable. Literature springs from the cultures of the people. New thrusts in those cultures during this period birthed new attitudes and achievements and consequently new voices. Women learned they could write and were given the freedom to the avenues of publication they needed. The postwar literary world was a society of new developments and accomplishments moving toward the achievements of the turn of the century.

# 9

# Music

American popular music has always triumphed despite a long tradition of opposition in high places. As early as the eighteenth century, Cotton Mather, the Puritan minister and cultural commentator of Colonial America, confessed in his diary his opposition to everyday music: "I'm informed that the minds and manners of many people about the country are much corrupted by foolish songs and ballads which the hawkers and peddlers carry to all parts of the country," he wrote, preferring religiously uplifting songs to the worldly music.

American popular tunes of the early nineteenth century were often borrowed from the British (as with "Yankee Doodle" and "The Star-Spangled Banner") or were composed by writers whose work was imitative of the British style. However, as early as the 1820s, African American material began to make its influence felt on American popular song. The fusion of musical traditions was furthered in the prewar years by Stephen Foster, who brought together black and white folk elements in his popular songs, and by the popularity of the minstrel show.

Before the Civil War, songs were disseminated in various ways. The most common means of distributing a song was by word of mouth. Though formal printed sheet music scores were popular with the musically trained, most Americans lacked the ability to read music and were more likely to learn songs by simple imitation. Thus, the most common means of song distribution were song sheets and songsters. Unlike sheet music, which contained the full musical score, song sheets were single printed sheets with lyrics but no musical notation except, perhaps, the name of the tune to which the lyrics were to be sung. Some of America's favorites songs, including "The Star-Spangled Banner" and "Battle Hymn of the Republic," were originally widely distributed as song sheets. Song sheets had been printed in the British Isles as early as the sixteenth century, but their popularity in the United States reached its peak during the Civil War. Song sheets often fit new lyrics to familiar tunes, "Yankee Doodle," and "Just before the Battle, Mother" being especially vulnerable to adaptation and parody. "The Last Rose of Summer" was parodied as "The Last Potato" a comical ode to the tuber. Other song sheets offered the lyrics of newly written popular songs, and as such they provide a glimpse of the topics that dominated Civil War popular culture: the evils of alcohol, the temperance movement, slavery, grief, and the extremes of fashion were all popular subjects in song. Song sheets reflected civilian attitudes toward the war ranging from unbridled patriotism to hesitancy to even occasional resistance. Many of the Civil War songs, like "Mother Kissed Me in My Dream," "The Children of the Battlefield," and "Lorena," were mawkishly sentimental.

The song sheets' counterpart was the songster or songbook. Like the song sheets, they contained only lyrics, but these inexpensive bound books, sometimes selling for just a few cents, usually contained from sixty to a hundred selections gleaned from folksongs, ballads, popular songs, and minstrelsy. They usually indicated the tune to which the song was to be sung, in lieu of a printed musical score. By 1860, these small songbooks were published in America by the hundreds, but they became even more popular during the war, as soldiers carried the slim volumes in their packs. Songs were also published in newspapers and magazines, especially in the South. In towns and in houses, songs were often accompanied by stringed instruments and, after the war, by the piano. The banjo was generally the folk instrument of choice, and it was the predominant instrument in minstrelsy and vaudeville.

Many Victorians believed that songs could enhance and stimulate intellectual activity and instill correct moral values. Music could make for a happier and more useful life on earth and even carry one toward heaven. One leading American proponent of this philosophy, William B. Bradbury (1816–1868) published 921 of his own hymns, more than three million copies of which had been sold by the end of the nineteenth century. His best-known was *Esther, the Beautiful Queen* (1856), a long musical drama based on the biblical Book of Esther. By the end of the war, 255,000 copies of *Esther* were in circulation.

During the war years and the sentimental decades that followed, popular music served as a cohesive force in American society. Songs often served as a form of self-entertainment or accompanied railroad construction, field work, and other tedious labor. Some workers accumulated large repertories, taking solace from hard labor in their singing. Everywhere the beneficial and useful influence exerted by music on the individual, and on society in general, was recognized. Song energized a an increasingly politicized and partisan population. The editor of *Songs of the People: The Union*

*Republican Campaign Glcc Book* (1868) stated unequivocally, "The Party that sings the loudest, longest, and oftenest is always sure to win." What was sound judgment for political campaigning was equally valid for boosting general spirits and morale.

Classical music during this period was largely reserved for the upper classes and therefore had limited distribution. Symphony orchestras, where they existed at all, were likely to be temporary organizations convened for a season with whatever freelance musicians might be available. In the larger cities, the new Italian operas of Giuseppe Verdi and the English operettas of Gilbert ad Sullivan were special favorites, but in general, classical music failed to attract much of a following outside the metropolitan areas, the proliferation of small-town "opera houses" (which were more likely to host melodramas and burlesque than opera) not withstanding. A few individuals sought to direct and cultivate the general public's musical taste, however. George Templeton Strong, a New York lawyer whose passion was the music of Beethoven, recognized the urgency of accommodating the growing middle class. After a night at the Academy of Music in New York, he wrote: "Nine-tenths of this assemblage cared nothing for Beethoven's music and chattered and looked about and wished it was over." But he felt the beneficial value of such music lay in educating the people: "It's well to bring masses of people into contact with the realities of music; it helps educate their sense of art, and Heaven knows they need it."

## STEPHEN FOSTER

Of all the popular composers of the period immediately preceding the Civil War, the favorite was Stephen Collins Foster (1826–1864). Because his music fit the sentiment of the period, it was popular during the war and the Reconstruction.

Foster was born near Pittsburgh and was a musical prodigy. He learned to play the guitar and flageolet (a kind of flute) and wrote high-quality ballads and songs that drew heavily on black and white folk traditions. Foster soon discovered that he could earn a living composing songs for minstrel shows, a popular form of entertainment in which white performers darkened their faces with burnt cork and performed in stereotypical "Negroid" fashion. After the success of his "Old Uncle Ned" and "Oh Susannah," Foster composed mainly for E. P. Christy's Minstrels, one of the most important blackface troupes of the period. Foster eventually wrote some 400 songs, usually favoring themes common to everyday life in both the North and the South during the period—such as love, beauty, and contentment—although many of his characters had black faces. Many of Foster's greatest minstrel-show hits, such as "Old Folks at Home" (often incorrectly called "Way Down upon on the Suwannee River," 1852), "My Old Kentucky Home" (1853), "Old Black Joe" (1860), "Camp Town Races"

(1852), and "Massa's in de Cold, Cold Ground" (1850) depict the South as a land of sunshine, nostalgia, contented whites, and loyal, happy-go-lucky slaves—the common themes of many minstrel-show songs. In fact, Foster knew very little about the South from personal experience. Foster's sentimental songs, such as "Jeanie with the Light Brown Hair," "Come Where My Love Lies Dreaming," "Beautiful Dreamer," "Gentle Annie," and "Our Bright Summer Days Have Gone" successfully exploited the sentimentality of the era. Despite his successes, Foster died in the New York Bowery an impoverished alcoholic, with three pennies and 35 cents of scrip in his pocket and the words "dear friends and gentle hearts," perhaps the title of a new song, in his pocket.

## BRASS BANDS AND MILITARY MUSIC

The early 1850s saw the flowering of brass band music in America. The all-brass band was predominant in America during that decade, but instrumentation was slowly being influenced by European immigrants, who introduced woodwinds to the ensembles. The New York Seventh Regiment Band introduced flutes, piccolos, and reed instruments as early as 1852. When Patrick S. Gilmore, the most popular and influential bandmaster of the Civil War era, introduced reed instruments into his brass band in 1859, it signaled the decline of the all-brass band.

The military used music to provide signals, sustain morale among the troops, and lend an air of formality to ceremonial occasions. Military music consisted of two distinct types: field music and band music. Field musicians, including company drummers, fifers, and buglers, signaled troops in daily routine as well as in battle. Company musicians were often too young to enlist as regular soldiers. Drummer boys as young as twelve or thirteen were celebrated in such popular parlor songs as Will Hays's "The Drummer Boy of Shiloh" (1863), the poignant story of a youngster not old enough to shave but old enough to beat the drum and stop a bullet.

Military bands generally were brass-and-percussion ensembles originally ranging from eight to twenty-four members and were usually attached to a regiment or brigade. Among the many unusual bands that entered military service was Frank Rauscher's cornet band from Germantown, Pennsylvania, composed of the colorfully uniformed Zouaves of General Charles Collis. Collis had the good fortune to be associated with Captain F. A. Elliott, a wool merchant, who kept the troops supplied with fresh, Turkish-style uniforms and fez hats, and he donated money for their purchase of band instruments. However, an unexpected glut of Union volunteer bands such as Rauscher's during the first year of the conflict caused the U.S. War Department to limit the number of ensembles, and the Confederacy soon imposed the same limit. Congress passed a bill on July 17, 1862, that ordered the mustering out of regimental bands. In October of the

same year, the War Department forbade the further enlistment of regi
mental bands. With ten companies to a regiment and two musicians generally allowed to each company, a regiment could assemble at most an ensemble of twenty men.

The musicians' meager pay was usually supplemented by contributions
from the unit's officers. The bandsmen also performed nonmusical, non-
combat duties, often carrying stretchers and assisting in field hospitals.
Gilmore's 24th Massachusetts Volunteer Infantry was required not only to
play in camp, but to follow the regiment into the field where the musicians
were put to work as hospital corpsmen. One member appears to have been
lost in action.

A full military brass band most often consisted of two or more E-flat cornets or saxhorns, two or more B-flat cornets or saxhorns, two alto horns,
two tenor horns, one baritone horn, one bass horn, and a percussion section
of snare drum, bass drum, and cymbals. A few bands included woodwind
instruments. The most common brass instruments in the bands of both sides
were saxhorns, an upright valved bugle with a backward-pointing bell that
directed the music to the troops parading behind the band. Levels of skill
varied widely among military musicians. While some musicians had
learned to play only after enlisting, others, like the members of the band of
the 25th South Carolina Infantry regiment, had been professional musicians
before the war.

Away from the front, military bands supplied music for ceremonies and
special events. Their repertoire ran the gamut from marches, patriotic
songs, and dance tunes to hymns, funeral dirges, and special arrangements
of overtures and other symphonic pieces. After the war, many military
bands regrouped as local civic bands. Patrick Gilmore went on to make
major contributions to the concert band by developing instrumentation that
allowed a large wind ensemble to handle a full orchestral score, with woodwinds substituting for the stringed instruments. At a time when full symphonic orchestras were still rare in America, concert bands like Gilmore's
filled a pressing need, attracting large followings and retaining their popularity into the early twentieth century.

## Songs of the Confederacy

The Confederacy did not have as many professional composers among
them, so they had to rely more on semiprofessional pieces and folk songs
and ballads.

A Confederate favorite was "The Bonnie Blue Flag." First published by
A. E. Blackmer & Brother in New Orleans, its origins are uncertain. Early
editions state the tune was "composed, arranged, and sung by Harry
Macarthy, 'The Arkansas Comedian.'" Other sources credit the lyrics to
Annie Chambers Ketchum, and the melody apparently was derived from

an old Irish tune called "The Jaunting Car." The song so fired up the Confederates that it became anathema to Yankees. After the fall of New Orleans, General Benjamin Butler (dubbed "The Beast of New Orleans" by the Confederates) reportedly fined its publisher $500, and anybody caught singing the song had to cough up $25.

Another of the Confederacy's favorite songs, "The Homespun Dress," was a sentimental ode to the privations Southern women had to endure for the sake of their cause. This song was supposedly written by a Lieutenant Harrington, who rode into Lexington, Kentucky, with Morgan's cavalry and was impressed by the quality and beauty of the ladies' homespun gowns. His song became popular, appealing to sentiment and promoting self-sacrifice, and was printed in numerous Civil war songbooks.

The most popular Confederate rallying songs of the conflict, however, was "Dixie." Over the years, authorship of this song has sometimes been incorrectly attributed to mythical origins, as in this claim from Francis F. Browne's *Bugle Echoes: Poems of the Civil War*: "The original for this popular Southern song, of which there were many variations during the War, is believed to be a Northern melody—an old Negro refrain, dating back to the time when slavery existed in New York. A certain Mr. Dixy or Dixie, owned large tracts of land on Manhattan Island, and many slaves, among whom the estate was known as Dixie's Land. It was felt that "Dixie belonged to slavery and therefore to the slave states."[1] But in fact, "Dixie" was composed in 1859 by Daniel D. Emmett for Dan Bryant's minstrel-show adaptation of the comedy *Pocohantas*. Emmett was Ohio-born and one of the first white entertainers to perform in blackface. A Copperhead (that is, a Northerner who was opposed to the war), he bitterly resented the way the Confederates appropriated his song for their own purposes. But he was never able to suppress their misuse of his piece. Originally titled, "I Wish I Was in Dixie's Land," it made its debut at Mechanics Hall, New York, on April 4, 1859. There is circumstantial evidence that Emmett first heard the tune in Ohio from two African American musicians, Ben and Lou Snowden.[2]

With its lively tune and sentimental words and the walk-around at the closing number, when the entire cast paraded across the stage, "Dixie" immediately became popular in all sections of the country. When it reached New Orleans in 1860, it became a favorite song onstage and off, and it grew to become the unofficial Confederate national anthem. Because of its seeming sympathy with southern sentiment, its appeal was universal throughout the South, and Southerners did everything possible to make "Dixie" their own song. Confederate citizens rewrote "Dixie" in at least 210 variations. Many were couched in terms of fire and valor. One popular southern version was written by Confederate General Albert Pike (1809–1891): "Southrons, hear your country call you! / Up, lest worse than death befall you! / To Arms! To Arms! To Arms! in Dixie Land!"

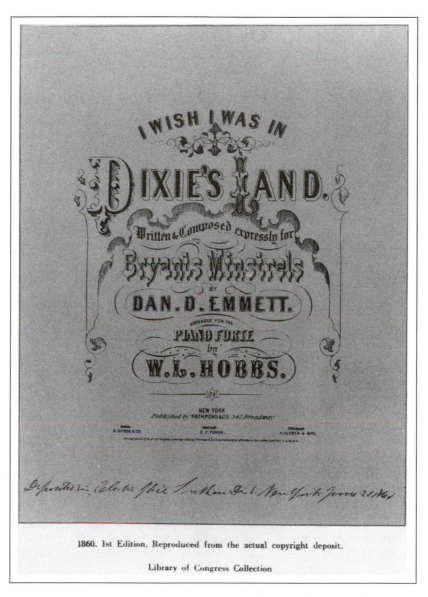

First edition of "Dixie," as composed for Bryant's Minstrels.
(Courtesy of the Popular Culture Library, Bowling Green
State University.)

Emmett's original version of "Dixie" was played at the inauguration of Jefferson Davis in Montgomery, Alabama, in February 1861. Ironically, the song was also a favorite of Abraham Lincoln's. As the war drew to its conclusion in Virginia in April 1865, Lincoln visited the Union camps below Richmond aboard the paddle-wheeler *River Queen* accompanied by a young French count who said he did not know "Dixie." When a band came aboard, Lincoln asked them to play the song, saying to the Frenchman: "The tune is now Federal property, and it's good to show the Rebels that with us in power, they will be free to hear it again. It has always been a favorite of mine, and since we've captured it, we have a perfect right to enjoy it." A week later, Lincoln ordered "Dixie" played as a peace offering upon Robert E. Lee's surrender at Appomattox.

At age eighty, Emmett was making triumphal tours with the Al G. Fields Minstrels and brought down the house every time he appeared, but popularity did not bring him wealth. Emmett had sold the copyright for "Dixie" to his publisher for $500, and he died a pauper.

## Songs of the Union

In the North, the heat of war generated numerous songs. Julia Ward Howe recast an old hymn, "Say, Brother, Will You Meet Us?" into the firebrand "Battle Hymn of the Republic." With its powerful patriotic and religious overtones, Howe's piece, like "Dixie," occasionally underwent transformation, the most memorable being "John Brown's Body" (lyrics anonymous, but attributed to Henry Howard Brownell, Thomas Brigham Bishop, and Charles S. Hall). Inspired by the hanging of John Brown on December 2, 1859, "John Brown's Body" was widely parodied in such songs as "Hang Abe Lincoln on a Sour Apple Tree," or, depending on the singer's point of view, "Hang Jeff Davis on a Sour Apple Tree."

"When Johnny Comes Marching Home" (1863), based on an Irish tune, has occasionally been revived in wartime. With its rollicking march tempo, the tune was adapted for numerous Civil War parodies. George F. Root's "Tramp, Tramp, Tramp, the Boys are Marching" (1864) captured the foot soldier's spirit, as did Henry Clay Work's "Marching through Georgia," one of the North's favorites.

## Music on the Home Front

On the home front, music was used to recruit volunteers, foster patriotism, and create public support for the war effort. Recruiting rallies relied on brass bands to attract crowds. Sheet music of the Civil War period often glorified the solders' life or related sentimental tales of fallen heroes and broken homes. Other popular songs, like "Kingdom Coming" (Henry Clay Work, 1862) and "Sixty-Three Is the Jubilee" (J. L. Greene and D. A. French,

1863), celebrated the advent of emancipation and showed the musical influences of blackface minstrel songs. Battles and leaders were commemorated in elaborate piano pieces, such as "General Bragg's Grand March" (Rivinac, 1861) and "Beauregard Bull Run Quickstep" (J. A. Rosenberger, 1862). More elaborate still was the "battle-piece," an extended and often quite bombastic orchestral depiction of a specific engagement.

Lamentations over the deaths and the sadness caused by the Civil War were numerous and heart-rending. Generally they bemoaned the absence of a family member who was away at war, leaving his loved ones heartbroken and sometimes financially destitute. One song flowing with tears over separation and death was "We Shall Meet but We Shall Miss Him" (words by George Frederick Root, music by H. S. Washburn, 1861). The subject is the man who has gone off to war, for whom "there will be one vacant chair" reserved for his spiritual presence at all future meetings of the family: "We shall meet but we shall miss him / There will be one vacant chair / We will linger to caress him / As we breathe our evening prayer." There was a national outpouring of grief following Abraham Lincoln's death, much of it expressed in such songs as "Farewell, Father, Friend and Guardian" and "Live but One Moment," the later based on the words spoken by Mary Todd Lincoln as her husband lay dying. The president's death left a lingering impression on song writers, who continued to pen memorial songs well into the 1870s and beyond.

One of the most popular sentimental songs of the Civil War was "Lorena." Written in 1857, the song remained largely unknown until the war years, when it became a favorite in both the North and South and was frequently parodied. Sometimes called "Lorena and Paul Vane," its lyrics were attributed to H. D. L. Webster and set to music by J. P. Webster, of no relation. In his headnote to the song, Vance Randolph quotes Dr. John Allen Wyeth's account of Southern appreciation of the song when Morgan's cavalry was returning from a raid in 1862: "Our spirits were high. As we passed the home of the Trappist Brotherhood, Lieutenant Frank Brady entertained us by singing 'Lorena,' a war-time poem which had been set to music and was then very popular. He told us that the author of the poem was an inmate of this Trappist home. If this were so and the self-imprisoned brother heard the sweet voice of the cavalier as he sang 'The years creep slowly by, Lorena,' what sad and tender memories it must have wakened!"[3] Another account makes Webster a Universalist preacher in Zanesville, Ohio.

Countless songs wafted throughout the North and South during the Civil War and Reconstruction. Septimus Winner (a popular songwriter of the day who also wrote under the pseudonyms Alice Hawthorne, Percy Cruger, Mark Mason, and Paul Stanton), composed "Listen to the Mocking Bird" and "Whispering Hope," both of which are still performed today. Among other Civil War- and Reconstruction-era songs still in circulation

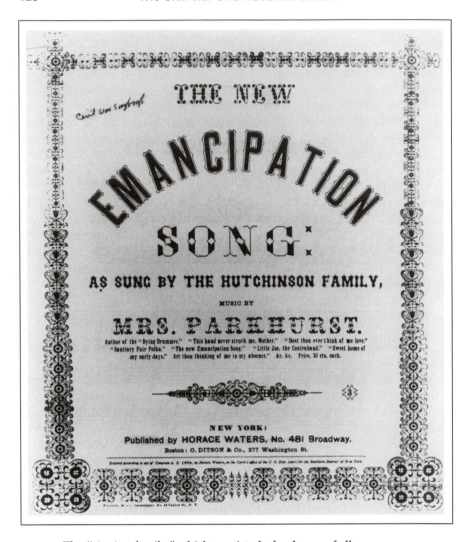

The "singing family," which consisted of a chorus of all age groups
from grandpa to the youngest child able to carry a tune, was a popular
mid-century phenomenon. The Hutchinson Family of New Hampshire,
a group of sixteen, was one such group. This song was copyrighted 1864.
Notice the many patriotic and sentimental songs by Mrs. Parkhurst.

are "Get Out of the Wilderness," later reworked as "The Old Gray Mare"
(1858); "The Yellow Rose of Texas" (1858); "Aunt Dinah's Quilting Party"
(Frances Kyle and L. J. Fletcher, 1860); "The Rock Island Line" (1862);
"When You and I Were Young, Maggie" (J. A. Butterfield and George Washington Johnson, 1866); "The Daring Young Man on the Flying Trapeze" (Al-

Frank Moore (1828–1904) was a Northerner who realized the historical value of popular materials. He collected popular print of the Revolution and material of both the North and the South during the Civil War, like *Anecdotes, Poetry, and Incidents of the War, North and South, 1860–1865*. (Courtesy of the Popular Culture Library, Bowling Green State University.)

LYRICS OF LOYALTY

ARRANGED AND EDITED BY

FRANK MOORE

NEW YORK
GEORGE P. PUTNAM
1864

BOWLING GREEN
STATE UNIVERSITY LIBRARY

fred Lee and George Leybourne, 1868); "Little Brown Jug" (R. A. Eastburn, a pseudonym of Joseph Eastman Winner, 1869); "Shoo Fly, Don't Bother Me" (Frank Campbell and Billy Reeves, 1868); "Reuben and Cynthia," now better known as "Reuben, Reuben, I've Been Thinking" (William Gooch and W. Harry Birch, 1871); "Silver Threads among the Gold" (Hart Pease Danks and Evan E. Rexford, 1873); "Grandfather's Clock" (W. C. Work, 1876); "I'll Take You Home Again, Kathleen" (Thomas P. Westendorf, 1876); "The Lost Chord" (Arthur Sullivan and Adelaide Procter, 1877); and "Where Is My Wandering Boy Tonight?" (Robert Lowery, 1877).

Frank Moore, an anthologizer of poetry and prose of the Civil War, was driven to preserve the popular songs of the period. He published five collections of songs of the period, including *Lyrics of Loyalty* (1864).

## WARTIME PARODIES

During the Civil War, both presidents were often lampooned in song. Often these songs carried double messages and were filled with innuendoes and symbols. Confederate President Jefferson Davis was the subject of the vitriolic "Jeff in Petticoats," which sprang from reports that he had fled Richmond disguised as a woman, ahead of advancing Union troops. During this period, hardly any insult could be greater than accusing a man of disguising himself in women's clothes. Such insults, then as now, could be created merely on rumor, and the facts in this case have long since become muddled.

Lincoln also appeared as the subject of countless song parodies set to folk melodies and minstrel-show tunes. One election-year parody of the folk song "Old Dan Tucker" declared, "Old Abe is coming down to fight / And put the Democrats to flight." Another song, "Lincoln and Liberty Too," was sung to the tune of "Rosin the Bow," an old melody popular in both the North and the South. "Old Abe Went to Washington" was set to the tune of "When Johnny Comes Marching Home," while "Brave Old Abe" used the Scottish tune "Auld Lang Syne." Not all the songs treated Lincoln approvingly. One that did not, sung to the tune of "Pop Goes the Weasel," claimed, "Old Abe is sick, old Abe is sick / Old Abe is sick in bed." Another, called "Old Honest Abe," characterized Lincoln as "an arrant fool, a party tool / A traitor, and a tory." "John Anderson, My Jo, John," an 1824 air often appropriated for political satires, turned up in "Old Abe, My Jolly Jo John," a Copperhead blast at the president in four stanzas. The English ballad "Lord Lovell" was also widely adapted for vitriolic attacks on the president.

For many Southerners and their sympathizers, the differences between Lincoln and Davis were summarized in four short lines, apparently sung by folk on all social levels: "Jeff Davis rides a white horse. / Lincoln rides a mule. / Jeff Davis is a gentleman, / and Lincoln is a fool."

## AFRICAN AMERICAN MUSIC

For slaves, singing was a way to ease their burdens, adapt and preserve some of their native musical traditions, and even communicate clandestinely. Because songs could contain hidden messages and symbols, slaves were sometimes forbidden to sing. For example, in Savannah a congregation of slaves attending a public baptism one Sunday was arrested, imprisoned, and punished with 39 lashes each for singing a song. The situation was rarely so draconian, however. Slaves' singing more often served as a source of entertainment for the plantation owners as well as their guests. Former slave Frederick A. Douglass reported that "slaves are generally expected to sing as well as to do work. A silent slave is not liked by masters or overseers.... This may account for the almost constant singing heard in the Southern states."[4] But as Douglass also pointed out, "it is a great mistake to suppose [slaves] happy because they sing. The songs of the slave represent the sorrows, rather than the joys, of his heart.... In the most boisterous outbursts of rapturous sentiment, there is ever a tinge of deep melancholy."[5]

Slaves often adapted songs from those they heard at the master's houses or in other contacts with whites. The fusion of white material with such African elements as syncopation, chanting, call-and-response, hand-clapping, and foot-stomping, was to have a profound influence on the development of American popular music, leading eventually to the development of such uniquely American musical styles as blues, ragtime, and jazz.

Since most slaves were illiterate and knew music only intuitively, many of their songs were lost. Others were only written down long after the war and were often heavily revised to appeal to the tastes of white audiences. A few are still extant. One, called simply "Civil War Chant," lists all the materials that Lincoln possessed to whip the Confederates, including food, clothes, powder, shot, and lead. Another popular slave song was "Old Jawbone," a ditty about eating and talking—and virtually anything else one wanted to do—which went on for as many stanzas as the singer wanted, always with the chorus: "Jawbone walk and jawbone talk / And Jawbone eat with a knife and fork." White patrols who roamed the plantations and villages looking for absent or runaway slaves were the subject of much derisive humor, especially in songs like "Run, Nigger, Run," which outlined ways of escaping and the terrible punishment if caught.

One form of slave song that did survive the war, although in highly altered form, was the black religious music known as the spiritual. Spirituals were being collected and studied by the time of the Civil War, and in 1873, Fisk University sent a group of spiritual singers on tour to raise money for the fledgling black university. The Fisk Jubilee Singers rewrote and rearranged the old spirituals for their white audiences, playing down the traditional African elements while introducing European harmonies and choral arrangements to add an element of "respectability." The formula worked, and the Fisk singers caused a national sensation on tour. They survived, with much turnover, well into the twentieth century.

At a time when few individual black performers and composers were able to rise above obscurity, James Bland made his mark on American popular music. Born to a middle-class African American family in New York, Bland studied composition and arrangement at Howard University. In 1874 Bland decided to leave his studies for a career on the stage after attending a performance by George Primrose, a popular white minstrel-show star. Within a year, Bland was managing his own minstrel troupe, and he went on to enjoy a long career as a singer and comedian with some of the best-known minstrel troupes, even touring to great acclaim in England and Germany. However, Bland's abilities as a performer have long been overshadowed by his popularity as a songwriter. Bland composed approximately 700 songs, among them "Carry Me Back to Old Virginny" (1875), which in 1940 was adopted by Virginia as its official state song; "In the

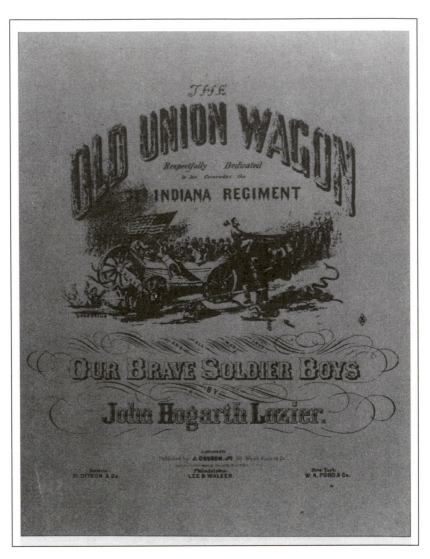

Cover for a collection of Union songs, showing Lincoln driving a
Union wagon through war. (Courtesy of the Popular Culture
Library, Bowling Green State University.)

Evening by the Moonlight" (1878); and "Oh, Dem Golden Slippers"(1879). Bland's work, however, exhibited little African American influence and was generally indistinguishable in content and form from the stereotypical minstrel songs being turned out by white composers. As musicologist Sam Dennison notes, "What is indisputable is Bland's genius in imitating white song types."[6]

## MUSIC ON THE FRONTIER

In the more remote parts of the nation, music sometimes developed very differently from in the large urban centers. The ways in which songs permeated the lives of Americans living on the frontier during the war and Reconstruction were recorded by Hamlin Garland. Born into a musical family, Garland recalled four songs that dominated his life on the fringes of American civilization. "Sweet Belle Mahone" (words and music by J. H. McNaughton) was published as sheet music and widely reprinted in songbooks as early as 1872. The fact that it was a sea song enhanced its romantic appeal for people thousands of miles from the ocean. "Maggie, Air Ye Weepin'?," had been published as early as 1822 and remained popular throughout the nineteenth century. A different kind of song altogether a song which was "O'er the Hills in Legions, Boys," a stirring song of pioneering. "The Rolling Stone" (collected as a folksong as early as 1852, according to the Frank C. Brown Collection of Folksong), deals with a debate between husband and wife over the desirability of giving up the established homestead, where life is relatively safe and satisfactory, and pioneering off to new lands where danger and uncertainty lurk. After fourteen verses, the wife finally prevails, and the family stays on the farm.

As the frontier expanded westward after the war, a new musical genre emerged as the songs of the Western laborers and cowboys were sanitized for public consumption. One of the earliest and longest-lived was "Home on the Range" (originally entitled "Western Home," and in print as early as 1874 in the publication *Kirwin Chief*, Kirwin, Kansas). Its authors, Daniel E. Kelley and Brewster Higley, idealized the territory in the most florid terms, depicting the American West as the land of milk and honey, hope and promise: "Oh! Give me a home where the buffalo roam / Where the deer and the antelope play / Where seldom is heard a discouraging word / And the sky is not cloudy all day." As living conditions became increasingly congested in the East after the war, the idealized West beckoned more and more strongly, and those people who could not or would not make the trip could use the wings of song to carry them there.

The wings of song have, in fact, always lifted people's spirits, hopes and aspirations. In America during the war, they accompanied the soldiers in the field and comforted the home folks in their loneliness. During the Reconstruction, which stimulated all kinds of professional, domestic, and home front entertainment, the floodgates of song opened, stimulated by increased opportunities, and the newly reestablished United States got down to the serious business of writing and singing popular songs.

# 10

# Performing Arts and Entertainment

The performing arts flourished in America in the years leading up to and following the Civil War. As cities grew and Americans found themselves with more leisure time available, a huge market was created for all sorts of staged entertainment. While the American legitimate theater became increasingly sophisticated, the working classes flocked to melodramas, minstrel shows, burlesque, vaudeville, and other easily accessible forms of popular theater. In outlying areas, the performing arts were often limited to traveling theater companies, circuses, medicine shows, or Lyceum and Chautauqua troupes.

## THEATER

Largely centered in the North, where the general populace continued at times to put personal pleasure before the harsh reality of a distant war, the theatrical world was not deeply affected by the Civil War. Some southern theaters, like the New Orleans Varieties Theater, operated throughout the war. Others in the South, closed at the outbreak of the conflict, had reopened by the early 1870s, although they often found it difficult to attract and retain the best actors.

Thousands of new theaters were built after the war, ranging from opulent classical structures in the major metropolitan areas to crude dance halls on the frontier. In New York City alone, twenty-five new theaters were built during the last third of the nineteenth century. The largest theaters, with seating capacities as high 2,500, were able to take advantage of the latest technologies in lighting and scenery management. Edwin Booth's theater was built in 1869 by James Renwick, Jr. (1818–1895), who had designed St.

Patrick's Cathedral and the Smithsonian Institution, and it boasted an ornate interior in the Second Empire style. Its stage was equipped with hydraulic lifts that provided rapid and uninterrupted changes of scenery, allowing scenes on one level to be changed while the play progressed on the main level. The Madison Square Theater, formerly Daly's Fifth Avenue, was another technological marvel, employing vertically shifting floors that allowed scenes to be changed within two minutes.

The coming of gaslights made innovations in theater lighting possible but posed a new threat. Gaslit theaters were especially vulnerable to fire, and some were destroyed. Ford's Theatre in Washington, D.C., seemed especially star-crossed. The first theater in Washington by that name had been an empty First Baptist Church, converted in 1861 by John T. Ford. It burned a year later. Ford rebuilt in brick with an increased seating capacity of 1,700 and reopened in August 1863. President Lincoln was shot there on April 14, 1865, while watching a light comedy by Tom Taylor titled *Our American Cousin*. Then, having been bought by the War Department and converted into an office building, part of it collapsed in the 1890s, killing twenty-two government employees. It was later restored and was reopened as a playhouse in January 1968.

## Shakespearean Plays

Americans in the early nineteenth century idolized the plays of William Shakespeare, and that adoration found its expression in entertainment of all kinds, for better or worse. The Shakespeare tradition was well established by the time of the Civil War. In Philadelphia between 1800 and 1835, twenty-one of Shakespeare's plays were produced on the legitimate stage, the seven most popular being produced 256 times. But in nineteenth-century America, Shakespeare's works were often used with complete democratic familiarity and lack of reverence. Mark Twain's rendition of a bungled production of Shakespeare in *The Adventures of Huckleberry Finn* rings true. John Hodges performed in minstrel shows as "Cool White, the renowned Shakespearean jester."

Americans viewed Shakespeare's characters as contemporary and his works as bristling with topical allusions. Shylock and Othello were held in contempt, probably because of their races, but when treated unfairly they received genuine sympathy. Jessica, Shylock's daughter, was always regarded as a lady. In minstrelsy, and later in burlesque and vaudeville, Shakespeare was treated with a lack of seriousness, a broad humor, a self-conscious wink at the audience, and a complete dedication to entertainment.

Shakespeare's reputation was widely invoked to defend the theater against charges of immorality. Edwin Booth and other prominent Shakespearean actors of the period were sometimes pictured as dangerous seducers, as in the song "Our Stage-Struck-Daughter" (1879), a great hit at Tony Pastor's Fourteenth Street Theater, which specialized in "straight, clean variety shows." Its front cover depicts two outraged parents who have just discovered that their daughter has thrown herself away to the theater. In their hands they hold the cause of this catastrophe, the picture of a book across which "Shakespeare" is written in large letters. The lyrics lament, "I have a stage-struck daughter. / She says she supports Edwin Boots, or Shoes … / In the character of Juliet / She broke poor Romeo's heart."

Shakespeare was a common topic in minstrel and vaudeville jokes and conundrums. One jokes tells how a Georgia young man asked his sweetheart if she had read *Romeo and Juliet.* She replied that she had read *Romeo* but she did not think she had read *Juliet.* Conundrums were more widely used: "When was Desdemona like a ship? When she was Moored." "What started the riot at the performance of *Hamlet* last night? When Ham [sic] held up the skull and said: 'Alas, poor Yorick! You were not the only dead head in the house.'" *Othello* was adapted for at least one vaudeville and one minstrel-show version, the latter written by the white minstrel star Thomas D. Rice, who to the delight of the audience once "jumped Jim Crow" (his popular rendition of a supposed African-American dance) after a legitimate performance of the play. Hooley's Minstrels produced a black-face version of *Macbeth,* a mixture of prose and song centering on the "fiend" Lady Macbeth. The general treatment is revealed in the reaction to the knocking at the gate, at which is sung: "Stop dat knocking / Oh, stop dat knocking / Oh, dey'll never stop dat knocking." *Hamlet* was the most widely adapted for the popular stage of Shakespeare's plays, just as it was the most widely staged in the legitimate theater. One version, *Hamlet Travestie, or Zouave Johnny's History of Denmark,* retold the story in terms of the brightly dressed volunteer regiments of the U.S. Army during the Civil War who called themselves Zouaves.

## Legitimate Theater

Until roughly the middle of the nineteenth century, American theatrical entertainment did not distinguish to a great extent between classical and popular drama. People of all classes generally were entertained at the same places by the same kind of productions. In 1849, however, an argument over whether an Englishman or an American should play Shakespeare incited the Astor Place Riot, in which twenty-two were killed and more than 100 seriously wounded. The result was an increasing segregation of theatrical entertainment by class and the elevation of the so-called legitimate theater as more suitable for the more affluent and better educated classes.

Classical drama remained popular throughout the Civil War and Reconstruction. New York was already the nation's theatrical center, and

Edwin Booth's Sixth Avenue theater was generally acknowledged as its finest legitimate theater. The assassination of President Lincoln by Booth's brother and fellow actor, John Wilkes Booth, did little to harm Edwin's reputation in the long run. His 1869 performance of Shakespeare's *Hamlet* played to a full house for 100 nights.

The end of the Civil War marked a turning point in American theater and theatrical production. More attention was paid to realism in props and setting, and technological advances allowed better lighting and increasingly elaborate sets. In the past, actors and actresses had supplied their own costumes, but following the war, professional costume designers were commissioned to provide greater authenticity. But perhaps the most important development in legitimate theater during this period was the emergence of the so-called star system. Until this time, stock companies, employing skilled but unknown actors, had been the standard means of production. In the 1850s and 1860s, however, a new class of featured players emerged. Stars like Edwin Booth, Edwin Forrest, Joseph Jefferson, and Thomas Keene developed loyal followings and were able to command huge sums—often as much as $500 per performance—far in excess of what the stock players received.[1] Traveling theater companies found large audiences after the war. Booth, Jefferson, and others traveled far afield in popular productions of Shakespearean plays as well as more modern plays like *Camille, Lucrezia Borgia, Oliver Twist,* and *Rip Van Winkle.*

## Melodrama

America looked upon the theater as entertainment as well as a means of moral instruction, and the melodrama—the most enduringly popular form of theater during the Civil War and Reconstruction—served that purpose well. Originating in the 1850s, the melodrama reflected the desires, needs, tastes, and morals of the working class in simple, unambiguous terms. Its appeal to the general public lay in its stereotyped, easily identifiable character types and in simple, formulaic plots that could be easily adapted to any setting, character, or event desired.[2] Virtuous maidens, villainous would-be seducers, and steadfast heroes abounded, and any moral lesson was likely to be overshadowed by sensational plot elements and extravagant overacting. Performances were often noisy affairs, with audiences loudly cheering the heroes and booing the villains while vendors roamed the aisles hawking peanuts to the crowd.[3]

Augustin Daly, whose Fifth Avenue Theater in New York was a leading venue of the period, galvanized his audiences with his melodramatic action and escape plots. In *Under the Gaslight* (1867), for example, he had a wounded soldier tied to a railroad track and let him escape only at the last moment. In *The Red Scarf,* his heroine was tied to a log facing an approaching buzz-saw. In *Saved from the Storm,* his endangered heroine was rescued by dogs at the last minute. With his intuitive understanding of the audience, Daly became one of the most effective theater managers in New York. Not an actor, but a former drama critic and successful playwright, Daly became an autocratic producer who took charge of all aspects of his company. He did not support established stars, choosing instead to make stars out of his ordinary stock-company actors, including Clara Morris (1846–1925), Fanny Davenport (1850–1898), and dozens of others. All remained loyal and dedicated to Daly throughout their careers. In 1879, Daly moved to his new Daly's Theatre on Broadway, where for the next twenty years he reigned almost supreme in the American popular theater.

Temperance melodramas like William Henry Smith's *The Drunkard, or the Fallen Saved* (1844) succeeded in reaching an audience who might otherwise have condemned theater as immoral.[4] The play stayed on the boards for the next twenty-five years and continued in road shows for an additional twenty, eventually incorporating all kinds of extravagant and irrelevant additions in an attempt to stay fresh and attract new audiences. One version included a thousand children parading across the stage singing temperance songs; another featured a quadrille of forty-eight dancers; and a California presentation featured a panorama, one of the more popular forms of entertainment outside the theater, extending to more than 3,000 square feet of canvas. Theatrical producers poured out other variations on the same theme, most notably a stage adaptation of Timothy Shaw Arthur's popular novel *Ten Nights in a Barroom and What I Saw There* (1854), with its terrifying picture of misspent time, wasted fortune, and lost opportunity, and its lachrymose songs like "One Glass More" and "The Drunkard's Warning."

Although melodrama often avoided difficult social issues, the various stage productions of *Uncle Tom's Cabin* were a notable exception. Based on Harriet Beecher Stowe's 1852 antislavery novel, two early adaptations appeared in Baltimore and New York City with little success. In September 1852, however, a new version starring George Aiken was an instant success, running for 100 performances in Troy, New York. Moved to New York City in 1853, it played for 200 consecutive days. By 1854, travelling companies had carried the play across the country, and it remained popular even after the war, with forty-nine road companies still performing it in the 1870s. Some actors spent their entire careers identified with the main characters. As with other popular plays of the period, *Uncle Tom's Cabin* underwent some improbable alterations over time. The plot was altered repeatedly, new characters were added, and any sort of spectacle that might attract a crowd—including jubilee singers, minstrel-show routines, dancers, panoramas, and even equestrian acts—was added. Excerpted highlights such as Little Eva's ascent to Heaven, Eliza crossing the ice (embellished by the addition of bloodhounds, which apparently had not occurred to Stowe), or Simon Legree's brutal beating of Tom, became standard vaudeville and minstrel-show fare. Road shows continued to perform various versions of the play until the 1930s.

After the war, Americans grew nostalgic for what they recalled as simpler times. That sentiment was capitalized upon by such playwrights as Denman Thompson, who in 1876 produced *The Old Homestead*, a wildly popular and unabashedly sentimental study of rural America.

The importance of melodramas in American cultural history has been seriously underestimated, for they embodied many of contemporary society's fundamental attitudes toward morality, democracy, and domestic life. To sneer at these plays, as recent drama critics have, as "full of moral cant and social claptrap," is to miss their point and their significance completely. They appealed to millions because they dealt in plain and simple terms with the lives and values of ordinary people.[5]

## MINSTRELSY

A distinctive form of African American humor was well established by the early nineteenth century.[6] By the 1840s, this form of humor would be appropriated, transformed, and commercially exploited by white performers wearing blackface makeup in the so-called minstrel show. White performers like George Washington Dixon and George Nichols had performed in blackface as early as the 1820s, but Thomas D. Rice, a minor actor, was the first to gain widespread popularity as a blackface performer. In a Louisville production of Robinson's *The Rifle* in 1829, Rice inserted a song-and-dance routine between acts that he claimed to have observed being performed by a crippled black stable hand. Rice's lyrics, in stereotypical "Negro" dialect, became the basis of his famous "Jump Jim Crow" routine: "Weel about and turn about and do jis' so. / Eb'ry time I weel about I jump Jim Crow." The actual year and place of Rice's observation have long been disputed, and some historians question whether the event took place at all, or was simply a product of Rice's talent for self-promotion.[7]

Rice took his Jim Crow act to New York in 1832, and the following year he produced a full-length "Ethiopian Opera" at New York's Bowery Amphitheatre. Among the many white performers who attempted to follow up on Rice's success was the team of Billy Whitlock, Frank Bower, Frank Pelham, and Dan Emmett (the latter the composer of "Dixie"), who in 1843 debuted as the Virginia Minstrels at the Bowery Amphitheatre. Like Rice, they presented a grossly distorted view of black Americans and the plantation system, and like Rice, they proved to be tremendously popular. Still more imitators followed, most notably the Ethiopian Serenaders, Bryant's Minstrels, and Edwin P. Christy's Minstrels. Christy finalized the form of the minstrel show with the group he founded in 1846, in which he placed the end men—a tambourine player ("Mr. Tambo") and a bones player ("Mr. Bones")—at opposite ends of a semicircle, with the master of ceremonies, or interlocutor, in the center. The interlocutor, usually in whiteface and attired in dress clothes, controlled the pace and content of the show. Assuming an exaggeratedly pompous demeanor, he functioned as straight man for the antics of the end men, projecting a stiffly patronizing and superior air.

The shows opened with a fast-paced walk-around, in which the entire company, dressed in flashy costumes and exaggerated blackface makeup, paraded on stage while singing a current hit song. Christy devoted the first half of his shows to singing, dancing, and joking. The second half introduced more serious skits, sentimental songs, "breakdown" dances, in which couples separated and danced, and special material improvised on the fly to suit the audience. Christy's Minstrels ran for 1,700 performances. Christy himself retired in 1856, but George Harrington, his chief comedian, changed his name to Christy and carried on the tradition for many years. Stephen Foster and many other important figures in nineteenth-century American popular culture began their careers appearing in or writing for Christy's and other minstrel shows.

In minstrelsy all things were equally vulnerable to mockery, from the end men's feigned ignorance to the white interlocutor's pomposity. Intended for white audiences, the jokes usually had no specific connection to black culture or social conditions. Blacks were used both as a source of humor and as objects of derision; the white audience might laugh *with* the blackface characters as they sprung their quips and puns, or *at* them when their misconceptions and malapropisms were smugly corrected by the interlocutor. In the prewar years, minstrel shows largely reflected the prevailing northern view of slaves as a mindless, happy-go-lucky lot basking in the comfort of idyllic plantation life.[8] Negative views of slavery were occasionally presented on the minstrel stage, particularly after the publication of *Uncle Tom's Cabin, or Life among the Lowly* by Harriet Beecher Stowe in 1852, but a more common reaction was to parody the novel in productions like *Uncle Dad's Cabin* and *Uncle Tom and His Cabin*. The Christy Minstrels, billing their parody as *Life among the Happy*, eliminated any mention of harsh treatment of slaves and cast the main character as laughably servile.[9]

The minstrel show waned in popularity during the Civil War. Those that survived sometimes presented a contradictory message, stressing reunification while continuing to extol the imagined virtues of the plantation system and romanticizing the South. Sentimental skits concerning whites' problems began to appear, although stereotypical blacks remained the primary characters. As the war progressed and a Union victory seemed likely, some shows demonstrated limited support for Emancipation. During Reconstruction, however, the minstrel show often became a platform from which to ridicule the newly freed slaves, especially any who aspired to a position of power. New stereotypes were invoked to reassure white audiences that blacks' innate ineptness ruled out any real threat to white dominance.[10] Minstrelsy remained popular well into the early twentieth century, and some all-black companies like the Rabbit's Foot Minstrels were later formed to play to black audiences in the South. By the end of Reconstruction, however, minstrelsy had begun to lose audiences to more modern variety shows, vaudeville, and other forms of popular entertainment.

## CONCERT SALOONS

One of the early centers of entertainment was the concert saloon, somewhat analogous to the speakeasy of the Prohibition era. The earliest was established in New York City by William Valentine in 1849. Initially flourishing in New York and other large cities, these saloon theaters soon spread to small towns as well. Initially called "free concert saloons" or "free-and-easies," they were later termed "concert rooms," "concert gardens," and "music halls" in an attempt at respectability.[11] Their counterpart in the western territories was the honky-tonk, a combination of beer hall, theater, and brothel that enjoyed great popularity among cowboys, miners, and laborers. Opened only in the evening, concert saloons offered risqué revues and other low-grade entertainment by bands, piano players, dancers, and singers, but the real attraction seems to have been the "abandoned women" who were employed to serve cheap drinks. The smallest of these establishments had a diminutive platform at one end for the entertainers, while the larger ones had regular auditoriums.

In 1861, New York City had forty-one such saloons on Broadway and in the Bowery. The entertainment varied widely. According to one New York journalist, the bill included acrobats, female vocalists ("the costume being thought far more important than the voice") and "a wind up of some outrageously absurd farce, replete with patriotic soldiers and comic Negroes, and screeching devotion to the flag, closing with a grand transparency of McClellan or of President Lincoln." The demand for such establishments grew so quickly that by 1872 there were seventy-five to eighty concert saloons serving thirsty New Yorkers. Few women would frequent such places. The sound was cacophonous, the female costumes risqué, the jokes and songs loose if not vulgar.

## BURLESQUE

Sexually suggestive theater was not limited to the concert saloon. Operating on a slightly more artistic level, burlesque featured a tantalizing combination of comedy, song, dance, and scantily clad women. The most notable early example was *The Black Crook,* which opened at New York's Niblo Gardens in 1866. A six-hour musical adaptation of the Faust legend, its main attraction was a chorus of 100 young women clad only in tutus and tights that were considered shockingly revealing by the day's standards. Mark Twain commented on the show, "The scenery and the legs are everything. Girls—nothing but a wilderness of girls ... dressed with a meagerness that would make a parasol blush. Clergymen were beside themselves; men's opera glasses sold like hot cakes."[12] European entrepreneurs were quick to notice and follow up on the success of *The Black Crook.* A Parisian opera company introduced the can-can, a high-kicking, leg-baring French cabaret dance, to America around 1867. It was followed in 1868 by Lydia Thompson's burlesque troupe of blond British showgirls. Frank and outspoken, Thompson and her showgirls were not allowed to work in the mainline theaters but attracted large audiences with their skits, comic songs, dances, and parodies of politics, meanwhile showing a lot of skin. Their production of *Ixion, or the Man at the Wheel* drew sell-out crowds. Lydia Thompson, recalling her American tours, claimed, "The entire male citizenry of your republic rose up and threw open their arms everywhere to us in a welcoming embrace."[13]

Burlesque's greatest practitioner was M. J. Leavitt, who combined the structure of the minstrel show with the bawdy atmosphere of the concert saloons and honky-tonks. Leavitt developed the standard burlesque format, alternating variety acts and crude humor with musical numbers featuring underdressed women. Guardians of public morality condemned these shows roundly, but there was no denying their widespread appeal.

## VAUDEVILLE

Vaudeville, a less risqué form of entertainment than burlesque, appealed to all ages and both sexes. Taken from the French term *voix de ville* ("voice of the people"), it combined elements from the legitimate theater with some of the tamer elements of burlesque. Tony Pastor (1834–1908) a deeply moral man trained in early theater and a prolific songwriter and entertainer, was among vaudeville's earliest and most significant pioneers. From 1861 to 1865, Pastor owned a concert saloon where he also performed. Tiring of that sort of material, he looked for other venues, and from 1865 to 1875, he staged and performed in his own variety show, where he tried to attract women in the audience. From 1875 onward, Pastor further cleaned up his shows, eventually becoming one of the most significant theater managers of the period.

Although Pastor and others produced vaudeville prototypes in the 1870s, vaudeville itself was largely a post-Reconstruction phenomenon. It was not until 1882 that B. F. Keith opened what is considered to be the first authentic vaudeville house, after which the vaudeville format was standardized. A typical bill of fare featured nine variety acts, including comic and sentimental skits, singers, dancers, jugglers, acrobats, and magicians, with an intermission scheduled at midpoint. Admission ranged from fifteen to fifty cents depending on the seat and the caliber of the company. Humor was often based on racial and ethnic stereotyping, with blacks, Jews, Irish, and, to a lesser extent, Germans, the favored targets. By the end of the nineteenth century, vaudeville had largely replaced minstrelsy as America's favorite form of stage entertainment.

## CROSS-DRESSING

One of the more unorthodox bits of popular theater during this period was the practice of cross-dressing. In various forms, the practice of theatrical cross-dressing was ancient at the time of the Civil War. The stage had been a site for male cross-dressing for centuries. On the Elizabethan stage, for instance, boys and young men played the roles of females. By the time of the Civil War, women had a stronger purpose for cross-dressing. According to Barnard Hewitt, "Feminism was on the march and some of the first victories were in the theatre." "Wearing the breeches," as cross-dressing was called, seemed threatening to both sexes. Men felt their role was being threatened, but many women were also made unsure of their role in society.

Several women gained notoriety for portraying males on stage, but Adah Isaacs Menken (ca. 1835–1868) was the most scandalous of them all. Growing up in the South, she led an unusual life and was married four times. She first appeared on the stage in a production of *Mazeppa, or The Wild Horse* in Albany, New York, in 1860, in which she appeared in flesh-colored tights tied to a snorting stallion. She further scandalized audiences by riding astride the horse rather than side-saddle, as was considered proper for women. Another female who scandalized American audiences in her cross-dressing and insistence on being treated equal to men was Lydia Thompson, manager of the "British Blondes" burlesque troupe.

After 1869, the number of women playing men's roles sharply declined. The four listed officially in that year were Minnie Madden Friske, Rose Coghlan, Clara Morris, and Fanny Buckingham. However, cross-dressing by both sexes continued on the burlesque and vaudeville stages well into the early twentieth century.

## CIRCUSES

The circus was one of the most popular forms of entertainment during the 1860s and 1870s. The early American circus was a direct descendant of the late-eighteenth-century British "hippodrama," a one-ring show featuring equestrian feats.[14] American circus companies adapted the single-ring show, combining it with individual novelty acts already in existence. A lion had been imported and exhibited in 1716, and a camel five years later, followed in the 1730s by monkeys and other trained animals. The ele-

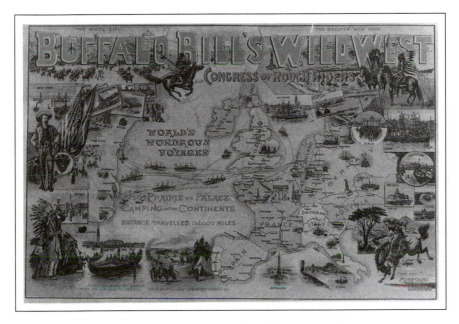

Advertisement of Buffalo Bill's Wild West Show.

phant, a key circus attraction, was first exhibited in America in 1796. The American public, still generally rural and unsophisticated, loved the sight of exotic animals. Early circuses were outdoor events, but in 1826, J. Purdy Brown introduced the large circus tent,[15] bringing together wild animals, clowns, acrobats, jugglers, and similar acts. The result was an exotic spectacle that in time added sideshows, concession booths, and stage spectaculars bearing such names as "The Queen of Sheba" and "Solomon and His Host." Many circuses followed the main event with a minstrel show that brought the latest songs, dances, and jokes to often remote locations.

With the opening of railroads, canals, and commercial navigation on the Ohio and Mississippi rivers in the 1820s and 1830s, circuses had greater freedom to travel. In 1856, Doc Spalding of the Spalding & Rogers Circus loaded his tents and animals onto nine special railroad cars and toured the western seaboard. That feat was topped after the war by the Dan Costell Circus, which toured from Baltimore to San Francisco from 1868 to 1869. Circuses generally traveled by railroad after the war, and towns located too far from the main lines generally had to content themselves with itinerant sideshows, medicine shows, and other lesser forms of entertainment.

Many new circus companies were formed during this period, including the George F. Bailey Circus, the W. W. Cole Circus, the Fayette Ludovic's Yankee Robinson Circus, the Mabie Brothers Circus, the Dan Rice

Circus, and Isaac Van Amburgh's various "Lion King" companies. The greatest surge of interest in the circus lasted from about 1870 into the early twentieth century. In 1871, P. T. Barnum agreed to let William Cameron Coup use his name for a two-ring circus, but the arrangement was terminated in 1875, after Barnum let other enterprises use his name as well. Barnum later joined James A. Bailey, who eventually took full control of the operation.

One outgrowth of the circus that would flower only after Reconstruction was the so-called wild west show, an outdoor pageant featuring scenes and events based loosely on the western frontier. Although the wild west show as such was not seen during the Civil War and Reconstruction eras, some of the elements from which it derived were already in place during those periods. Circuses had exhibited Native Americans as sideshow attractions early as 1820. Rodeos and other exhibitions of cowboy skills were also popular, as were traveling frontier melodramas. In the early 1870s, the pioneer scout William F. ("Buffalo Bill") Cody began to tour in melodramas based on his frontier exploits, but it was not until 1883 that he staged the first full-fledged wild-west show. In its final form, "Buffalo Bill's Wild West" reached the peak of its popularity a decade later.[16]

## MEDICINE SHOWS

Fueled by the tremendous growth of the patent medicine industry, the medicine show evolved as a major form of American entertainment during the Civil War and Reconstruction. In small towns and remote areas bypassed by the circuses and traveling theater companies, the medicine show often attracted huge and gullible crowds. Although the traveling medicine men often bestowed the title "doctor" or "professor" upon themselves, few had any legitimate credentials, and the tonics and elixirs they peddled were often little more than colored water laced with alcohol, flavorings, and possibly cocaine or other dangerous drugs. The shows varied widely in size and format, but all featured a facile and convincing pitchman and testimonial speeches by satisfied customers. The largest companies staged elaborate tent shows.

Hamlin Garland gives an interesting account in his *Son of the Middle Border* of one medicine show he witnessed, which consisted of three performers: a man with long black hair and a very tall white hat, a short nondescript man who was handing out bottles at a dollar each, and a young, indifferent-looking girl who played the guitar. They sang conventional ballads and songs as well as their own parodies. As Garland recounted forty years later, "The medicine they peddled was of doubtful service, but the songs they sang, the story they suggested, were of priceless value to us who came from the monotony of the farm, and went back to it like bees laden with the pollen of new intoxicating blooms."[17]

THE

# HUMBUGS OF THE WORLD.

AN ACCOUNT OF HUMBUGS, DELUSIONS, IMPOSITIONS,
QUACKERIES, DECEITS AND DECEIVERS
GENERALLY, IN ALL AGES.

BY

## P. T. BARNUM.

"Omne ignotum pro mirifico."—" Wonderful, because mysterious."

Title page of P. T. Barnum's explanation of human nature.
(Courtesy of the Popular Culture Library,
Bowling Green State University.)

# THE LECTURE CIRCUITS

The performing arts were not limited to pure entertainment. American audiences also packed theaters to hear lectures by prominent authors, humorists, and intellectuals of the day. Illustrated lectures accompanied by the "magic lantern," an early form of slide projector, which was a lighted candle in a box projecting a transparency, were also very popular.

Thousands assembled to hear such nationally known speakers as P. T. Barnum, Henry Ward Beecher, Frederick Douglass, Ralph Waldo Emerson, and Bayard Taylor speak on current issues and events. The British author Charles Dickens toured the United States delivering well-attended dramatic readings, and native humorists like Mark Twain and Artemus Ward drew overflow crowds. The demand for such speakers become so great that several lecture bureaus, such as the James Redpath Agency in Chicago, were established to schedule speaking tours. Women, despite some resistance and ridicule, emerged as popular public speakers during this period. Susan B. Anthony enjoyed great success on the lecture circuits for more than forty-five years. Other popular female speakers included Lucretia Mott, Elizabeth Cady Stanton, Sojourner Truth, and Frances E. Willard.

Smaller towns had little hope of booking such prominent celebrities, but they were well served by the Lyceum-Chautauqua movement that began in the 1830s. The National American Lyceum (1831) developed from the exploratory work of such persons as Josiah Holbrook and others who almost immediately joined him in lecturing on such subjects as the arts, sciences, history, religion, and public affairs. The response was enthusiastic, and after the war the Lyceum was continued in the Chautauqua movement, which was begun by John Heyl Vincent and Lewis Miller in 1874 at a Methodist Episcopal camp meeting in Chautauqua, New York. The model was soon copied elsewhere as summer Chautauqua communities sprung up in many remote locations.

After the war, the nation was hungry for entertainment. The war years had drawn country folk to larger communities and energized town and city people to want more of the kind of entertainment the war years had begun. In order to attract larger crowds, prices on all forms of entertainment came down to affordable levels. The aim of entertainment was to find the kind that was either open and risque, as in the minstrelsy, or appealing to respectable people and dedicated to educating in one way or another The result was a springing up of entertainment of all sorts in all the cities. With the spread of entertainment came the growth of the city and with the growth of the city developed the demand for entertainment. It was an ever-widening circle.

# 11

# Travel and Transportation

The mid-nineteenth century witnessed a nation on the move, first in the flood of settlers migrating westward, later in the mass troop movements of the Civil War, and then, after the war, in the growing tourist trade. Travel in the 1860s was still a time-consuming, arduous, and sometimes dangerous task, not be undertaken lightly. By the 1870s, however, with technological improvements and increased leisure time available to them, more and more Americans began to travel for pure pleasure.

By the 1860s, most major urban thoroughfares were paved with brick or cobblestone. The predominant form of urban mass transportation was the stage or omnibus, a slow-moving twelve-passenger horse-drawn vehicle. Passengers entered through the rear, deposited their ten-cent fare, and sat on unpadded benches for a jarring ride over the brick or cobblestone paving. The horse-drawn trolley, introduced in the 1850s, was a marked improvement. Larger than the stages, holding up to forty passengers, they traveled smoothly on steel rails at twice the stages' speed. At its peak, the Boston trolley system operated 108 cars. Service began at 6:45 A.M. and continued through the evening. Drivers were paid $1.75 per day for a twelve-hour workday. Horses were the primary means of personal transportation, and city alleys were lined with livery stables and blacksmith shops. The trolley lines, along with the first commuter railroads, enabled cities to expand outward, giving rise to the suburb and the commute.

As city traffic became increasingly unmanageable, an engineer named Alfred Beach turned his vision underground. In 1870, he opened the Beach Pneumatic Transit demonstration line, the forerunner of the modern subway system, to the public in New York City. Entry to the small under-

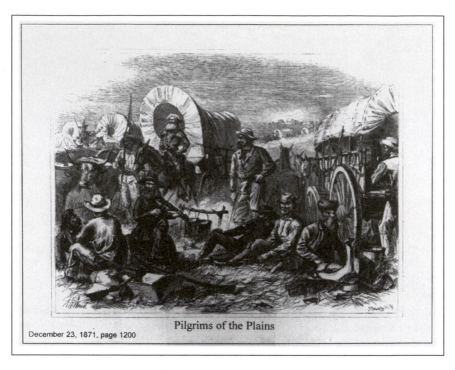

Pilgrims of the Plains

December 23, 1871, page 1200

The assumed pleasures of traveling to the West.
(From *Harper's Weekly*)

ground station was gained through the basement of Devlin's Clothing Store, at the southwest corner of Broadway and Warren Street. A single car propelled by compressed air ran on rails through a short tunnel for a total distance of about 300 feet, or about a block. Beach failed to attract investors, however, and to make matters worse, the line was opposed by Boss Tweed and other corrupt New York politicians, many of whom had financial interests in surface transportation. The stock market panic of 1873 put an end to Beach's line, which had never extended beyond a block. Although the Beach Pneumatic Transit line was a failure, the idea refused to die, and in the 1890s it inspired proposals for what would become the modern subway system.

While headway was being made in urban transportation, the means of travel remained primitive in the outlying small towns and rural areas. Streets were sometimes planked over or covered with loose gravel in the towns, but elsewhere they were often little more than rutted dirt lanes, muddy in winter and dusty in summer. The main means of local transportation was the mule or horse, either ridden or pulling a carriage or wagon.

## TURNPIKES AND TRAILS

Long-distance travel by road usually entailed following the turnpikes, private and state-subsidized toll roads of widely varying quality. The best roads boasted a macadamized surface composed of crushed stone in a binder of asphalt, tar, or similar material. The sixty-two-mile Lancaster Pike in Pennsylvania was the first long-distance macadamized road, and others soon followed, but many turnpikes remained simple packed dirt or gravel outside of the major metropolitan areas. Tolls were collected every few miles, based on the number of passengers, type of conveyance, and quantity and nature of any cargo.

Several great trails carried settlers westward from the Mississippi and Missouri Rivers. The best known, the 2,000-mile Oregon Trail, was scouted in the early 1840s from the Missouri River to Oregon Country. Between 1841 and 1869, the trail carried at least 350,000 people, most of them in long wagon trains. The favored vehicle was the Conestoga wagon, a four-by-ten-foot wooden wagon with arched canvas top, drawn by a team of horses, mules, or oxen. The Mormon Trail paralleled the Oregon Trail for some distance but differed markedly in the favored means of transportation. Many Mormon emigrants, too poor to afford draft animals, favored small hand carts.

By the time of the Civil War, western emigration had slowed markedly, and the Oregon Trail and other overland routes were improved and converted to commercial use by freight carriers and stagecoach lines. By 1860, stagecoach lines like the Western Stage Company and the Central Overland and Pike's Peak Express Company ran regular service from the Missouri River to Nebraska, Colorado, and points west. Wells, Fargo & Company consolidated many of the smaller stage companies in 1866, offering a "reduced" fare of $300 from Omaha, Nebraska, to Sacramento, California. A stagecoach trip was arduous at best. Demas Barnes, traveling west of Denver by stage in August 1865, complained:

Coaches will be overloaded, it will rain, baggage will be left to the storm, passengers will get sick, a gentleman of gallantry will hold the baby, children will cry, nature demands sleep, passengers will get angry, the drivers will swear, the sensitive will shrink, rations will give out, potatoes become worth a gold dollar each, and not to be had at that, the water brackish, the whiskey abominable, and the dirt almost unendurable.[1]

Because journeying by stagecoach was so inconvenient and uncomfortable, travelers turned to rail travel as quickly as possible. By 1869, with the coming of coast-to-coast rail service, the overland stage routes fell into disuse.

## WATERWAYS

Canals provided the first viable use of waterways for travel and commerce. They were an obvious great advantage over road travel. Standard travel on land was by horse and buggy, mule or horse and wagon. Both vehicles and animals entailed various degrees of upkeep and cleanup. Horses and mules dropped their offal all over the streets, making it necessary for men and boys to clean up the pathways for all pedestrian traffic. Animals were kept in stables where they had to be protected somewhat against the weather and constantly cared for. Well-to-do owners tried to beautify their horses by driving matched pairs and foursomes in handsome carriages, but they were at best living animals. Work animals of the poor were often mistreated, underfed, and abandoned when they could no longer survive abuse. During the war, they had in extreme case been eaten but after the war they were more likely to be abandoned. As early as the late eighteenth century, George Washington's Patowmack Company had built short canals skirting the falls and rapids on the Potomac River near Washington, D.C. The Erie Canal, the most successful of all, was opened October 25, 1825, inaugurating a national canal-building fad.

The canal systems were well known, and because they were more comfortable than land travel they became favored as a means of travel. Because they were "domesticated," as it were, that is, running near the people, they played large parts in folklore and folksongs. Their shortcomings and discomforts were well known and tolerated because they had to be but these deficiencies were also the subject of many folksongs both comical and generic. One, "The E-rie Canal," tells about a "dreadful storm" that was experienced on the canal one night and its destructive results. Another song was more like a brief sketch of life on the Erie Canal, indicating the neighborliness and comradeship that grew up on that waterway:

### The Erie Canal

I've got a mule, her name is Sal,

Fifteen miles on the Erie Canal.

She's a good old worker and a good old pal,

Fifteen miles on the Erie Canal.

We've hauled some barges in our day,

Filled with lumber, coal and hay,

And we know ev'ry inch of the way

From Albany to Buffalo.

Refrain:

Low bridge, ev'ry body down!

Low bridge, for we're going through a town,

And you'll always know your neighbor

You'll always know your pal,

If you've ever navigated on the Erie Canal.

But a means of transportation as unsatisfactory as the canal had to give way to something more efficient, and did so with the advent of the steamboat and then the railroad.

Navigable rivers like the Ohio, the Missouri, and the Mississippi, provided access to the continent's central interior, at first to canoes, flatboats, keelboats, and arks, and later to steam-powered riverboats. Travel on the open waterways always presented some dangers. On the Ohio and Mississippi rivers, shifting sandbars and changing channels could ground or damage the steamboats, and floods presented such extra hazards such as treacherous cross-currents, submerged obstructions, and floating logs and debris. A steamboat pilot had to memorize the river from end to end. Whether side-wheelers or sternwheelers, the steamboats were awkward, boxlike craft that required ample space and time to maneuver. With their high, flat profiles, they were constantly at the mercy of the winds. A tailwind might help propel the boat, but a headwind could almost stop any forward progress. Handling such crafts was not an easy task. Pilots depended on the leadsman's cry of "mark twain"—taken by the aspiring young river pilot Samuel Clemens as his pseudonym—to guide them to water that was at least two fathoms (twelve feet) deep. Clemens apprenticed as a pilot under Horace Bixby, who soon realized that his imaginative student wasn't suited to the steady discipline of memorizing a river's course.

By the outbreak of the Civil War, the interior rivers were crowded with watercraft of all kinds, from rafts and canoes to steamboats. The steamboat was the most dramatic phenomenon on the river, first appearing in the distance in a plume of smoke and sparks, its docking often a social event. The pilots were elite characters, "starchy boys ... and greatly envied by the youth of the West," as Mark Twain described them. In *Life on the Mississippi*, Twain recalled, "The steamboats were finer than anything on shore. Compared with superior dwelling-houses and first-class hotels in the valley, they were indubitably magnificent, they were 'palaces.'" The most common steamboat on the Mississippi was the packet, consisting of a single first-class deck with the rest of the space uncomfortably cramped. The boat's crews were often made up of slaves and low-paid transient laborers. Luxury boats were much less common, but the best, like the *J. M. White*, the *Robert E. Lee*, and *Natchez*, were as fast as they were glamorous. The main cabins boasted filigree woodwork, and the furniture, china, and linens were specially made for the individual boats. Up to 400 passengers could be accommodated on the promenade decks and galleries, with seating provided for 200 or more for meals. On the top deck were spacious, well-furnished staterooms and sometimes even a bridal suite.

Steamboat races were run, sometimes with tragic results. Pushed beyond their capacity, the boilers could explode, killing the workers and others in the immediate vicinity and burning and drowning many passengers. Mark Twain's younger brother, Henry, was fatally wounded in the explosion of the *Pennsylvania* in 1858. The worst steamboat disaster on the river occurred on April 27, 1865, when the boilers on board the steamboat *Sultana* exploded near Memphis, Tennessee. The boat was overloaded with discharged Union soldiers, and 1,700 of its 2,300 passengers perished, the greatest marine disaster in U.S. history.

Traffic on the Mississippi reached its peak in 1860, with roughly 1,000 steamboats plying the river above New Orleans. However, the heavy and profitable traffic on the Mississippi, the gateway to the West, was soon to be reduced and then closed by the war. Travel was then necessarily shifted to the railroad systems, energizing their rapid development and spelling the decline of the steamboat. By the time Mark Twain recounted his days as a river pilot in *Life on the Mississippi* in 1883, the steamboat was already an anachronism. "A strangely short life for so majestic a creature," he lamented.

## RAILROADS

The American railroad system has been one of the most powerful forces in changing the face of America. Its mystique was immediate as was its saturation of society. In a big country with vast spaces between centers of population, the railroad tracks symbolized a connecting rod. They were order imposed upon chaos. The train appeared on them from nowhere and left on them for everywhere. The engine was a belching dragon that conquered all. Breathing fire and steam and whistling like a dragon, it seemed bigger than life. The mystique of the railroad during the Civil War period is perhaps best caught in the ethereal poem of Emily Dickinson, one of the major though unrecognized poets of the time, who wrote in an unpublished poem what must have been the sentiments of most of the people:

> I like to see it lap the Miles—
>
> And lick the Valleys up—
>
> And stop to feed itself at Tanks—
>
> And then—prodigious step

Around a Pile of Mountains—

And supercilious peer

In Shanties—by the sides of Roads—

And then a Quarry pare

To fit its Ribs

And crawl between

Complaining all the while

In horrid—hooting stanza—

Then chase itself down Hill—

And neigh like Boanerges—

Then—punctual as a Star

Stop—docile and omnipotent

At its own stable door—(c. 1862)[2]

The rigors of early rail travel are obvious from a timetable issued by the Richmond, Fredericksburg & Potomac Railroad Company in 1836. It noted that the trip from New Orleans to New York required twelve days and thirteen hours, although on the return trip the time was shaved to twelve days and eight hours. Predating the construction of connecting long-distance rail lines, the journey required travel by rail as well as by steamboat: "Of the whole distance between Blakeley [N.C.] and Baltimore, 126 miles is traveled upon Rail Roads, over fifty miles by steamboat." For the convenience of the passengers, carriages and horses would be "safely and expeditiously transported, enabling those traveling in them, with the additional use of the Potomac Steamboat and the Petersburg Rail Road, to accomplish without fatigue to their horses, the journey between Washington and Blakely, N.C. in two days." In a disclaimer that sounds terribly modern, the sheet announced, "All possible care will be taken of baggage, but it will be carried only at its owner's risk."

By 1850, railroads were supplanting other means of travel. Travel by wagon or coach was at the mercy of the weather, and roads were often muddy or even impassable. Riverboats, although inexpensive to ride, were slow and sometimes dangerous. Canals in the north and east could be used only from May to November, and traffic moved at a leisurely pace in the mule-drawn boats. Manufacturers and merchants, in a hurry to get raw materials and move finished goods, were willing to pay railroads four to five times the cost of the slower means of transportation. Early railroad travel, though by no means comfortable, was less uncomfortable than other means. "Train boys," generally from eight to eighteen years old, roamed

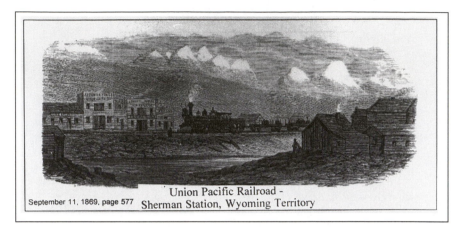

September 11, 1869, page 577 Union Pacific Railroad -
Sherman Station, Wyoming Territory

A realistic illustration of railroad works in the West. (From *Harper's Weekly*.)

the aisles hawking snacks, magazines, and newspapers. Some train boys went on to greater things. Thomas Alva Edison (1847–1931) worked as a train boy on the Grand Trunk Line, departing from Port Huron, Michigan, on the 7 A.M. train to Detroit. He spent his day reading science in the Detroit Public Library, then took the return train out of Detroit at 6 P.M. At the age of thirteen, Edison was already publishing and selling his *Weekly Herald* onboard, and he also kept a small laboratory hidden in a corner of the train.

As rail mileage increased and locomotive technology improved, personal travel and freight transportation by rail increased dramatically. From 1850 to 1860, rail mileage grew from 9,021 to 30,626 miles. Railroad lines fairly well covered the northeastern states and were expanding rapidly. Though he used a much longer route for political purposes, newly elected president Abraham Lincoln could have traveled from Springfield to Washington, D.C., with a rail trip of only 966 miles, using only three different railroad lines.

The lack of standardized time caused scheduling problems for railroads and their passengers. There were over 100 different local times throughout the United States. Philadelphia's time was five minutes slower than New York City's, but five minutes faster than Baltimore's. When it was noon in Chicago, it was 12:31 in Pittsburgh, 12:24 in Cleveland, 11:48 in Dubuque, and 11:27 in Omaha. Michigan was cursed with twenty-seven local times, Wisconsin with thirty-eight, Illinois with twenty-seven, Indiana with twenty-three. On a trip from coast to coast, the time-conscious traveler would have to adjust his watch twenty times. This chaos was remedied on November 18, 1883, when railroad officials in Chicago divided the continental United States into four time zones and all clocks were set to railroad time. The public generally accepted the standardization with a sigh of relief.

Another roadblock to the development of rail travel was the sanctity of the Sabbath. Railroads at first were forbidden to run on Sundays, but to maintain their financial development, they needed to operate every day of the week. The conflict between commerce and religion was initially resolved by having the carriers convey only those passengers who were not going to church anyway. An 1850 timetable contained one sly example of railroaders' effort to circumvent the prejudice against running on Sunday: "Persons purchasing tickets for Sunday trains will be required to sign a pledge they will use the ticket only if they are not going to church otherwise."

Track gauges—the inside distance from one rail to the other—were not fully standardized until 1886. President Lincoln recommended a 5-foot gauge to be used on the government-subsidized Union Pacific and Central Pacific lines, but the recommendation was ignored, and the 4 foot, 8.5-inch gauge became standard. Standard engines cost from $8,000 to $10,000 and used the 4–4–0 drive configuration: two sets of four drive wheels under the fire box and cab. Narrow-gauge lines, with gauges running from 2 feet to 3.5 feet, were common, especially on logging and mining lines in mountainous regions where narrow right-of-ways made the standard gauge impractical. In 1876, there were eighty-one narrow-gauge roads operating in twenty-six states.

Despite such obstacles, railroads developed quickly in the North. Development lagged in the South, however. When the Civil War began in April 1861, the South had less than 9,000 miles of track in place, much of it poorly constructed, while the Union could boast 22,000 miles (Heidler and Heidler, 1999). Most of the 170 Southern railroads were locally owned and operated short lines, and lack of a standard gauge often precluded connections. The railroads were largely unstandardized and unregulated under the Confederate States' decentralized administrative system, and by the end of the war much of the southern rail industry lay in ruins.

Railroads became the dominant form of long-distance travel after the Civil War, especially with the completion of the transcontinental railroad in 1869. The Railroad Act of 1862 had put government support squarely behind the transcontinental railroad and helped create the Union Pacific Railroad, which subsequently joined with the Central Pacific at Promontory Point, Utah, on May 10, 1869, and completed the linking by rail of the continent.

Passenger cars became increasingly luxurious as the decade progressed. Comfortable sleeping cars were a long time in development. Passengers initially slept in their seats, but as early as 1838, Charles McGraw was granted a patent for a sleeping car, and apparently some such cars were placed in use that year between Baltimore and Philadelphia. The first major advance in sleeping cars, however, did not come until George Pullman introduced his "palace sleeping car" in 1865, equipped with mahogany paneling, plush carpet, mirrors, and gaslights. Pullman had run his first long, clumsy sleepers on the line from Bloomington, Indiana, to Chicago, on September 1, 1858. His first sleepers were equipped with simple berths—made up with blankets and pillows, but no sheets—that provided little privacy for modest travelers. In 1864, however, Pullman was granted a patent for an improved upper berth and cushions, and he set to work designing the most elegant sleeper seen to that time. It was built too large to pass through the average station, but misfortune saved the day when first lady Mary Todd Lincoln insisted on riding in Pullman's coach for the last leg of the president's funeral trip, from Chicago to Springfield. Stations had to be renovated to accommodate the sleeper, but the Pullman sleeper's fame was assured.

Other improvements in passenger comfort and convenience soon followed. The hotel car, combining a sleeping car with a diner, was introduced in the same year. Full-fledged dining cars appeared two years later, followed by the luxuriously furnished parlor car in 1875. The sexes were segregated to some extent, with ladies' cars provided for unescorted women and smoking cars reserved for the men. Passenger fares averaged about 3 cents per mile but ranged from a low of 1.33 cents to a high of 6.25 cents. Direct, nonstop, coast-to-coast Pullman service was introduced in 1870. Porters, as gracious and helpful as folklore and tradition have pictured them, tended to the passengers' comfort.

By the mid-nineteenth century, the publication of railroad maps, timetables, and guides had become a growth industry. The *New York Tribune* endorsed the *American Railway Guide* of 1851, for example, saying, "Whoever has it in his possession can take his breakfast quietly, without depending on a tardy hack driver to land him in season at the depot." Some early timetables provided city maps and useful information on canal and steamboat schedules and attractions such as opera houses and music halls in certain parts of the country. Many carried advertising, especially for destinations served by a particular line, as well as short stories, humor, and advice. Sleeping car passengers were urged to refrain from swearing, spitting on the floor, and wearing boots in bed.

The coming of the railroad to the more remote regions created a new phenomenon, the railroad town. Railroad companies often promoted construction and settlement of new towns on their lands along their right-of-ways, sometimes luring potential settlers to the desired locations with free or reduced fares. By the late 1860s, most Western railroads were operating profitable land departments, and a few even maintained immigration bureaus in Europe to lure foreign settlers to American railroad land. The Burlington and Missouri River Railroad Company offered free room and board to potential buyers for millions of acres of their land in Iowa and Nebraska and even offered financing of 6 percent on ten-year loans. Speculators published land grant maps to advertise railroad lands for sale to the public, often grossly exaggerating the quality of the land for sale and misrepresenting its proximity to civilization. One such town that owed its existence solely to the coming of the railroad was Cheyenne, the future capital of Wyoming. The early railroad towns were often lawless, free-wheeling settlements notorious for their saloons, brothels, and bawdy entertainment. Many served as little more than temporary camps for railroad construction workers and other transients, fading from the landscape once the work was completed. Others, like Cheyenne, grew and prospered as important transportation hubs.

The railroad fair, with its displays of the latest engines and rolling stock, was a popular event during this period. In the West, towns and cities vied with one another to lure the railroads, and the opening of a new line was always cause for public celebration. Trains were also favored in publicity stunts. In 1876, author Grace Greenwood (Sara Jane Lippincott) attempted to call attention to women's equality with men at the Centennial Exposition in Philadelphia by riding on a cowcatcher, the projecting device at the front of the engine intended to sweep animals and other obstruction from the track. She did not care for the experience, however. "I shall never do that again," she said as she swung down from the cowcatcher in a cloud of steam.

By the 1870s, the railroads employed tens of thousands of workers in one of the most tightly organized industries in the country. Rail workers sometimes faced inordinate risks. Cars were coupled and uncoupled manually by the brakeman, who had to stand between the cars and risk losing fingers and hands in the process, a common accident. Braking was done manually from the top of the car. As a result, many state legislatures during this period passed laws holding the railroads liable for worker injury and death if it resulted from the railroads' negligence. In response, the railroads issued detailed handbooks specifying standard and duties for each position and creating a rigid chain of command. Engineers and mechanics earned respectable salaries, up to $3.50 per day, while daily pay for unskilled laborers averaged $1.50.

Railroad travel was generally safer than travel by stage or wagon, but it was not free from risk. The first recorded U.S. train robbery took place on October 6, 1866, on the Ohio and Mississippi Rail Road near Seymour, Indiana, when two armed robbers collected $13,000 from the passengers. The most notorious train robbers were Frank and Jesse James, Cole Younger, and their gang. The Jameses, who began their career by robbing banks, staged their first train robbery on July 21, 1873, near Adair, Iowa. The public's attitude toward train robbers was sometimes ambivalent, fueled by bitterness toward the rich and powerful railroad owners and their perceived indifference toward the public.

The realities of travel overnight, as illustrated by *Frank Leslie's Illustrated Weekly*, and protection on the train from robbers, also from the *Illustrated Weekly*. (Courtesy of the Central Pacific Railroad Photographic History Museum.)

## RECREATIONAL TRAVEL

Postwar society had the money, leisure time, and curiosity to indulge a newfound interest in travel. Travel literature and a rudimentary tourism industry evolved to guide those who could afford to travel, and to provide a vicarious experience to those who could not. Nathaniel Hawthorne's *Marble Faun* (1860), a travel guide disguised as fiction, lured people to the art treasures of Europe.

The wealthy increasingly took to the waterways for pure pleasure. The New York Yacht Club was organized in 1844, and the end of the war marked the beginning of what Bernard Mergen has termed "ostentatious yachting by American millionaires."[3] By the 1870s, exclusive yacht clubs spread along both coasts, the Gulf of Mexico, and the Great Lakes. *The Aquatic Monthly and Nautical Review,* one of the first journals devoted exclusively to recreational sailing and rowing, appeared in 1872.

The voyage of the *Quaker City* was the first voyage of an American ship to Europe undertaken exclusively for pleasure. Its most illustrious passenger was Mark Twain, who based his *Innocents Abroad* (1869) on the experience. Twain cursed his fellow tourists as "the d——dest, rustiest, ignorant, vulgar, slimy, psalm-singing cattle that could be scraped up in seventeen states." Henry James saw American tourists as helpless in the hands of corrupt, though superior, European civilization. Americans needed to develop self-confidence and self-reliance, a message Ralph Waldo Emerson had been preaching for decades.

One promising form of transportation to appear in the 1860s was the velocipede. This forerunner of the bicycle, developed in Paris by Pierre Lallement and Pierre Michoux, had its pedals mounted on the front wheel. Although inefficient and difficult to handle, it enjoyed some success in the United States. French cycling instructors gave the sport a high-class air, and bicycles were promoted at the 1876 Centennial Exposition in Philadelphia. Continual improvements in design and construction would eventually lead to the great bicycling craze of the 1890s.

Recreational ballooning was also popular. As early as 1835, John Wise had sold rides in his hot-air balloon, the *Meteor.* Wise continued to operate until 1879, when he was lost in a ballooning accident over Lake Michigan. Wise's rival, Thaddeus Lowe, piloted the *Enterprise,* which served as the model for several balloons Lowe built for the Union army during the Civil War. Lowe's balloons were constructed of varnished silk and, unlike Wise's hot-air model, were filled with hydrogen or other gases.

## MAIL SERVICE

Then, as now, businesspeople realized that success depended on speed, especially in mail service. Although the railroad seemed to be a logical way to speed mail delivery, early service was uncertain and unscheduled. Those in commerce and the general public saw a desperate need for improved services, not only in predictable schedules but in reduced postal rates.

As early as 1834, two brothers, B. D. and L. B. Earle, operated a mail service on the railroad between Providence and Worcester, Massachusetts. In 1839, a competitive service was opened by William Harnden, who in announcing his service first used the word "express." These services carried newspapers, news dispatches, and other items that need to be transported quickly from place to place. Also hidden in their dispatch cases were letters that for one reason or another were best not trusted to the tender mercies of the post office. Early express companies would carry a letter from New York to Boston for 12.5 cents, half the cost of the post office. Post-masters naturally responded to the new competition, and in 1845 federal postal rates were reduced to 5 cents for up to 300 miles, or 10 cents for any-where in the United States. The express companies persisted, however. In 1852, American Express expanded service to the West Coast through Wells, Fargo & Company, and Adams & Company opened its business in Cali-fornia. Both companies flourished, becoming the leading express services after the war.

One improvement introduced by the in U.S. mail service was the sort-ing of mail on the moving cars, allowing delivery to stations along the route while in transit. To speed up service, trains did not stop at all stations, in-stead relying on a long metal arm that would reach out and grab the mail pouch from a pole alongside the track as the express roared by. Another improvement was the creation of the Railway Mail Service. Conceived in 1862 by W. A. Davis, a clerk in the St. Joseph, Missouri, post office, it stretched first out of Chicago and the Midwest. The service succeeded and was further refined by George B. Armstrong, assistant postmaster in Chicago. In July 1864, with the enthusiastic support of Postmaster General Montgomery Blair, Armstrong introduced their service on the Galena Di-vision of the Chicago and North Western Rail Road. It worked and through the years became one of the most successful railroad mail services.

Having no postal infrastructure, the Confederacy initially continued to use the U.S. mail service—including using U.S. stamps and facilities—for a month and a half after the bombardment of Fort Sumter on April 12, 1861. However, the U.S. government suspended mail service to and from the Confederate States on May 31, 1861, forcing Richmond to quickly establish a postal service. Service between the United States and the Confederate States, though haphazard, was still possible through private carriers such as the American Letter Express Company, with offices in Nashville and Louisville. To use this service, a Confederate citizen enclosed a letter in an envelope with a U.S. stamp and ten cents. The letter was taken across the Ohio and deposited in the U.S. mail.

The Civil War and Reconstruction periods were the morning of the de-velopment of new forms of travel. Geographical and psychological condi-tions drove the new need. Life was reaching out across the vast distances of the nation and people wanted to investigate. In order to do so, they had to have faster and more comfortable means of transportation. The results were a nation that left behind the old horse and buggy, converted to faster and more complicated means, and accompanied this new transportation with new means of communication. Between the Civil War and the end of Reconstruction, or at least the end of the nineteenth century, more inven-tions came about than during any other similar period before or after.

# 12

# Visual Arts

Americans during the mid-nineteenth century often found their artists and sculptors lacking in originality. Critics faulted the tendency of American visual artists to copy the latest trends and styles of western Europe. "America has yet morally and artistically originated nothing," Walt Whitman lamented in 1871. "She seems singularly unaware that the models of persons, books, manners, etc., appropriate for former conditions and for European lands are but exiles and exotics here." Yet Whitman's verdict, albeit a rallying cry for greater artistic endeavors in the United States, might have been too harsh. By the early 1860s, American themes began to dominate the visual arts. The Civil War and the settlement of the West, among other historical events, fired the imagination of American artists of all kinds. How artists strove to record these moments both for immediate consumption and for posterity forms one of the most compelling stories of the nation's history. Their media included all forms of visual communication, some soon to be made obsolete by technology, and some remaining with us today.

## DIORAMAS AND PANORAMAS

Credit for the development of the diorama, popular at mid-century, is given to Louis Daguerre, inventor of the daguerreotype, and his partner Charles-Marie Bouton. Introduced in Paris in 1822, the diorama was a kind of three-dimensional peep show consisting of sculptured figures or other objects placed in a box in front of a backing cloth, with colored transparent or translucent curtains used to create an illusion of depth. Viewed through a small aperture, they were crude forerunners of the more elaborate, adaptable, and effective cycloramas that became popular at the beginning of the twentieth century.

Among the many other forms of visual entertainment of the time was the panorama, popular for at least half a century. The panorama consisted of a large painting on canvas that was unrolled across one or more walls before an audience. At first only silent pictures, they were later improved by the addition of a commentator and musical accompaniment. Originating in England in 1787, panoramas were introduced to America in 1814 by a painting 165 feet long and between 11 and 12 feet tall, and they became immensely popular. In 1848, Benjamin Russell, with a house painter named Caleb Parrington, recorded his adventures aboard the American whaler *Kutusoff* in an extended series of paintings more than a quarter of a mile long, which he exhibited for a fee of twenty-five to fifty cents.

The Mississippi River provided the inspiration for several attractive panoramas, most notably one based on the adventures of a Philadelphia archeologist named Montroville Wilson Dickeson. Measuring 348 feet by 7.5 feet, it was painted on muslin and weighed only 100 pounds. Another very popular panorama, by Carl Christian Anton Christianson, depicted the Mormons' 1,300-mile exodus to Salt Lake City. Also successful was "Stevens' Great Tableau Painting Representing the Indians Massacre in Minnesota in 1862."

Despite their appeal, and perhaps because of their bulk and the difficulty in viewing them, panoramas declined in popularity soon after the Civil War.

## TABLEAUX VIVANTS

*Tableaux vivants* ("living pictures") were an artistic genre that catered to the prurient interests of mid-nineteenth century Americans while pretending to do otherwise. Sometimes called "artist models," they were introduced into the United States from France in 1831. Well established in New York by the late 1840s, *tableaux vivants* featured partially draped females framed as still pictures. Theater owners sometimes pushed the limits of the law in posing and uncovering their models. Riots erupted when unruly members of the audience tried to get to the women, who escaped through trapdoors. In 1847, a Dr. Collyer, one of the leading exhibitors, presented a full living picture company. The enormity of the presentation led to its suppression. *Tableaux vivants* continued to be shown throughout the Civil War and Reconstruction period and into the twentieth century.

## LITHOGRAPHY

Lithography, invented by a Bavarian named Alois Senefelder around 1795, was a simple printmaking process utilizing limestone slabs as the printing medium. The process was introduced in the United States America by Bass Otis, a pupil of the artist Gilbert Stuart, around 1820, and it revolutionized American popular art. Relatively cheap to produce, lithographs made popular art widely available to the general public.

Nathaniel Currier (1813–1888) was among the early artists to adapt and perfect the lithographic process. At age fifteen, he apprenticed with William and John Pendleton, owners of a Boston printing firm, and in 1834 he founded his own lithographic company. Currier was catapulted to fame with his print, "The Ruins of the Merchants Exchange," issued four days after the fire of December 16–17, 1835. Disaster scenes were to become a stock-in-trade for Currier. His print of the burning of the steamboat *Lexington* in Long Island Sound, on January 13, 1840, was distributed in the New York papers three days later in what has been called "perhaps the first illustrated extra in history."

James Merritt Ives (1824–1895) married Currier's sister-in-law and in 1852 was hired as Currier's bookkeeper. Because of his keen sense of the public's desires and sensibilities, Ives was made a partner in 1857. Thus was formed a partnership that catered successfully to the wishes of the public. Published before the perfection of commercial color printing, Currier & Ives's lithographs were printed in black and white. The more expensive editions were colored by hand by a line of young women, each of whom was responsible for applying her assigned color before passing the print to the next in line. One woman stood at the end of the table and finished off any touches needed to turn the lithograph into a realistic work of art.

Altogether Currier & Ives produced approximately 7,000 to 8,000 lithographs. The prints ran the gamut from natural disasters, wrecks, and fires to Mexican-American and Civil War land and naval battles, whalers and clipper ships, railroads, Barnum's attractions, farm and country life, Indians, and the West. Although their prints reflect virtually every aspect of American life of the time, they were often highly romanticized, a fault that becomes especially evident when the prints are compared to photographs of the period. In most of these prints they merely followed the popular trends, picturing what they perceived in the spirit of the times. Their depictions of African Americans, for example, adhered to the popular stereotypes of the happy slave, grinning and contented, joyful to be protected in slavery from the horrors of freedom and the mastery of one's own fate.

## GENRE PAINTING

Departing from the classical traditions that dominated the fine arts, American genre painters depicted everyday people and events, usually in a near-photographic style. Sometimes referred to as romantic realism, their work often addressed, in veiled but intended ways, important social and political issues of the day. Genre painters fused political commentary with a simple form of sentimental pictorialism that was readily grasped and appreciated by the general public.

William Sidney Mount (1807–1868) is considered the father of American genre painting. He created cheerful, sometimes comic pictures of life on rural Long Island during the first half of the nineteenth century. Although overtly simple, Mount's scenes were often commentaries on political events. His racially integrated cast of characters, based not on slaves but on free blacks, was unusual for its time. Mount portrayed whites and free blacks interacting socially and produced a popular set of prints depicting cosmopolitan black musicians. Mount's family had held slaves on Long Island in the early 1800s, and that experience probably influenced his sentimental portrayal of African Americans. Nevertheless, he largely avoided the prevailing stereotypical portrayal of southern blacks.

Among the most popular American genre artists were James H. Beard, John G. Brown, Winslow Homer, Thomas LeClear, and Charles Caleb Ward. The most financially successful was Brown, the favorite artist of William Jennings Bryan. Brown's subjects were the children of the streets of New York, the visual equivalent of Horatio Alger's novels. Eastman Johnson captured the essence of a more innocent form of childhood, and Homer captured the essence of everyday life. E. L. Henry was best known for his paintings of small-town life in antebellum rural America.

## SCULPTURE

The nineteenth century is usually credited as the period that saw the flowering of American sculpture. Early America was awash in sculptured objects, although many of them, intended to be strictly utilitarian, were not perceived as sculpture. Considered folk or commercial art, such pieces were not accorded much respect by serious students of art at the time of their creation. During the early nineteenth century, however, American sculpture underwent a transformation from folk art to high art. Monuments of all kinds, from tombstones to statues, were rising all around.

Among the most famous American sculptors of the antebellum and Civil War periods were Horatio Greenough and Hiram Powers. Greenough was educated at Harvard and served his early apprenticeship in Italy, at that time the preeminent center for sculpture in the western world. While there in 1832, he received a commission to carve a statue of George Washington to be mounted in the rotunda of the United States Capitol. Influenced by his Italian mentors, as well as by Thomas Jefferson's earlier insistence that the father of his country should be represented in classical Roman terms, Greenough created a statue that quickly became a laughingstock when it was displayed in the Capitol. It was larger than life, a half-nude Roman emperor, seated on his throne, right hand raised, left hand displaying a Roman short sword, toga lying below bared upper torso across his lap. The sculpture was unexpected, unappreciated, and unacceptable. Philip Hone, a self-appointed authority on art and culture, derided it roundly: "It looks like a great Herculean, warrior-like *Venus of the bath* ... undressed, with a huge napkin lying in his lap and covering his lower extremities, and he, preparing to perform his ablutions, is in the act of consigning his sword to the care of the attendant."[1] The statue was eventually relegated to an obscure corner of the Smithsonian Institution.

Greenough's misjudgment aside, Americans still adored marble statuary in the classical style, but they preferred that the work be more realistic, warmer, and less austere. Hiram Powers's "Greek Slave" (1843), which now resides in the Corcoran Gallery in Washington, D.C., met those demands nicely, somehow satisfying the elite and the general public alike. It had been successfully displayed for two years in Europe and therefore came to America with all the weight of approval by recognized arbiters of taste. The statue was a life-size rendering of a young, seminude Greek female slave. Tens of thousands saw and approved the nicely executed figure. This appreciation was clearly the voice of a frustrated yet culturally aspiring and developing public. The sculptor was careful to explain that it was "not her person, but her spirit" that was unclothed. Another critic, Caroline Kirkland, gushed with appreciation, "Men take off their hats, ladies seat themselves silently, and almost unconsciously; and usually it is minutes before a word is uttered. All conversation is carried on in a hushed tone and everybody looks serious on departing." This almost reverential appreciation of the sculpture reflected the harsh realities of the period. People remembered that the Turks, in their campaigns against the Greeks, had held Greek women in slavery; others saw a parallel to black slave women. But it also seems likely that prurient interests were being satisfied by this and similar statuary.

One sculptor whose work departed from the classical tradition and flourished during Reconstruction was John Rogers. Rogers, after a period of wandering, settled in Chicago and worked in various mechanical jobs. In 1859, he created a little plaster group called "Checker Players" that met with instant approval. In 1860, he moved to New York and through the years cast figures of an idealized American past in such works as "Peddler at the Fair," "Frolic at the Old Homestead," "Fetching the Doctor," "Fighting Bob," and "School Days."

Though the Civil War to a certain extent interrupted the production of sculpture, such organizations as the Cosmopolitan Art Association continued to encourage and distribute sculpture and associated arts.

## PHOTOGRAPHY

Louis Daguerre developed the first practical photographic process in France in 1837, and the daguerreotype soon took America by storm. *Godey's*

*Lady's Book* in 1849 commented that daguerreotypists were "limning faces at a rate that promises soon to make every man's home a Daguerrean gallery."[2] However, Daguerre's process was slow, requiring exposure times of up to several minutes, and it created rather dim, mirrorlike positive images on sensitized metal plates that did not lend themselves to copying. The development of the wet-plate process in the 1840s, combined with the invention of the albumen paper print in the 1850s, allowed photographers to produce a permanent glass negative from which multiple, inexpensive paper prints could be made. The new negative-positive process created a huge demand for photographs of all kinds.

Unlike paintings and sketches, cameras captured their subjects without embellishment by the artist. In an oft-repeated story, President Lincoln is said to have visited a photographer during the Civil War. When told that he looked very natural, Lincoln quipped, "Yes, that is my objection. The cameras are painfully truthful." Studio portraits taken during the Civil War era were stiffly posed, often against painted backdrops depicting ancient ruins, majestic scenery, or exotic locales. To keep their subjects from moving during the long exposures, thus blurring the shot, photographers routinely resorted to a head clamp that can sometimes be seen in the finished picture. Photomontages, combining bits of imagery from multiple negatives, enjoyed a brief vogue; one of the most popular depicted George Washington welcoming President Lincoln to heaven. The less posed and contrived photographs of the period, many of them captured by traveling photographers in the course of documenting the war, often reveal a way of life that appears casual and homespun to the modern viewer.

Stereoscopic photography and color tinting, processes developed in the previous decades, became popular during the Civil War. Stereographs employed two photographs of the same view, one shot from the position of the left eye and other from the right, and mounted side-by-side on a cardboard card. When viewed through the dual-lens stereoscope, the images blended to produce a realistic three-dimensional effect. One proponent of stereographs gushed that the resulting images were the next best thing to being on the actual spot of the photograph, because the "mind feels its way into the very depths of the picture." By the end of the war, Alexander Gardner and the E. & H. T. Anthony Company, then the largest marketers of stereographs, had produced a combined 2,500 stereoscopic images, many of which remained in circulation in various editions into the twentieth century. Similarly, color tinting added a degree of realism to standard monochrome photographs. Tinting artists used watercolors to add color, ranging from a bit of highlighting on the face to a full colorization. The process was time-consuming and resulted in higher prices for the customer. In a catalogue published by the E. & H. T. Anthony Company in 1868, color views cost $6 a dozen, while black-and-white views in the same quantity cost only $4.50.

The most popular photographic form of the period was the *carte-de-visite*. It was a small card—about twice as large as the modern business card—and was often left as a calling card or traded with friends and acquaintances. Collecting *cartes-de-visite* of national celebrities became a national fad in the early 1860s. During January 1861 alone, E. & H. T. Anthony printed a thousand *cartes-de-visite* a day of Major Robert Anderson, a central figure in the attack on Fort Sumter.

The larger cabinet cards, measuring about four by six inches, were introduced in 1867. As subject and photographer were quick to discover, the larger format made the sitter's imperfections more obvious, and hand-retouching became a common practice. Cabinet cards were proudly displayed in elaborate family albums. By 1870, E. & H. T. Anthony offered more than 500 album styles, many of them sporting gilt edges, engraved metal clasps, and mother-of-pearl inlays.

Mathew Brady' studios were undoubtedly the most famous producers of these cards, although countless other photographers operated across the country during the period. Brady (1823–1896) went into the business of photography early, opening his Daguerrean Miniature Gallery in New York in 1844. Exploiting the booming popularity of daguerreotypes, Brady soon became among the most fashionable portrait photographers of the day, admired as much for his engaging personality as for his great professional skill. Brady photographed many notables of his day, including P. T. Barnum, Walt Whitman, and Mark Twain. But his most popular subject was Abraham Lincoln, whom Brady photographed often.

Handicapped by failing vision, Brady turned much of his later work over to a team of capable assistants, many of whom—most notably Alexander Gardner and George N. Barnard—left Brady to pursue their own careers during the course of the Civil War. The postwar years brought Brady little financial reward for his previous efforts and expenditures. In debt because of his wartime operations, he sold his collection to the federal government for $25,000. Although a large sum of money at the time, the payment failed to save Brady from several later bad business decisions. Impoverished and nearly blind, he died in the charity ward of New York Presbyterian Hospital in 1896.

The Confederacy also had its photographers—notably George S. Cook, J. D. Edwards, and A. D. Lytle—who worked mainly in portraiture.

## CAPTURING THE IMAGES OF THE CIVIL WAR
### Photographers

Photography and illustrated journalism brought the realities of warfare home to Americans during the Civil War as in no previous conflict. During the Mexican-American War (1846–1848), artists rarely visited the sites of the conflict, and only a handful of primitive photographs were taken. Instead, painters and illustrators produced their work in studios in the United States, based largely on secondhand reports and far removed from the sweat and blood of military life. The result was a heroic image of war that emphasized dash and color. "I used to read stories about the Mexican war, and earnestly wished I was a man," Major James Connolly, a Union volunteer, admitted during the summer of 1863, "so that I could go to war like the men in the pictures, wearing a nice blue coat and red pants, flourishing a great yellow sword over my head, and dashing into the thickest of the fight on a furious, coal black horse." After fighting in the thick of several battles in Kentucky and Tennessee, Connolly found that his image of war had changed. The sight of men killed and wounded at his side made the prospect of further battle not romantic and stirring but "very unenchanting."

Photography was the most important visual medium in recording the Civil War experience because of its ability to reproduce lifelike images of soldiers and battlefields. The process of picture-taking during the Civil War was daunting. A photographer or his assistant had to coat the glass photographic plate with various chemicals, including silver nitrate. The procedure occurred in a hooded wagon that served as a portable darkroom. Once coated, the wet plates were rushed to the camera, which had already been positioned on a heavy tripod or other support and focused upon the intended subject. The photographer then pulled a black cape over his head and the camera and exposed the plate. At best, exposure times ranged from ten to thirty seconds, making pictures possible only of landscape, still objects, and unmoving people and animals. With the negative completed, photographers took their product back to the portable darkroom for development. They had to move carefully and quickly, keeping the plate wet while avoiding airborne dust, debris, and insects that could ruin the negative. Additionally, development of the plate needed to be completed with twenty to thirty minutes, or the image would be lost.

Despite the many obstacles they faced, Civil War–era photographers compiled a magnificent chronicle of the conflict. Not all campaigns were photographed, especially those that occurred in the South (where photographic supplies were in short supply) or in remote and inhospitable terrain. Still, photographers recorded pictures of weapons, soldiers, camps, and ships. No accurate records exist regarding how many pictures were taken during the war, although various scholars have estimated that anywhere from several hundred thousand to one million photographs were shot. The overwhelming majority of these were portraits, either individual or group. High-ranking officers sometimes received more than their share of attention from photographers, but company officers and enlisted soldiers also were well documented.

Mathew Brady was among the most famous Civil War photographers. With the outbreak of the Civil War, Brady left his fashionable photographic studios after winning permission from the Lincoln administration to chronicle the operations of the Union army at his own expense. "I felt I had to go," Brady explained later of his decision to journey to the front lines. "A spirit in my feet said 'go' and I went." Brady and his associates eventually amassed 5,700 negatives of war subjects, primarily in the eastern theater.

Brady was at his best when detailing the daily life of Union soldiers in the East. In camp, he captured images of soldiers at work and at play. In one picture, Brady or one of his assistants, apparently perched on a hilltop, photographed a regiment in parade formation. The image is striking because the muskets and fixed bayonets of the men form row upon row of bristling steel. In another photograph, Brady photographed the Roman Catholic soldiers of the 69th New York State Militia participating in an outdoor mass, eagerly gathered around the priest, who holds an open Bible. Brady took few photographs of actual battle. Long exposure times required photographer and subject to remain stationary, and no one was so foolish as to stand still during combat. Brady, however, got as close to battle as possible. In one notable incident, he came under Confederate long-range fire while making a picture of a federal artillery battery outside Petersburg, Virginia, in 1864. The resulting picture was only one of a handful that showed Union troops preparing to go into action.

Alexander Gardner, Timothy O'Sullivan, and George Barnard were other famous photographers of the Union war effort. Gardner and O'Sullivan, born in 1821 and 1840, respectively, worked as Brady's assistants at the start of the war. They left during late 1862, however, angered that their pictures appeared in print under their boss's name (albeit a common practice at the time). The two photographers worked together for the remainder of the war, with Gardner serving as studio owner. Their photographs of bloated corpses following the battle of Gettysburg, Pennsylvania (July 1–3, 1863) shocked a nation that until that time still thought of battle as noble and picturesque. One of the most graphic photographs of the series, O'Sullivan's "A Harvest of Death," served a "useful moral," according to Gardner. He explained that the brutal starkness of the picture showed, like no other visual medium could, "the blank horror and reality of war." Gardner and O'Sullivan continued their photographic careers after the conclusion of the Civil War. In 1866, Gardner published his *Photographic Sketchbook of the War*. Although the book appeared under Gardner's name, O'Sullivan received credit for forty-four of the 100 prints. In later years, both men carried their cameras across the American West, photographing Native Americans and white settlers.

George Barnard won wartime fame as the photographer of the Union army in the western theater. Born in 1819, Barnard also served as one of Brady's many assistants at the start of the war. He soon left, and by 1863 he was working independently. His most notable photographs recorded the campaigns of General William Tecumseh Sherman during 1864 and 1865. Barnard took haunting shots of Atlanta and Columbia, South Carolina, both of which were ravaged by fire during Confederate retreats and Union advances in the March to the Sea. In 1866, Barnard published sixty-one of his pictures in *Photographic Views of Sherman's Campaign*. Barnard continued to practice his art into the early 1890s, working in various cities across the East. He died in 1902, after retiring to Cedarville, New York.

Photographers were less common in the Confederacy. In large part, the deficiency resulted from lack of supplies. The Union navy blockaded Confederate ports, forcing any materials, military or otherwise, to enter through smuggling operations. Although no exact data exist on the priority placed by Southern officials upon the import of nonmilitary items, photographic equipment and supplies likely ranked low. Some photographers in the South, like George Cook, circumvented the problem of the blockade by obtaining supplies directly from the North. Such enterprising spirits, however, were few. The overwhelming majority of southern photographers had to use their supplies sparingly, if not close shop altogether. To a lesser extent, photography in the wartime South was hindered by a scarcity of manpower. The Confederate States imposed conscription during the spring of 1862, exempting only owners of large plantations. As a result, many photographers and their assistants found themselves carrying muskets and bayonets rather than their usual cameras and wet plates. Whether through lack of supplies or lack of manpower, as one northern photographic journal noted with satisfaction in 1863, there was "very little photography in Jeffdom for the past two years."

Southern photographers achieved their greatest wartime successes following the bombardment of Fort Sumter, off Charleston, South Carolina, on April 12, 1861. The attack was the opening military battle of the Civil War, and the federal garrison surrendered after enduring two days of Confederate artillery fire. Many Southern photographers rushed to record the Confederate triumph. Some photographed the artillery batteries that shelled the fort. In a picture circulated widely throughout the South, Osborn & Durbec, a Charleston-based photography company, captured the battery that reportedly fired the first shot of the war. Other photographers ventured inside the ruins of the surrendered stronghold. In another well-known picture, one photographer recorded the image of Confederate soldiers and civilians milling about several captured federal artillery pieces. Another cameraman snapped the Confederate national flag, better known throughout the South as the Stars and Bars, waving in triumph above the fort.

## Illustrators

While photographers brought the Civil War home to the American public on glass plates, sketch artists and editorial cartoonists did the same on paper. Illustrated journalism in the United States received its trial by fire during the fighting that raged between 1861 and 1865. Newspaper artists had been sent to sketch many historical events during the late 1850s and early 1860s. In a notable example, artists from *Frank Leslie's Illustrated Newspaper* drew pictures of the Heenan-Sayers heavyweight championship fight in England in 1860. The issue in which the drawings subsequently appeared was a hit, selling 347,000 copies. War, however, proved to be a new experience for American newspaper artists. Among the several dozen artists who accompanied the Confederate and Union armies during 1861, only Thomas Nast previously had seen battle. Nast had served as a sketch artist for the *New York Illustrated News* during the wars for Italian unification in 1860. Otherwise, American illustrated journalists were as green as the soldiers they attempted to portray.

Northerners dominated illustrated journalism, as they did photography. This was not because they inherently were more skilled in the art. Rather, Confederates again suffered from lack of supplies and manpower. In the fall of 1862, Ayers & Wade, Richmond publishers, founded the *Southern Illustrated News*. The founders proclaimed the publication as a "News and Literary Journal for Southern Families." Despite such lofty objectives, the paper struggled to remain financially viable because of a lack of skilled labor. "Engravers Wanted," one of their advertisements pleaded during the summer of 1863. "Desirous, if possible of illustrating the 'News' in a style not inferior to the 'London Illustrated News,' we offer the *highest salaries* ever paid in this country for good engravers." No qualified applicants came forward, despite the monetary inducement. Illustrations were rare in the southern press, usually limited to a roughly drawn political cartoon or portrait of a Confederate general. One northern editor delighted in calling attention to the "wonderfully bad" illustrations of his southern counterpart. The *Southern Illustrated News* did not survive the war, going out of business during the late winter of 1864.

Sketch artists who accompanied the Union armies confronted many professional obstacles. One source of frustration was that their talent often was served poorly by the newspaper printing process. Wartime artists sketched various military events with whatever tools were at hand, including pencil, crayon, watercolors, and pen and ink. Illustrators had an advantage over photographers in this respect, because they could record action scenes, most notably marches and battles, on the spot. Once an artist had completed a piece, he rushed the product to the home office of his newspaper, where the process often ran into difficulties. Engravers copied the drawing onto thick blocks of wood. They next carved away negative areas, leaving raised surfaces to imprint ink on the news page. Unfortunately, engravers often lost the sensitive lines and details of the artist. The result often was a highly stylized picture that bore slight resemblance to the original. "Those who draw their conceptions of the appearance of the rebel soldiery from *Harper's Weekly*," one critic of Union newspaper illustrations scoffed during mid-war, "would hardly recognize one on sight."

Another hardship confronted by sketch artists was daily life in the field. Men who drew pictures for their wartime careers shared the same physical hardships and discomforts of the soldiers whom they covered. They marched when the armies marched and ate what the armies ate. Henri Lovie, an artist for *Frank Leslie's Illustrated Newspaper,* served in both the eastern and western theaters. After covering the Shiloh Campaign during early April 1862, Lovie complained that "riding from ten to fifteen miles daily, through mud and underbrush, and then working until midnight by the dim light on an attenuated tallow 'dip,' are among the least of my *desagremens* and sorrows." He explained, "I am deranged about the stomach, ragged, unkempt, and unshorn, and need the conjoined skill and services of the apothecary, the tailor and the barber, and above all the attentions of home." Lovie retired from professional illustration during late 1863 in part to enter private business, but also to recover from the physical wear and tear of his wartime service.

Newspaper artists also had to overcome the initial suspicions and prejudices of Union soldiers. Some fighting men believed that journalists were giving valuable aid to the enemy through their detailed drawings and maps. George Alfred Townsend of the *New York Herald* was making a map of the Cedar Mountain battlefield in Virginia during the late summer of 1862 when a wary soldier asked the artist if he was including the nearby federal positions. When Townsend applied in the affirmative, the soldier ordered the artist to stop his work. In another instance, W. R. McComas of *Frank Leslie's Illustrated Newspaper* asked General Sherman if he could accompany his command during late 1861. "You fellows makes the best spies that can be bought," Sherman is said to have indignantly responded. "Jeff Davis owes more to you newspapermen than to his army." Newspaper artists eventually overcame such suspicions regarding their loyalty, as much through their hard work as through soldiers' enjoyment of the artists' published work.

Despite obstacles at the home office and on the front lines, sketch artists played a vital role in illustrating what military life was like for the northern soldier. In a high compliment, Ulysses S. Grant, the general-in-chief of the Union army during 1864 through 1865, praised the historical importance of the wartime work done by illustrated journalists. "We are the men who make history," the general is said to have told one artist, "but you are the men who perpetuate it." Artists such as Winslow Homer, Alfred Waud, and Theodore Davis were among the most popular Union artists because of their ability to depict realistically the many and varied aspects of military life. Homer arguably was the most distinguished of the three because of his skill in capturing moments of human interest. "Prisoners at the Front" (1865) is among Homer's most acclaimed wartime pieces. The picture portrays a Union officer studying three Confederate prisoners. In addition to displaying uniforms and equipment, each figure depicts different regional characteristic. One Confederate, for example, represents the cavalier tradition of the Old South, with ramrod posture and defiant glare.

## Cartoonists

Newspaper cartoonists played a different role in the Union war effort than sketch artists, using caricature, exaggeration, and satire to explain why the North was fighting. Their task was difficult. Though intended to cut and slash, cartoons usually disguised their serious messages under a veneer of humor. In part, cartoonists had their work cut out for them because political debate continued in the North throughout the war. Many Northerners thought they were fighting only to preserve the Union, while others fought also to end slavery. Some in the North believed that President Lincoln exercised too much central control, while others argued that he wielded too little. The task of newspaper cartoonists was made all the more difficult because of the duration and human cost of the war. Many Northerners experienced flagging spirits at some point during the fighting, but especially during the first three years. Morale fell as the casualty lists grew without any end to the fighting in sight.

The cartoons carried in the Northern popular press were particularly unrestrained. Many of the most vitriolic attacks were against the South and its president, Jefferson Davis. Cold, austere, and leader of a despised cause, Davis was ridiculed in every possible way by cartoonists. In the early days of the secession, when southern leaders were having trouble establishing a permanent capitol for the Confederacy, *Frank Leslie's Illustrated Newspaper* pictured Davis and his cabinet on an alligator labeled "Davis's Great Moving Circus," with the caption, "Davis's Vagrant Acrobats on a Professional Tour through the Southern Cities."

In 1863, when the future of the Confederacy looked increasingly bleak, *Harper's Weekly* for August 22 pictured Davis addressing a group of armless veterans. The cartoon was titled "Jeff Davis's Last Appeal to Arms," and was captioned "Fellow Citizens—the Victory is within your reach. You need but stretch forth your hands to grasp it" Three months earlier, the same magazine had addressed the dire food shortages in the South with a cartoon of Davis and General P. G. T. Beauregard titled "The Food Question Down South," with a caption reading, "Jeff Davis: 'See, see! The beautiful Boots just come to me from the dear ladies of Baltimore!' Beauregard: 'Ha! Boots? Boots? When shall we eat them? Now?'" One of the most pointed criticisms of Davis' ineptitude appeared in *Harper's Weekly* (April 1, 1865). Davis stands with a speech in his hand as three soldiers are relaying the news of the day. One says, "Schofield has whipped Bragg and is moving on Goldsboro." Another says, "Sherman has cleaned out South Carolina and is marching on Raleigh!" The third announces, "Sheridan is only 10 miles from Richmond!" To which Davis replies, "Our country is now environed with perils which it is our duty calmly to contemplate."

*Harper's Weekly* ran a scathing cartoon in the summer of 1863, when Davis was accused of encouraging the abuse of captured Union soldiers and blacks in the Confederacy. In retaliation, Lincoln prepared his General

JEFF DAVIS'S LAST APPEAL TO ARMS.

"Fellow Citizens — the Victory is within your reach. You need but STRETCH FORTH YOUR HANDS TO GRASP IT."—(Address of Jeff Davis to his Soldiers.)

*Frank Leslie's Illustrated Weekly's* caricature of the ineptitude of President Davis in the final hours before his defeat.

JEFF DAVIS "CALMLY CONTEMPLATING."

"Our country is now environed with perils which it is our duty calmly to contemplate."— *Extract from Davis's last Message.*

Unionists insisted that while the confederacy collapsed around him, Davis clothed himself in high rhetoric. (From *Harper's Weekly*, April, 1865)

Order No. 252, which stated that "for every United States soldier killed in violation of the laws of war, a rebel soldier shall be executed; and for every one enslaved by the enemy or sold into slavery, a rebel soldier shall be placed at hard labor on the public works." The *Harper's* cartoon showed Lincoln holding a rebel boy by the scruff of the neck and waving his stick at Davis, who was chasing a boy slave with a whip. Lincoln's comment was, "Look here, Jeff Davis! If you lay a finger on that boy to hurt him, I'll lick this *ugly cub of yours* within an inch of his life!" Davis never triumphed in the northern press.

Interestingly, Robert E. Lee was only minimally caricatured. He was looked upon as a soldier who served his conscience and was generally for-

The reelection of
Lincoln in November
1864 brought joy to
most of the North.
Here Lincoln, who
was frequently referred
to as being very "long,"
is made by the *Harper's*
cartoonist "a little longer."
This comparison was
used frequently in
cartoons to tease Davis
about how much the
"longer" Lincoln was
going to plague him.

Long ABRAHAM LINCOLN a Little Longer.

*Harper's Weekly* rejoices after the November 1864 election returns

given for fighting against his country instead of his home state of Virginia.
But Lee was the subject of "Prospects of the Southern Sambo," one of the
most brutal cartoons published by *Frank Leslie's Illustrated Newspaper*. It
shows a slave tied to a post and being beaten by a white man, to which Lee
responds, "Hold on there, driver. We want Sambo to fight for Liberty and
Independence. You can thrash him as much as you like when he comes
back."

Lincoln, though pictured in the hostile press as every kind of fool and
monster, generally received far more favorable coverage in the North than

did Davis. Whenever there was a chance to demonstrate Lincoln's superiority over Davis, the triumph was clear and definite. In one cartoon in *Frank Leslie's Illustrated Newspaper* (December 24, 1864), Lincoln is shown grappling Davis around the neck and saying, "Now, Jeffy, when you think you have had enough of this, say so, and I'll leave off." A more dignified portrayal of Lincoln becomes apparent after his election to a second term in 1864. A *Harper's Weekly* cartoon pictured a pencil-thin president standing the height of the page with the caption, "Long Abraham a Little Longer."

The popular press of the war filled their sheets with numerous cartoons and illustrations about the heroes of both cultures. What they did for the Lincoln and Davis administrations they continued to do for political friends and foes during the Reconstruction.

This period in the visual arts, as in all other forms of communication, was the breakthrough in all the visual arts. Private collections of artifacts and rather modest expressions of art developed into public displays, and new media to express the spirit and expressions of Americans. It was a period when America began to free itself from European domination and to flex its own muscles.

# Comparative Values of Money

In the Union between 1850 and 1865, workers' real wages fell by 20 percent and the overall cost of living rose 70 percent.

In the Confederacy during the same period, the Confederate dollar fell to 1,850 for one federal greenback.

The cost of feeding a small family rose from $6.55 to $68.25 per month. The costs of most items was staggering: meat, 50 cents per pound; butter, 75 cents per pound; coffee, $1.50 per pound; tea, $10.00 per pound; boots, $30.00; men's shoes, $18.00; women's shoes, $15.00; shirts, $6.00, house rent, $1,000 annually; room and board for one per month, $30–$40; sheets, $15.00; cornmeal, $8.00 per bushel; chickens, $5.00 each; turnip greens, $18.00 a bushel; bacon, $1.50 per pound; bread, 20 cents a loaf; flour, $30.00 per hundredweight.

The cost of some forms of entertainment during the conflict remained low, only to rise after the war. An American playwright could be paid $500 for an original play and $200 for a subsequent adaptation. John Wilkes Booth was paid $20 a week for playing a supporting role in *Beauty and the Beast*.

Slaves could cost from $1,000 to $2,000, while a white overseer would receive $200 to $500 per year in salary.

Gambling, a near-obsession with those who could afford large stakes, drew huge sums. Tens of thousands of dollars were won or lost in a night. Gamblers lost or won plantations, crops, slaves, everything they owned but family.

(Information from Dorothy Denneen Volo and James M. Volo, *Daily Life in Civil War America* [Westport, Conn.: Greenwood, 1998].)

# Notes

## CHAPTER 1

1. For a succinct overview of American economic, territorial, and population growth during the mid-nineteenth century, see McPherson, *Battle Cry of Freedom: The Civil War Era* (New York: Oxford Univ. Press, 1988), 6–46.

2. The ill-preparedness of the American military for war during early 1861 is described in McPherson, *Battle Cry of Freedom*, 312–14.

3. For a discussion of the number men who served in the Union and Confederate armies, see McPherson, *Battle Cry of Freedom*, 306–7. See also Thomas L. Livermore, *Numbers and Losses in the Civil War in America, 1861–65* (Boston: Houghton Mifflin Co., 1900). Reprint, introduction by Edward E. Barthell, Jr. (Bloomington: Indiana University Press, 1957).

4. The financial and casualty figures cited above are taken from *Writing the Civil War: The Quest to Understand*, James M. McPherson and William J. Cooper, Jr., eds. (Columbia: University of South Carolina Press, 1998), 2.

5. The mobilization of military manpower in the Union and Confederacy is described in James I. Robertson, Jr., *Soldiers Blue and Gray* (Columbia: University of South Carolina Press, 1998), 11–14. The standard overview of the mobilization of the Union army is Fred Albert Shannon, *The Organization and Administration of the Union Army, 1861–1865*, 2 vols. (Cleveland, Ohio: Arthur H. Clark Co., 1928).

6. The local orientation of American life prior to the outbreak of the Civil War is discussed in Philip S. Paludan, *"A People's Contest": The Union and the Civil War, 1861–1865* (New York: Harper and Row, 1988), 10–15.

7. The literature on why Civil War soldiers fought is extensive. Works that stress the importance of ideology in the decision of soldiers to volunteer include: James M. McPherson, *For Cause and Comrades: Why Men Fought in the Civil War* (New York: Oxford University Press, 1997) and *What They Fought For, 1861–1865* (Baton Rouge: Louisiana State University Press, 1994); and Reid Mitchell, *Civil War Soldiers: Their Expectations and Their Experiences* (New York: Viking, 1988). For works

that play down the role of ideology in soldiers' motivations to enlist, see: Gerald F. Linderman, *Embattled Courage: The Experience of Combat in the American Civil War* (New York: Free Press, 1987); and Bell Irwin Wiley, *The Life of Billy Yank* (Indianapolis: Bobbs Merrill, 1952).

8. New Jersey soldier quotation taken from McPherson, *Battle Cry of Freedom*, 309.

9. Thomas Taylor to Antoinette Taylor, May 23, 1861, in McPherson, *For Cause and Comrades*, 19.

10. Mississippi soldier quotation taken from McPherson, *Battle Cry of Freedom*, 310.

11. John Lee Holt to Ellen Holt, May 2, 1862, in McPherson, *For Cause and Comrades*, 21.

12. William Wyckoff to Frances Ives, June 1861, in McPherson, *For Cause and Comrades*, 22.

13. John A. Gillis, diary entry, November 11, 1861, in McPherson, *For Cause and Comrades*, 23.

14. The emphasis upon honor and duty in Confederate letters is explored in McPherson, *For Cause and Comrades*, 23–24. For a detailed explanation of the importance of honor in antebellum southern society, see Bertram Wyatt-Brown, *Southern Honor: Ethics and Behaviour in the Old South* (New York: Oxford University Press, 1982).

15. Samuel D. Sanders to Mary Sanders, March 22, 1862, in McPherson, *For Cause and Comrades*, 23.

16. Hugh L. Honnell to sister, December 17, 1861, in McPherson, *For Cause and Comrades*, 23.

17. Alfred Hough to Mary Hough, October 28, 1863, in McPherson, *For Cause and Comrades*, 13.

18. Edward W. Cade to Allie Cade, November 19, 1863, in *A Texas Surgeon in the C.S.A.*, John Q. Anderson, ed. (Tuscaloosa: University of Alabama Press, 1957), 67–68.

19. For a description of northern reactions to the Emancipation Proclamation in the army and on the homefront, see McPherson, *Battle Cry of Freedom*, 557–67.

20. Lucius Hubbard to Mary Hubbard, September 8, 1862, in "Letters of a Union Officer: L. F. Hubbard and the Civil War," N.B. Martin, ed. *Minnesota History* 35 (1957): 314–15.

21. B. W. H. Parson to A. A. Shafer, March 24, 1863, in McPherson, *For Cause and Comrades*, 125.

22. Alexander Caldwell to brother, January 11, 1863, in McPherson, *For Cause and Comrades*, 121.

23. Charles Brewster to mother, March 4, 1862, in *When This Cruel War Is Over: The Civil War Letters of Charles Harvey Brewster*, David W. Blight, ed. (Amherst: University of Massachusetts Press, 1992), 92.

24. The occupation of Union soldiers is detailed in Wiley, *Billy Yank*, 303–4, while the occupation of Confederate soldiers is detailed in Bell Irwin Wiley, *The Life of Johnny Reb, the Common Soldier of the Confederacy* (Baton Rouge: Louisiana University Press, 1978), 330. Data on the occupations of American men in 1860 are taken from McPherson, *Battle Cry of Freedom*, 608. Drawing from the 1860 federal census, McPherson lists the following occupational categories and percentages of all males:

farmers and farm laborers, 42.9 percent; skilled laborers, 24.9 percent; unskilled laborers, 16.7 percent; white-collar and commercial, 10 percent; professional, 3.5 percent; and miscellaneous and unknown, 2 percent.

25. Examinations of the ages of Union and Confederate soldiers are found in Wiley, *Billy Yank,* 303; and Wiley, *Johnny Reb,* 330–31.

26. Data on literacy rates among Union and Confederate soldiers are taken from Wiley, *Billy Yank,* 304–6; Wiley, *Johnny Reb,* 335–37; and McPherson, *For Cause and Comrades,* 11. McPherson claims that "Civil War armies were the most literate in history to that time."

27. The geographic distribution of Union and Confederate soldiers is taken from McPherson, *For Cause and Comrades,* 179–80.

28. Soldiers' sense of pride in their army and their disparagement of others is discussed in Wiley, *Billy Yank,* 321–23; and Wiley, *Johnny Reb,* 340.

29. Unidentified Alabama soldier to Miss Annie Rouhlac, in Wiley, *Johnny Reb,* 340.

30. Henry L. Abbott to Josiah Gardner Abbott, September 11, 1861, in Henry Livermore Abbott, *Fallen Leaves: The Civil War Letters of Major Henry Livermore Abbott,* Robert G. Scott, ed. (Kent, Ohio: Kent State University Press, 1991), 44.

31. Wiley, *Billy Yank,* 307. Wiley claims that the "overwhelming majority of Yanks, probably more than three fourths of them, were native Americans." The best books on the experience of foreign-born soldiers in the Union army are William Burton, *Melting Pot Soldiers: The Union's Ethnic Regiments* (2d ed., New York: Fordham University Press, 1998); and Ella Lonn, *Foreigners in the Union Army and Navy* (Baton Rouge: Louisiana State University Press, 1951).

32. Wiley, *Billy Yank,* 307–8. Wiley places the number of Germans in the Union army at 200,000, and the number of Irish at 150,000.

33. The standard history of the Irish Brigade is David P. Conyngham, *The Irish Brigade and Its Campaigns,* Lawrence F. Kohl, ed. (New York: Fordham University Press, 1994).

34. Peter Welsh to Mary Welsh, February 3, 1863, in *Irish Green and Union Blue: The Civil War Letters of Peter Welsh,* Lawrence F. Kohl and Margaret Cosse Richard, eds. (New York: Fordham University Press, 1986), 65.

35. For brief summaries of the careers of the ethnic regiments of the Union army, see Burton, *Melting Pot Soldiers.*

36. The best scholarly treatments of the black military experience during the Civil War are: Noah Trudeau, *Like Men of War: Black Troops in the Civil War, 1862–1865* (Boston: Little, Brown, and Co., 1998); Joseph T. Glatthaar, *Forged in Battle: The Civil War Alliance of Black Soldiers and White Officers* (New York: The Free Press, 1990); and Dudley Taylor Cornish, *The Sable Arm: Negro Troops in the Union Army, 1861–1865* (New York: Longmans, Green and Co., 1956).

37. For the numbers and the service of African Americans in the Union army, see Wiley, *Billy Yank,* 313–16.

38. *Atlantic Monthly* quotation taken from McPherson, *Battle Cry of Freedom,* 686.

39. A description of the Federal attack upon Battery Wagner is found in Glatthaar, *Forged in Battle,* 135–42. The history of the 54th Massachusetts is detailed in Luis F. Emilio, *History of the Fifty-fourth Regiment of Massachusetts Volunteer Infantry, 1863–1865* (Boston: Boston Book Co., 1891).

40. The best book on women serving as soldiers in the Union and Confederate armies is Elizabeth D. Leonard, *All the Daring of the Soldier: Women of the Civil War Armies* (New York: W.W. Norton, 1999).

41. The number of women who served in the Union and Confederate armies is taken from Daniel E. Sutherland, *The Expansion of Everyday Life, 1860–1876* (Fayetteville: University of Arkansas Press, 2000), 2.

42. Indiana soldier quotation taken from Wiley, *Billy Yank,* 339.

43. Union general quotation taken from Sutherland, *Expansion,* 2.

44. The life and career of Sarah Emma Edmonds is briefly detailed in Patricia L. Faust, ed., *Historical Times Illustrated Encyclopedia of the Civil War* (New York: Harper & Row, 1986), 236; and Wiley, *Billy Yank,* 337.

45. For descriptions of the daily drill of Civil War soldiers, see Robertson, *Soldiers Blue and Gray,* 47–52.

46. Ibid., 117–21.

47. Confederate officer quotation taken from Wiley, *Johnny Reb,* 53.

48. Union newspaper reporter quotation taken from Wiley, *Billy Yank,* 257.

49. The rates of venereal disease among Union soldiers is taken from Wiley, *Billy Yank,* 261.

50. A recent study that explores the religious faith of Civil War soldiers is Steven E. Woodworth, *While God Is Marching On: The Religious World of Civil War Soldiers* (Lawrence: University Press of Kansas, 2001).

51. Robertson, *Soldiers Blue and Gray,* 186–89.

52. Robert McAllister to Ellen McAllister, April 11, 1864, in Robert McAllister, *The Civil War Letters of General Robert McAllister,* James I. Robertson, Jr., ed. (New Brunswick, N.J.: Rutgers University Press, 1965), 405.

53. Wilbur Fisk, *Hard Marching Every Day: The Civil War Letters of Private Wilbur Fisk, 1861–1865,* Emil Rosenblatt and Ruth Rosenblatt , eds. (Lawrence: University Press of Kansas, 1992), 200–201.

54. For examples of religious revivals in the Confederate army, Larry J. Daniel, *Soldiering in the Army of Tennessee: A Portrait of Life in a Confederate Army* (Chapel Hill: University of North Carolina Press, 1991), 115–25; and Bell I. Wiley, *The Plain People of the Confederacy* (reprint; Columbia: University of South Carolina Press, 2000), 28–29.

55. The best study regarding Union soldiers and their abilities to withstand the strains of combat is Earl J. Hess, *The Union Soldier in Battle: Enduring the Ordeal of Combat* (Lawrence: University Press of Kansas, 1997).

56. McPherson, *For Cause and Comrades,* 30.

57. Charles B. Haydon, diary entry, July 12, 1861, in *For Country, Cause, and Leader: The Civil War Journal of Charles B. Haydon,* ed. Stephen W. Sears (New York: Ticknor and Fields, 1993), 45.

58. Illinois sergeant quotation taken from Wiley, *Billy Yank,* 70.

59. Augustus Van Dyke to his wife, September 21, 1862, in Hess, *The Union Soldier,* 26.

60. James Binford to "Carrie and Annie," August 13, 1862, in McPherson, *For Cause and Comrades,* 33.

61. Texas soldier quotation taken from Wiley, *Johnny Reb,* 32.

62. Cyrus Stone to Parents, September 23, 1862, in Wiley, *Billy Yank,* 83.

63. William Hamilton to mother, December 24, 1862, in Wiley, *Billy Yank,* 83.

64. Wiley, *Yank*, 35; Faust, *Encyclopedia of the Civil War*, 773.

65. Wiley, *Billy Yank*, 272–73; Wiley, *Johnny Reb*, 176–82.

66. Robertson, *Soldiers Blue and Gray*, 167–69. The numbers of female nurses cited above is taken from Chuck Lawliss, *The Civil War: Unstilled Voices* (New York: Crown Publishers, 1999), 20.

67. Robertson, *Soldiers Blue and Gray*, 169.

68. Books that detail the activities and experiences of women during the Civil War are becoming numerous. Among the best and the most recent include: Drew Gilpin Faust, *Mothers of Invention: Women of the Slaveholding South in the American Civil War* (Chapel Hill: University of North Carolina Press, 1996); Catharine Clinton and Nina Silber, eds., *Divided Houses: Gender and the Civil War* (New York: Oxford University Press, 1992); and George C. Rable, *Civil Wars: Women and the Crisis of Southern Nationalism* (Urbana: University of Illinois Press, 1989).

69. Kate Stone, *Brokenburn: The Journal of Kate Stone, 1861–68,* John Q. Anderson, ed. (Baton Rouge: Louisiana State University Press, 1955), 17.

70. Ella Gertrude Clanton Thomas, *The Secret Eye: The Journal of Ella Gertrude Clanton Thomas, 1848–1889,* Virginia Ingraham Burr, ed. (Chapel Hill: University of North Carolina Press, 1990), 240.

71. Margaret Easterling to Jefferson Davis, December 3, 1862, in Faust, *Mothers of Invention*, 241.

72. North Carolina mother quotation taken from Wiley, *Plain People*, 68.

73. For a description of the Grand Review of the Union army in Washington, D.C., during May 1865 and its larger social implications, see Stuart McConnell, *Glorious Contentment: The Grand Army of the Republic 1865–1900* (Chapel Hill: University of North Carolina Press, 1992), 1–17.

74. The two Union soldier quotations cited are taken from William J. Miller and Brian C. Pohanka, *An Illustrated History of the Civil War: Images of an American Tragedy* (Alexandria, Va.: Time-Life Books, 2000), 414.

75. Alabama woman quotation taken from Miller and Pohanka, *Illustrated History*, 421.

76. Allan Nevins, "The Emergence of Modern America, 1865–1878," in *A History of American Life*, vol. 8, Arthur M. Schlesinger and Dixon B. Fox, eds. (New York: Macmillan, 1927), 405–7.

77. For a brief but detailed summary of the many changes in American life during the postwar era, see Eric Foner, "Reconstruction," in *The Reader's Companion to American History*, Eric Foner and John A. Garraty, eds. (Boston: Houghton Mifflin Company, 1991), 917–24.

78. Richard Taylor to Samuel L. M. Barlow, December 13, 1865, in McPherson, *Battle Cry of Freedom*, 861.

79. George Ticknor quotation taken from Morton Keller, *Affairs of State: Public Life in Late Nineteenth Century America* (Cambridge, Mass.: Harvard University Press, 1977), 2.

80. The political importance of the Fourteenth Amendment is described in Eric Foner, *A Short History of Reconstruction, 1863–1877* (New York: Harper & Row, 1990), 114–17. Quotation from civil rights group taken from ibid., 127.

81. The numbers of blacks holding political office during Reconstruction is listed in Eric Foner, "Reconstruction," 919.

82. Foner, *A Short History*, 193.

83. Ibid., 93–97.

84. Congressman quotation taken from Thomas A. Bailey and David M. Kennedy, *The American Pageant: A Short History of the Republic* (8th ed., Lexington, Mass.: D.C. Heath and Company, 1987), 464.

85. The standard work on the role of the Ku Klux Klan in the Reconstruction South is Allen W. Trelease, *White Terror: The Ku Klux Klan Conspiracy and Southern Reconstruction* (Baton Rouge: Louisiana State University Press, 1995).

86. Group of blacks quotation taken from Bailey and Kennedy, *The American Pageant*, 473.

87. Paul Johnson, *A History of the American People* (New York: Harper Collins, 1997), 507. Johnson writes that the "great Civil War, the central event of American history, having removed the evil of slavery, gave birth to a new South in which whites were first-class citizens and blacks citizens in name only."

88. The economic and steel production figures cited above are taken from Johnson, *A History of the American People*, 531, 552. For a brief description of the importance of iron and steel to the economic development of the United States, see John S. Gordon, "Iron and Steel Industry," in *Reader's Companion*, 574–75.

89. The wages of American farmers and workers are taken from *Historical Statistics of the United States*, vol. 1, Series D 705–714, "Farm Laborers—Average Monthly Earnings, with Board, by Geographic Divisions: 1818 to 1918," 163; and Series D 728–734, "Daily Wages of Five Skilled Occupations and of Laborers, in Manufacturing Establishments," 165. The monthly pay of Union soldiers is taken from Wiley, *Billy Yank*, 49.

90. The data on the cost of living and consumer prices cited above are taken from *Historical Statistics of the United States*, vol. 1, Series E 183–186, "Cost of Living Indexes (Federal Reserve Bank of NY): 1820 to 1926," 212; and Series E 52–63, "Wholesale Price Indexes (Warren and Pearson), by Major Product Groups: 1749 to 1890," 201.

91. Nevins, *Emergence*, 300–301.

92. Sutherland, *Expansion*, xi.

93. Nevins, *Emergence*, 342.

94. Typewriter manufacturer quotation taken from Sutherland, *Expansion*, 206.

95. Ibid., 205–07.

96. Nevins, *Emergence*, 69–71; Sutherland, *Expansion*, 178–79.

97. Sutherland, *Expansion*, 159–62.

98. The population data cited are taken from *Historical Statistics of the United States*, vol. 1, Series A 1–5, "Area and Population of the United States: 1790 to 1970," 8.

99. Michael R. Haines, "Birthrate and Morality," in *Reader's Companion*, 103–5; Johnson, *American People*, 513.

100. Johnson, *American People*, 513–14.

101. Nevins, *Emergence*, 48.

102. Johnson, *American People*, 515; John Bodnar, "Immigration," in *Reader's Companion*, 534–35.

103. The population data cited above are taken from *Historical Statistics of the United States*, vol. 1, Series A 57–72, "Population in Urban and Rural Territory, by Size of Place: 1790 to 1970," 12.

104. For a brief description of the American push westward during the postwar era, see Johnson, *American People*, 515–23.

105. English visitor quotation taken from Sutherland, *Expansion*, 79.

106. The information on American religious activity is taken from Nevins, *Emergence*, 343–44; and Sutherland, *Expansion*, 79–81, 95–96. The standard history of American religion is Sydney A. Ahlstrom, *A Religious History of the American People* (New Haven, Conn.: Yale University Press, 1972).

107. Churchgoer quotation taken from Sutherland, *Expansion*, 87.

108. For a discussion of the debate between science and religion, see Nevins, *Emergence*, 286–89.

# CHAPTER 2

1. The only scholarly examination of the world of youth during the Civil War era is James Marten, *The Children's Civil War* (Chapel Hill: University of North Carolina Press, 1998). For general overviews of American childhood and family life, see: Steven Mintz and Susan Kellogg, *Domestic Revolutions: A Social History of American Family Life* (New York: Free Press, 1988); and Robert H. Bermner, ed., *Children and Youth in America: A Documentary History*, vol. 1, *1600–1865* (Cambridge, Mass.: Harvard University Press, 1970).

2. The figures from the U.S. census cited above are taken from *Historical Statistics of the United States*, Series A, 119–134, "Population, by Age, Sex, Race, and Nativity," 15.

3. Marten, *The Children's Civil War*, note 5, 244.

4. Ibid., 2. Readers seeking more detailed treatment regarding the experiences of drummer boys and underage soldiers should see: Jim Murphy, *The Boys' War: Confederate and Union Soldiers Talk about the Civil War* (New York: Clarion, 1990); and Francis A. Lord and Arthur Wise, *Bands and Drummer Boys of the Civil War* (New York: Yoseloff, 1966). Murphy's book is heavily illustrated and intended for young readers.

5. The infrequency that soldiers received furloughs to go home is detailed in Robertson, *Soldiers Blue and Gray*, 79–80.

6. Joshua Chamberlain to Daisy Chamberlain, May 1863, in Alice Rains Trulock, *In the Hands of Providence: Joshua L. Chamberlain and the American Civil War* (Chapel Hill: University of North Carolina Press, 1992), 113.

7. Isaac Austin Brooks to unidentified recipient, October 13, 1861, in *Yankee Correspondence: Civil War Letters between New England Soldiers and the Home Front*, Nina Silber and Mary Beth Sievans, eds. (Charlottesville: University of Virginia Press, 1996), 60.

8. Josiah Patterson to sons, December 13, 1861, in *"Dear Mother: Don't Grieve about Me. If I Get Killed, I'll Only Be Dead." Letters from Georgia Soldiers in the Civil War* (Savannah: Library of Georgia, 1990), 88–89.

9. Henry Hitchcock to Mary Hitchcock, November 11, 1864, in Marten, *The Children's Civil War*, 84.

10. James Hall to Jesse and Mary Hall, June 11, 1861, in Marten, *The Children's Civil War*, 84.

11. Confederate soldier quotation taken from Marten, *The Children's Civil War*, 86.

12. The different types of souvenirs sent by soldiers to their families is detailed in Marten, *The Children's Civil War*, 79–82.

13. The push in the Confederacy to produce new schoolbooks is described in Marten, *The Children's Civil War*, 52–54; and George C. Rable, *The Confederate Republic: A Revolution against Politics* (Chapel Hill: University of North Carolina Press, 1994), 179–80.

14. *Columbia Daily Southern Guardian,* July 15, 1861, in Marten, *The Children's Civil War,* 55.

15. Marten, *The Children's Civil War*, 32.

16. The Confederate textbook quotations given above are taken from Rable, *The Confederate Republic,* 181–83.

17. The quotations from the Confederate arithmetic text are taken from Marten, *The Children's Civil War*, 56–57.

18. Ibid., 59–61.

19. Velma Maia Thomas, *Freedom's Children: The Passage from Emancipation to Great Migration* (New York: Crown Publishers, 2000), 6.

20. The descriptions of the contents and circulation figures of the five *Freedman's* books are taken from Marten, *The Children's Civil War*, 61–63.

21. *Our Children* quotation taken from Marten, *The Children's Civil War*, 40.

22. *Child's Index* quotation taken from Marten, *The Children's Civil War*, 51.

23. The descriptions of children's magazines in the Union and the Confederacy are taken from Marten, *The Children's Civil War*, 33–52.

24. Marten, *The Children's Civil War*, 16.

25. For examples of children incorporating the war into their play, see James Marten, "Stern Realities: Children of Chancellorsville and Beyond," in *Chancellorsville: The Battle and Its Aftermath,* Gary W. Gallagher, ed. (Chapel Hill: University of North Carolina Press, 1996), 226–28.

26. Julia Taft Bayne, *Tad Lincoln's Father* (reprint; Lincoln: University of Nebraska Press, 2001), 56–59.

27. The increased workloads taken up by children during the Civil War is discussed in Marten, *The Children's Civil War*, 167–77.

28. Theodorick Montfort to David Montfort, November 14, 1861, in *Rebel Lawyer: Letters of Theodorick W. Montfort, 1861–1862,* Spencer B. King, Jr., ed. (Athens: University of Georgia Press, 1965), 34–35.

29. Marten, *The Children's Civil War,* 173.

30. Michigan youth quotation taken from Marten, *The Children's Civil War,* 174.

31. Children's public support for the war, especially through fund-raising, is detailed in Marten, *The Children's Civil War,* 177–85.

32. The experiences of Sue Chancellor and her family are described in Marten, "Stern Realities," 219–43.

33. Opie Read story taken from Marten, *The Children's Civil War*, 103.

34. Cornelia MacDonald, diary entry, March 1862, in *A Woman's Civil War: A Diary, with Reminiscences of the War, from March 1862,* Minrose C. Gwin, ed. (Madison: University of Wisconsin Press, 1992), 35–36.

35. Albertus McCreary story taken from Marten, *The Children's Civil War*, 106.

36. Ibid., 211–20.

37. The three Confederate youth quotations are taken from Marten, "Stern Realities," 225 and 223.

38. The observation about changing attitudes toward American adolescence following the end of the Civil War is taken from Joseph F. Kett, *Rites of Passage: Ado-*

*lescence in America, 1790 to the Present* (New York: Basic Books, 1977), 111–13; and Sutherland, *Expansion*, 110–11.

39. The expansion of common school education after the conclusion of the Civil War is described in Ellen Condliffe Lagemann, "Education," in *Reader's Companion*, 313–17. For a general overview of the rise of public education in the United States, see Lawrence A. Cremin, *American Education: The National Experience, 1783–1876* (New York: Harper and Row, 1980).

40. Oscar Handlin and Mary F. Handlin, *Facing Life: Youth and the Family in American History* (Boston: Little, Brown and Co., 1971), 115.

41. Sutherland, *Expansion*, 104–5; Lagemann, "Education," 326.

42. Ellen Condliffe Lagemann, "McGuffey's *Reader*," in *Reader's Companion*, 713.

43. Sutherland, *Expansion*, 101.

44. The two McGuffey's readers quotations are taken from Sutherland, *Expansion*, 101.

45. The two textbook quotations are taken from Dorothy Denneen Volo and James M. Volo, *Daily Life in Civil War America* (Westport, Conn: Greenwood Press, 1997), 277.

46. D. L. Leonard, "Women as Educators," *Chicago Schoolmaster* 5 (October 1872): 276; quoted in Kett, *Rites of Passage*, 130.

47. Kett, *Rites of Passage*, 129–30.

48. Lagemann, "Education," 315; Volo and Volo, *Daily Life in Civil War America*, 273. Volo and Volo write that in one Pennsylvania school district during 1861, male teachers received pay of $24.20 per month, while female teachers received pay of $18.11 per month.

49. Kett, *Rites of Passage*, 20–21; 126–28.

50. American Social History Project, *Freedom's Unfinished Revolution: An Inquiry into the Civil War and Reconstruction* (New York: New Press, 1996), 176.

51. Foner, *A Short History*, 43–45; Lagemann, "Education," 316.

52. Dorothy Sterling, *The Trouble They Seen: The Story of Reconstruction in the Words of African Americans* (New York: De Capo Press, 1994), 14–15.

53. Lagemann, "Education," 324–27. For a history of women in higher education, see Barbara Miller Solomon, *In the Company of Educated Women: A History of Women and Higher Education in America* (New Haven, Conn.: Yale University Press, 1985).

54. Kett, *Rites of Passage*, 133–34.

55. John S. Haller, Jr. and Robin M. Haller, *The Physician and Sexuality in Victorian America* (Urbana: University of Illinois Press, 1974), 195–97; Kett, *Rites of Passage*, 134.

56. Advice writer quotation taken from Haller and Haller, *The Physician and Sexuality*, 197.

57. Kett, *Rites of Passage*, 134–35; Haller and Haller, *The Physician and Sexuality*, 197–98.

58. Kett, *Rites of Passage*, 140–41.

59. Haller and Haller, *The Physician and Sexuality*, 27–28.

60. Kett, *Rites of Passage*, 141–42.

61. Ibid., 36.

62. The two previous quotations cited are taken from Sutherland, *Expansion*, 114–15.

63. Ibid., 113.

64. Kett, *Rites of Passage*, 45.

65. Sutherland, *Expansion,* 54. Sutherland writes that among the twenty million Americans sixteen years of age and older during 1870, fourteen million "lived as man and wife."

66. Ellen K. Rothman, *Hands and Hearts: A History of Courtship in America* (New York: Basic Books), 287. Rothman writes that "Until the Second World War, Americans continued to marry at the age and rate characteristic of the nineteenth century. The median age at first marriage in 1900 was 21.9 for women and 25.9 for men...."

67. Etiquette writer quotation taken from Rothman, *Hands and Hearts,* 171.

68. Wilson Carpenter, journal entry, January 1875, in Rothman, *Hands and Hearts,* 172.

69. For changing American wedding customs during the mid- and late nineteenth century, see Rothman, *Hands and Hearts,* 168–76; and Sutherland, *Expansion,* 119–20.

70. Nevins, *Emergence,* 215.

71. Sutherland, *Expansion,* 125–26.

72. Nevins, *Emergence,* 216.

73. Haller and Haller, *The Physician and Sexuality,* 117. Haller and Haller write that during the "first half of the nineteenth century, druggists reported more purchases of abortive drugs than contraceptive devices and germicides."

74. Ibid., 113–24.

75. Quotation taken from Sutherland, *Expansion,* 122.

76. Ibid., 120–23.

# CHAPTER 3

1. The Franklin and Chamberlain quotations are taken from Frank Presbrey, *The History and Development of Advertising* (Garden City, N.Y.: Doubleday, 1929), 136–37, 191.

2. Daniel J. Boorstin, *The Americans: The Democratic Experience* (New York: Random House, 1973), 146.

3. Books that examine the rise of advertising during the mid-nineteenth century are few. The best include: Presbrey, *History and Development;* E. S. Turner, *The Shocking History of Advertising!* (New York: Dutton, 1953); and James P. Wood, *The Story of Advertising* (New York: Ronald Press Co., 1958).

4. For the importance of the Hoe rotary press to newspaper publishing, see Bernard A. Weisberger, *Reporters for the Union* (Boston: Little, Brown and Company, 1953), 19.

5. Louis M. Starr, *Bohemian Brigade: Civil War Newsmen in Action* (New York: Alfred A. Knopf, 1954), 6; Weisberger, *Reporters,* 6.

6. J. Matthew Gallman, *The North Fights the Civil War: The Home Front* (Chicago: Ivan R. Dee, 1994), 31.

7. Weisberger, *Reporters,* 6.

8. For the development and growth of the penny press, see Presbrey, *History and Development,* 196–204; and Weisberger, *Reporters,* 16.

9. Starr, *Bohemian Brigade,* 54, 242.

10. Ibid., ix.

11. The standard, though now dated, biography of Bennett is Oliver Carlson, *The Man Who Made News: James Gordon Bennett* (New York: Duell, Sloan and Pearce, 1942).

12. Frederic Hudson, *Journalism in the United States from 1690 to 1872* (New York: Harper and Brothers, 1872), 470.

13. The implementation of daily newspaper advertisements is discussed in Boorstin, *The Americans,* 143–45.

14. Hudson, *Journalism in the United States,* 468.

15. The adherence among newspapers to the agate rule is described in Boorstin, *The Americans,* 138–39.

16. Bonner's use of iteration is detailed in Presbrey, *History and Development,* 236–40.

17. Ibid., 242.

18. The use of gimmicks and stunts to increase newspaper advertisements is described in Presbrey, *History and Development,* 237; and Wood, *Story,* 161–62. Wood places the amount that Bonner paid Beecher for *Norwood* at $20,000.

19. For a description of the Stanley expedition, see Presbrey, *History and Development,* 260.

20. *New York Tribune,* August 13, 1859, in Presbrey, *History and Development,* 259.

21. Advertising agencies and their work are described in Presbrey, *History and Development,* 261–75; and Boorstin, *The Americans,* 148–50.

22. For Rowell's autobiography, see George P. Rowell, *Forty Years an Advertising Agent, 1865–1905* (1906; reprint, New York: Garland, 1985).

23. Frank B. Noyes, speech at the Sphinx Club, 1905, in Presbrey, *History and Development,* 278–79.

24. The attempts of the Union and Confederacy to finance their war efforts are described in McPherson, *Battle Cry of Freedom,* 437–50.

25. The quotations for the sale of Union and Confederate war bonds are taken from Wood, *Story,* 175–76, 179.

26. *Columbus (Georgia) Enquirer,* April 29, 1862, in Wood, *Story,* 177.

27. *Springfield (Massachusetts) Republican,* April 1864, in Wood, *Story,* 174.

28. *Columbus (Georgia) Enquirer,* April 29, 1862, in Wood, *Story,* 178.

29. *Springfield Republican,* February 23, 1864, in Wood, *Story,* 175.

30. The various headlines from wartime advertisements are taken from Wood, *Story,* 174–75, and 179–80.

31. The growth of department stores during the mid- and late nineteenth century is traced in Boorstin, *The Americans,* 101–9.

32. The use of display type in newspaper advertisements is described in Presbrey, *History and Development,* 244–48.

33. *New York Daily Tribune,* November 6, 1865, in Presbrey, *History and Development,* 249.

34. For Barnum's autobiography, see Phineas T. Barnum, *The Life of P. T. Barnum, Written by Himself,* intro. by Terence Whalen (Urbana: University of Illinois Press, 2000).

35. *New York Herald,* August 17, 1842, in Presbrey, *History and Development,* 216.

36. *Cincinnati Gazette,* September 9, 1879, in Presbrey, *History and Development,* 223.

37. *New York Herald,* April 13, 1869, in Wood, *Story,* 170.

38. The public controversy created by the publication of personal ads is detailed in Turner, *Shocking History,* 146–49.

39. *Round Table* 6 (November 23, 1867): 337, in Frank Luther Mott, *A History of American Magazines, 1865–1885* (Cambridge, Mass.: Harvard University Press, 1938), 5:5.

40. The data on magazine numbers and publishing are taken from Mott, *American Magazines*, 5:5.

41. *Literary World* 3 (December 1, 1872): 104, in Mott, *American Magazines*, 5:8.

42. The magazine circulation figures cited are taken from Mott, *American Magazines*, 5:6–9.

43. Ibid., 8–9.

44. The circulation figures for *Youth's Companion* are taken from Mott, *American Magazines*, 3:6. A description of *Youth's Companion* is found in R. Gordon Kelly, *Mother Was a Lady: Self and Society in Selected American Children's Periodicals, 1865–1890* (Westport, Conn.: Greenwood Press, 1974), 11–15.

45. The Standard Oil Company advertisement is taken from an 1869 issue of *Youth's Companion*, in Presbrey, *History and Development*, 472.

46. Ibid., 473.

47. The quotations for Warner's Safe Kidney and Liver Cure and St. Jacob's Oil are taken from an unidentified Cincinnati newspaper, in Presbrey, *History and Development*, 295.

48. For a discussion of patent medicine advertisements, see Presbrey, *History and Development*, 289–97.

49. The two quotations are taken from Mott, *American Magazines*, 3:17.

50. The two Powers quotations are taken from Presbrey, *History and Development*, 306, 308.

51. Descriptions of Powers's life and career are found in Presbrey, *History and Development*, 302–9; and Wood, *Story*, 231–33.

52. The story of the Ivory Soap slogan is told in Turner, *Shocking History*, 142.

53. Presbrey, *History and Development*, 248.

54. The Sapolio advertisement is taken from *Frank Leslie's Illustrated Weekly*, 1869, in Presbrey, *History and Development*, 250.

55. Ibid., 473.

56. Mott, *American Magazines*, 4:37–38; and Presbrey, *History and Development*, 285–86.

57. For a description of Ward's start with publishing mail-order catalogues, see Boorstin, *The Americans*, 121–24.

58. Ibid., 122–23.

59. Ibid., 123–24.

60. The advertisements cited are taken from Presbrey, *History and Development*, 287.

61. *New York Tribune*, December 8, 1875, in Presbrey, *History and Development*, 285.

62. Bradley and Company quotation taken from unidentified mail-order catalogue, in Presbrey, *History and Development*, 288.

63. George Wakeman, *Galaxy* magazine, 1867, in Presbrey, *History and Development*, 255.

# CHAPTER 4

1. Richard Guy Wilson, "Architecture," in *Concise Histories of American Popular Culture*, M. Thomas Inge, ed. (Westport, Conn.: Greenwood Press, 1982), 32.

2. Ibid., 32.

3. Daniel E. Sutherland, *Expansion*, 31.

4. Pamela H. Simpson, *Cheap, Quick, and Easy: Imitative Architectural Materials, 1870–1930* (Knoxville: University of Tennessee Press, 1999), 30.

## CHAPTER 5

1. Sutherland, *Expansion*, 55.
2. Jeanette C. Lauer and Robert H. Lauer, "The Battle of the Sexes: Fashion in Nineteenth Century America," *Journal of Popular Culture 13, no.* 4 (Spring 1980): 583.

## CHAPTER 6

1. Quoted in John Mariani, *America Eats Out* (New York: William Morrow, 1991), 41.
2. Richard B. Harwell, *The Confederate Reader* (New York: Longmans, Green & Co., 1957), 238–89.
3. Ibid., 209–10.
4. Boorstin, *The Americans*, 123.
5. Andrew F. Smith, *Popped Culture: A Social History of Popcorn in America* (Columbia: University of South Carolina Press, 1999), 20.
6. Mariani, *America Eats Out*, 71.

## CHAPTER 7

1. Robert Crego, *Sports and Games of the 18th and 19th Centuries* (Westport, Conn.: Greenwood Publishing, 2003), 194.
2. Ibid., 195.
3. The standard work on American leisure activities is Foster Rhea Dulles, *America Learns to Play: A History of Popular Recreation, 1607–1940*, 2d ed. (New York: D. Appleton-Century, 1940)
4. Dulles, *America Learns*, 183–84.
5. Ibid., 184.
6. Ibid., 184.
7. Sutherland, *Expansion*, 239.
8. Wiley, *Johnny Reb*, 159.
9. Robertson, *Soldiers Blue and Gray*, 88; Wiley, *Billy Yank*, 170.
10. James A. Hall to Joe Hall, April 18, 1864, in Wiley, *Johnny Reb*, 159.
11. Edward L. Edes to father, April 3, 1864, in Wiley, *Billy Yank*, 170.
12. Dulles, *America Learns*, 188.
13. The three quotations are taken from Dulles, *America Learns*, 189.
14. Sutherland, *Expansion*, 240.
15. Nevins, *The Emergence*, 220.
16. Dulles, *America Learns*, 189–90; Nevins, *Emergence*, 220.
17. Dulles, *America Learns*, 190; Sutherland, *Expansion*, 240.
18. Nevins, *Emergence*, 219–20.
19. Robert H. Walker, *Life in the Age of Enterprise, 1865–1900* (New York: G. P. Putnam's Sons, 1967), 156.
20. Dulles, *America Learns*, 191.

21. *The Nation,* vol. 3, August 9, 1866, in Nevins, *Emergence,* 223.

22. Rule book quotation taken from Dulles, *America Learns,* 191.

23. Song quotation taken from Sutherland, *Expansion,* 76.

24. Croquet rule book quotation taken from Dulles, *America Learns,* 191.

25. The practice of "spooning" is described in Dulles, *America Learns,* 192.

26. Magazine quotation taken from Dulles, *America Learns,* 192.

27. Nevins, *Emergence,* 223; Dulles, *America Leans,* 192.

28. Dulles, *America Learns,* 197–98; Allen Guttmann, "Football," in *Reader's Companion,* 407–8.

29. Dulles, *America Learns,* 197–98.

30. Walker, *Age of Enterprise,* 152–53.

31. North Carolina boy quotation taken from Sutherland, *Expansion,* 243.

32. Ibid.

33. Nevins, *Emergence,* 219.

34. Sutherland, *Expansion,* 243.

35. Wichita resident quotation taken from Sutherland, *Expansion,* 243.

36. The percentage figures on Union and Confederate cavalry are taken from Robertson, *Soldiers Blue and Gray,* 19.

37. A. E. Rentfrow to sister, February 11, 1862, in Wiley, *Johnny Reb,* 38.

38. Sutherland, *Expansion,* 244.

39. Dulles, *America Learns,* 144–46.

40. Walker, *Age of Enterprise,* 151–52.

41. For a description of gander-pulling, see Dulles, *America Learns,* 161. Dulles also writes that the "Dutch settlers in New York had practiced this sport, and there was to be a later version of it on the western prairies."

42. North Carolina observer quotation taken from Dulles, *America Learns,* 161.

43. Wiley, *Johnny Reb,* 160–61.

44. Nevins, *Emergence,* 223.

45. *Scientific American,* January 9, 1869, in Nevins, *Emergence,* 224.

46. Dulles, *America Learns,* 194–96.

47. Ibid., 192–93.

48. Ibid., 193–94.

49. Newspaper quotation taken from Dulles, *America Learns,* 172.

50. Sutherland, *Expansion,* 237.

51. Ibid., 82.

52. Nevins, *Emergence,* 344–45. Beecher's drawing power at the pulpit declined sharply during the mid-1870s, after he went on trial for his alleged intimacies with a married woman.

53. Foreign observer quotation taken from Sutherland, *Expansion,* 81.

54. For discussions of black religious enthusiasm, see Thomas, *Freedom's Children,* 4–5; and Sutherland, *Expansion,* 96–97.

55. Black woman quotation taken from Sutherland, *Expansion,* 97.

56. For the importance of independent churches to the black community during Reconstruction, see Foner, *A Short History,* 40–42.

57. The information and quotations on camp meetings are taken from Sutherland, *Expansion,* 84–85.

58. Nevins, *Emergence,* 346.

59. Nevins, *Emergence,* 338; "Woman's Christian Temperance Union," in *Reader's Companion,* 1157–58; and Walker, *Age of Enterprise,* 143.

60. Walker, *Age of Enterprise,* 141.

61. Sutherland, *Expansion,* 237.

62. Walker, *Age of Enterprise,* 140–41.

63. "Granger Movement," in *Reader's Companion,* 464–65.

64. Descriptions of the social affairs of the Granger movement are taken from Sutherland, *Expansion,* 237–38.

65. Granger member quotations are taken from Sutherland, *Expansion,* 238.

66. Michael H. Fitch, *Echoes of the Civil War as I Hear Them* (New York: R. F. Fenno & Company, 1905), 343–44.

67. Civil War veteran quotation taken from Hess, *The Union Soldier,* 160.

68. Linderman, *Embattled Courage,* 270. The best studies of the activities of the Grand Army of the Republic are: Stuart McConnell, *Glorious Contentment: The Grand Army of the Republic, 1865–1900* (Chapel Hill: University of North Carolina Press, 1992); and Mary K. Dearing, *Veterans in Politics: The Story of the G.A.R.* (Baton Rouge: Louisiana State University Press, 1952).

69. For differing perspectives on veterans' wartime memories, see Linderman, *Embattled Courage,* 266–97; and Hess, *The Union Soldier,* 158–90.

70. The importance of holiday celebrations in American civic life is detailed in Mary P. Ryan, *Civic Wars: Democracy and Public Life in the American City during the Nineteenth Century* (Berkeley: University of California Press, 1997), 234–44.

71. McConnell, *Glorious Contentment,* 11.

72. *New Orleans Bee,* July 4, 1865, in Ryan, *Civic Wars,* 236.

73. Confederate veteran quotation taken from Sutherland, *Expansion,* 263.

74. Exposition director quotation taken from Sutherland, *Expansion,* 265–66.

75. Descriptions of the exhibits at the Centennial Exposition are found in Sutherland, *Expansion,* 263–64; and Nevins, *Emergence,* 306–10.

76. Attendance figures at the Centennial Exposition are taken from Nevins, *Emergence,* 306–7; and Sutherland, *Expansion,* 265.

77. Centennial Exposition visitor quotations taken from Sutherland, *Expansion,* 264, 266.

78. *New York Tribune* quotation taken from Ryan, *Civic Wars,* 235.

79. A description of the 1870 fireworks display in New York City is found in Ryan, *Civic Wars,* 243–44.

80. American writer quotation taken from Walker, *Age of Enterprise,* 172.

# CHAPTER 8

1. Fahs, Alice, *The Imagined Civil War: Popular Literature of the North and South, 1861–1865* (Chapel Hill: University of North Carolina Press, 2001), 2.

2. Nye, Russel B., *The Unembarrassed Muse: The Popular Arts in America* (New York: Dial, 1970), 23.

3. Fahs, *Imagined Civil War,* 3.

4. Ibid., 229.

5. Ibid., 47.

6. Nye, *The Unembarrassed Muse,* 27.

## CHAPTER 9

1.  Francis F. Browne, *Bugle-echoes: Collection of Poetry of the Civil War Northern and Southern* (New York: White, Stokes & Allen, 1886), 3.
2.  David S. Heidler and Jeanne T. Heidler, eds., *Encyclopedia of the American Civil War: A Political, Social, and Military History* (Santa Barbara, Calif.: ABC-CLIO, 1999), 607.
3.  Vance Randolph, *Ozark Folksongs: Collected and Edited for the State Historical Society of Missouri* (Columbia, Mo: State Historical Society, 1946–50), 4: 257–59.
4.  Frederick A. Douglass, *My Bondage and Freedom* (New York: Miller, Orton & Mulligan, 1855), 97.
5.  Ibid., 99.
6.  Mel Watkins, *On the Real Side: Laughing, Lying, and Signifying* (New York: Simon & Schuster/Touchstone, 1994), 116.

## CHAPTER 10

1.  Sutherland, *Expansion,* 245.
2.  Don B. Wilmeth, "Stage Entertainments," in *Concise Histories of American Popular Culture,* M. Thomas Inge, ed. (Westport, Conn: Greenwood Press, 1982), 385.
3.  Sutherland, *Expansion,* 246.
4.  Wilmeth, "Stage Entertainments," 385.
5.  Nye, *The Unembarrassed Muse,* 160.
6.  Watkins, *On the Real Side,* 81.
7.  Ibid., 84.
8.  Ibid., 93.
9.  Ibid., 94.
10. Ibid., 97.
11. Ann Anderson, *Snake Oil, Hustlers and Hambones: The American Medicine Show* (Jefferson, N.C.: McFarland, 2000), 84.
12. Quoted in Sutherland, *Expansion,* 248.
13. Ibid.
14. Don B. Wilmeth, "Circuses and Outdoor Entertainment," in Inge, *Concise Histories,* 65.
15. Ibid., 66.
16. Ibid., 68.
17. Hamlin Garland, *A Son of the Middle Border* (New York: Grosset and Dunlap, 1917), 169.

## CHAPTER 11

1.  Quoted in W. Turrentine Jackson, *Wells Fargo in Colorado Territory* (Denver: Colorado Historical Society, 1982), xi–xii.
2.  Thomas H. Johnson, ed., *The Complete Poems of Emily Dickinson* (Boston: Little, Brown, 1960), 286.
3.  Bernard Mergen, "Leisure Vehicles, Pleasure Boats, and Aircraft" in *Concise Histories,* 187.

## CHAPTER 12

1. Carl Bode, *Antebellum America* (Carbondale: University of Southern Illinois Press, 1959), 94.

2. Richard N. Masteller, "Photography," in *Concise Histories of American Popular Culture,* M. Thomas Inge, ed. (Westport, Conn.: Greenwood Press, 1982), 255.

# Suggested Reading

Allmendinger, Blake. *Ten Most Wanted: The New Western Literature*. New York: Routledge, 2000.

Ames, Kenneth. *Winterthur Portfolio* 70 (1975): 23–50.

Anderson, Ann. *Snake Oil, Hustlers and Hambones: The American Medicine Show*. Jefferson, N.C.: McFarland, 2000.

Anderson, Norman. *Ferris Wheels: An Illustrated History*. Bowling Green, Ohio: Bowling Green State University, Popular Press, 1992.

Ayers, Edward I. *The Promise of the New South: Life after Reconstruction*. New York: Oxford University Press, 1992.

Barlow, Ronald S. *The Vanishing American Outhouse: A History of Country Plumbing*. New York: Viking, 2000.

Barnum, Phineas T. *The Life of P. T. Barnum, Written by Himself*. Introduction by Terence Whalen. Urbana: University of Illinois Press, 2000.

Baur, John E. *Christmas on the American Frontier, 1800–1900*. Caldwell, ID: Caxton, 1961.

Bloom, Lynn Z. "It's All for Your Own Good: Parent-Child Relationships in Popular American Child-Rearing Literature, 1820–1970." *Journal of Popular Culture* 10, no. 3 (Summer 1976): 191–98.

Bode, Carl. *Antebellum America*. Carbondale: University of Southern Illinois Press, 1959.

Boller, Paul F., Jr. *Presidential Anecdotes*. New York: Oxford University Press, 1981.

Boorstin, Daniel J. *The Americans: The Democratic Experience*. New York: Random House, 1973.

Botkin, B. A. *A Treasury of American Folklore*. New York: Crown, 1945.

Brown, Dee. *The Year of the Century*. New York: Scribner's, 1966.

Brown, Frank C. *The Frank C. Brown Collection of North Carolina Folklore*. Durham, N.C.: Duke University Press, 1952.

Brown, Richard D. *Modernization: The Transformation of American Life, 1600–1865*. New York: Hill and Wang, 1976.

Browne, Francis F. *Bugle-echoes: Collection of the Poetry of the Civil War, Northern and Southern.* New York: White, Stokes & Allen, 1886.

Browne, Ray B. *Lincoln-Lore: Lincoln in the Popular Mind,* Rev. ed. Bowling Green, OH: Bowling Green State University, Popular Press, 1999.

———. "Popular and Folk Songs: Unifying Force in Garland's Autobiographical Works." *Southern Folklore Quarterly* 25, no. 3 (September 1961): 153–66.

Caplan, Jane. *Written on the Body: The Tattoo in European and American History.* Princeton, N.J.: Princeton University Press. 2000.

Cartmell, Robert. *The Incredible Scream Machine: A History of the Roller Coaster.* Bowling Green, Ohio: Bowling Green State University, Popular Press, 1987.

Cashin, Joan E., ed. *The War Was You and Me: Civilians in the American Civil War.* Princeton, N.J.: Princeton University Press, 2002.

Cook, James W. *The Arts of Deception: Playing with Fraud in the Age of Barnum.* Cambridge, Mass.: Harvard University Press, 2000.

Crane, Diana. *Fashion and Its Social Agendas: Class, Gender, and Identity in Clothing.* Chicago: University of Chicago Press, 2000.

Crego, Robert. *Sports and Games of the 18th and 19th Centuries.* Westport, Conn.: Greenwood Publishers, 2003.

Cremin, Lawrence A. *American Education: The National Experience: 1783–1876.* New York: Harper & Row, 1980.

Davis, Burke. *The Civil War: Strange & Fascinating Facts.* New York: Wings Books, 2000.

Denney, Robert E. *Civil War Medicine: Care and Comfort of the Wounded.* New York: Sterling, 1994.

Denning, Michael. *Mechanic Accents: Dime Novels and Working-Class Culture in America.* New York: Verso, 1987.

Dizard, Jan E., Robert Merrill Muth, and Stephen P. Andrews, Jr. *Guns in America.* New York: New York University Press, 1999.

Douglass, Frederick A. *My Bondage and Freedom.* New York: Miller, Orton & Mulligan, 1855.

Dulles, Foster Rhea. *A History of Recreation: America Learns to Play.* Englewood Cliffs, N.J.: Prentice-Hall, 1965.

During, Simon. *The Cultural Studies Reader.* New York: Routledge, 1993.

Emmet, Boris, and John E. Jeuck. *Catalogues and Counters: A History of Sears, Roebuck and Company.* Chicago: University of Chicago Press, 1950.

Fahs, Alice. *The Imagined Civil War: Popular Literature of the North and South, 1861–1865.* Chapel Hill: University of North Carolina Press, 2001.

Foner, Eric. *Reconstruction: America's Unfinished Revolution, 1863–1877.* New York: HarperCollins, 1988.

Foy, Jessica H., and Thomas J. Schlereth. *American Home Life, 1880–1930: A Social History of Spaces and Services.* Knoxville: University of Tennessee Press, 1992

Fraser, Antonia. *A History of Toys.* New York: Delacorte Press, 1966.

Fuller, Wayne E. *The American Mail: Enlarger of the Common Life.* Chicago: University of Chicago Press, 1972.

Funderburg, Ann Cooper. *Chocolate, Strawberry, and Vanilla: A History of American Ice Cream.* Bowling Green, OH: Bowling Green State University Popular Press, 1995.

Garland, Hamlin. *A Son of the Middle Border.* New York: Grosset and Dunlap, 1917.

Gibbons, Herbert Adams. *John Wanamaker.* New York: Harper and Bros., 1917.

Glassie, Henry. *Vernacular Architecture.* Bloomington: Indiana University Press, 2000.

Goodrich, Carter. *Government Promotion of American Canals and Railroads, 1800–1890.* New York: Columbia University Press, 1960.

Gowans, Alan. *The Unchanging Arts.* Philadelphia: J. B. Lippincott, 1971.

Grabau, Warren E. *Ninety-Eight Days: A Geographer's View of the Vicksburg Campaign.* Knoxville: University of Tennessee Press, 2000.

Groce, W. Todd. *Mountain Rebels: East Tennessee Confederates and the Civil War, 1860–1870.* Knoxville: University of Tennessee Press, 2000.

Grodinsky, Julius. *Transcontinental Railway Strategy, 1869–1893: A Study of Businessmen.* Philadelphia: University of Pennsylvania Press, 1962.

Gutjarh, Paul C. *An American Bible: A History of the Good Book in the United States, 1777–1880.* Stanford: Stanford University Press, 1999.

Gwin, Minrose C. *A Woman's Civil War, A Diary with Reminiscences of the War, from March 1862.* Madison: University of Wisconsin Press, 1992.

Haller, John S., Jr. "From Maidenhood to Menopause: Sex Education for Women in Victorian America. " *Journal of Popular Culture* 6, no. 1 (Summer 1972): 49–70.

Harwell, Richard B. *The Confederate Reader.* New York: Longmans, Green and Co., 1957.

Hattaway, Wakelyn. *Shades of Blue and Gray Series.* Columbia: University of Missouri Press, 2001.

Heidler, David S., and Jeanne T. Heidler. *Encyclopedia of the American Civil War: A Political, Social, and Military History.* Santa Barbara, Calif.: ABC-CLIO, 1999.

Hibbard, Don. "American Genre Painting in Post-Civil War America: Changing American Dreams." *Journal of Popular Culture* 10, no. 3 (Winter 1976): 593–600.

Holbrook, Stewart H. *The Story of American Railroads.* New York: Crown, 1947.

Holzer, Harold. *Prang's Civil War Pictures.* New York: Fordham University Press, 2001.

Holzer, Harold, Gabor S. Boritt, and Mark E. Neely, Jr. *The Lincoln Image.* Chicago: University of Illinois Press, 1984.

Hower, Ralph M. *History of Macy's of New York, 1858–1959.* Cambridge: Harvard University Press, 1943.

Hudson, Frederic. *Journalism in the United States from 1690–1872.* New York: Harper and Bros., 1873.

Hume, Janice. *Obituaries in American Culture.* Jackson: University of Mississippi Press, 2000.

Inge, M. Thomas. *The Frontier Humorists.* New York, and Hamden, Conn.: Archon Books, 1975.

———, ed. *Concise Histories of American Popular Culture.* Westport, Conn.: Greenwood Press, 1982.

Inscoe, Kenzer. *New Perspectives on Unionists in the Civil War.* Athens: University of Georgia Press, 2001.

Johnson, Nan. *Gender and Rhetorical Space in American Life, 1866–1910.* Carbondale: Southern Illinois University Press, 2002.

Kammen, Michael. *In the Past Lane: Historical Perspectives on American Culture.* New York: Oxford University Press, 1997.

———. *Mystic Chords of Memory: The Transformation of Tradition in American Culture.* New York: Alfred Knopf, 1991.

Katzman, David. *Seven Days a Week: Women and Domestic Service in Industrializing America.* New York: Oxford University Press, 1970.

Kelly, R. Gordon. *Mother Was a Lady: Self and Society in Selected American Children's Periodicals, 1865–1890.* Westport, Conn.: Greenwood Press, 1974.

Koppelman, Susan. "A Preliminary Sketch of the Early History of University Women's Short Stories." *Journal of American Culture* 22, no. 2 (Summer 1999): 1–6.

Kytle, Elizabeth. *Home on the Canal.* Cabin John, Md.: Seven Locks Press, 1983.

Laderman, Gary. *The Sacred Remains: American Attitudes toward Death, 1799–1883.* New Haven, Conn.: Yale University Press, 1996.

Landau, Sarah Bradford, and Carl W. Condit. *Rise of the New York Skyscraper 1865–1913.* New Haven, Conn.: Yale University Press, 1996.

LaPorte, Dominique. *History of Shit.* Cambridge, Mass.: MIT Press, 2000.

Lauer, Jeanette C., and Robert H. Lauer. "The Battle of the Sexes: Fashion in Nineteenth Century America." *Journal of Popular Culture* 13, no.4 (Spring 1980): 581–89.

Leach, MacEdward. *The Ballad Book.* New York: Harper's, 1955.

Leavitt, Sarah A. *From Catherine Beecher to Martha Stewart: A Cultural History of Domestic Advice.* Chapel Hill: University of North Carolina Press, 2002.

Lebhar, Godfrey M. *Chain Stores in America, 1859–1959.* New York: Chain Store Publishing Co., 1959.

Lehuu, Isabelle. *Carnival on the Page: Popular Print Media in Antebellum America* Chapel Hill: University of North Carolina Press, 2000.

Leonard, Elizabeth D. *Yankee Women: Gender Battles in the Civil War.* New York: Norton, 1994.

Levine, Lawrence W. *Highbrow/Lowbrow: The Emergence of Cultural Hierarchy in America.* Cambridge, Mass.: Harvard University Press, 1988.

———. *The Opening of the American Mind: Canons, Culture, and History.* Boston: Beacon Press, 1996.

Lingenfelter, Richard E., Richard A. Dwyer, and David Cohen. *Songs of the American West.* Berkeley: University of California Press, 1968.

Litwicki, Ellen M. *America's Public Holidays 1865–1920.* Washington, D.C.: Smithsonian Press, 2000.

Macher, James L. and Philip Goldstein. *Reception Study: From Literary Theory to Cultural Studies.* New York: Routledge, 2001.

Mariani, John. *America Eats Out.* New York: William Morrow, 1991.

Marsh, John L. "Drama and Spectacle by the Yard: The Panorama in America." *Journal of Popular Culture* 10, no. 3 (Winter 1976): 581–92.

Marten, James. *The Children's Civil War.* Chapel Hill: University of North Carolina Press, 1998.

Martinez, J. Michael, William D. Richardson, and Ron McNinch-Su. *Confederate Symbols in the Contemporary South.* Gainesville: University of Florida Press, 2000.

Mattingly, Carol. *Appropriate[ing] Dress: Women's Rhetorical Style in Nineteenth-Century America.* Carbondale: Southern Illinois University Press, 2002.

McCaghy, Charles H., and Arthur G. Neal. "The Fraternity of Cockfighters: Ethical Embellishments of an Illegal Sport." *Journal of Popular Culture* 8, no. 3 (Winter 1974): 557–69.

McCrossen, Alexis. *Holy Day, Holiday: The American Sunday.* Ithaca, N.Y.: Cornell University Press, 2000.

McNeil, W.K. "Popular Songs from New York Autograph Albums 1829–1900." *Journal of Popular Culture* 3, no. 1 (Summer 1969): 46–56.

McPherson, James M., and William J. Cooper, eds. *Writing the Civil War: The Quest to Understand.* Columbia: University of South Carolina Press, 1998.

McPherson, James M. *Ordeal by Fire: The Civil War and Reconstruction.* New York: Knopf, 1982

———. *The Battle Cry of Freedom: The Civil War Era.* New York: Oxford University Press, 1988.

Meredith, Roy. *Mr. Lincoln's Camera Man.* New York: Dover, 1974.

———. *The World of Mathew Brady.* New York: Brook House, 1976.

Merish, Lori. *Sentimental Materialism: Gender, Commodity Culture, and Nineteenth-Century American Literature.* Durham: Duke University Press 2000.

Mitgang, Herbert. *Abraham Lincoln: A Press Portrait.* New York: Fordham University Press, 2000.

Montell, William Lynwood. *Ghosts across Kentucky.* Lexington: University Press of Kentucky, 2000.

Moore, Frank. *Anecdotes, Poetry, and Incidents of the War, North and South 1860–1865.* New York: Arundel, 1882.

———. *The Civil War in Song and Story, 1860–1865.* New York: P. F. Collier, 1882.

———. *Lyrics of Loyalty.* New York: G. P. Putnam, 1864.

Moseley, Caroline. "The Maids of Dear Columbia: Images of Young Women in Victorian American Parlor Song." *Journal of American Culture* 6, no. 1 (Spring 1983): 3–17.

Mosier, Jennifer L. "The Big Attraction: The Circus Elephant and American Culture." *Journal of American Culture* 22, no. 2 (Summer 1999): 7–19.

Mullenix, Elizabeth Reitz. *Wearing the Breeches: Gender on the Antebellum Stage.* New York: St. Martin's Press, 2000.

Murdock, Catherine Gilbert. *Domesticating Drink: Women, Men, and Alcohol in America, 1870–1940.* Baltimore: Johns Hopkins University Press, 2000.

Myers, Dowell. *Housing Democracy: Linking Demographic Structure and Housing Markets.* Madison: University of Wisconsin Press, 1990.

Nadelhaft, Jerome. "Wife Torture: A Known Phenomenon in Nineteenth Century America." *Journal of American Culture* 10, no. 3 (Fall 1987): 39–60.

Nye, Russel B. *The Unembarrassed Muse: The Popular Arts in America.* New York: Dial, 1970.

O'Brien, Jerry. "Everybody Chases Butterflies: The Theme of False Hope in *The Gilded Age.*" *Journal of American Culture* 6, no. 1 (Spring 1983): 69–75.

Pearson, Edmund. *Dime Novels; or, Following an Old Trail in Popular Literature.* Port Washington, N.Y.: Kennikat Press, 1968.

Pendergrast, Mark. *Uncommon Grounds: The History of Coffee and How It Transformed Our World.* New York: Basic Books, 1999.

Perry, Sandra. "Sex and Sentiment in America of What Was Really Going on Between the Staves of Nineteenth Century Songs of Fashion." *Journal of Popular Culture* 6, no. 1 (Summer 1972): 32–48.

Peters, Harry T. *Currier & Ives: Printmakers to the American People.* Garden City, N.Y.: Doubleday, Doran & Co., 1942.

Peterson, Merrill. *Lincoln in American Memory.* New York: Oxford University Press, 1994.

Pfanz, Harry W. *Gettysburg—The First Day*. Chapel Hill: University of North Carolina Press, 2001.

Presbrey, Frank. *The History and Development of Advertising*. Garden City, N.Y.: Doubleday, 1929.

Raitz, Karl. *The National Road*. Baltimore: Johns Hopkins University Press, 1996.

Randolph, Vance. *Ozark Folksongs, Collected and Edited for the State Historical Society of Missouri*. 4 vols. Columbia, Mo.: State Historical Society, 1946–50.

Restad, Penne L. *Christmas in America: A History*. New York: Oxford, 1995.

Riis, Jacob A. *How the Other Half Lives: Studies among the Tenements of New York*. New York: Scribner's, 1929.

Rippa, S. Alexander. *Education in a Free Society: An American History*. New York: Longman, 1984.

Roth, Leland M. *A Concise History of American Architecture*. New York: Harper and Row, 1980.

Rowell, George P. *Forty Years an Advertising Agent, 1865–1905*, 1906; reprint, New York: Garland, 1985.

Rugh, Susan Sessions. *Our Common Country: Family Farming, Culture and Community in the Nineteenth-Century Midwest*. Bloomington: Indiana University Press, 2001.

Sampson, Henry. *History of Advertising from the Earliest Times*. London: Chatto and Windus, 1974.

Sandburg, Carl. *Abraham Lincoln: The Prairie Years and the War Years*. New York: Harcourt, Brace, 1954.

Saum, Lewis O. *The Popular Mood of America, 1860–1890*. Lincoln: University of Nebraska Press, 1990.

Scharnhorst, Gary F. "The Boudoir Tales of Horatio Alger, Jr." *Journal of Popular Culture* 10, no. 1 (Summer 1976): 215–26.

Schmidt, Leigh Eric. *Consumer Rites: The Buying and Selling of American Holidays*. Princeton: Princeton University Press, 1995.

Schroeder, Fred E. H. *Front Yard America: The Evolution and Meanings of a Vernacular Domestic Landscape*. Bowling Green, OH: Bowling Green State University, Popular Press, 1993.

Schwartz, Barry. *Abraham Lincoln and the Forge of National Memory*. Chicago: University of Chicago Press, 2000.

Shaw, Ronald E. *Erie Water West: A History of the Erie Canal 1792–1854*. Lexington: University of Kentucky Press, 1966.

Shepard, Leslie. *The History of Street Literature*. Detroit: Singing Tree Press, 1973.

Siegel, Adrienne. "When Cities Were Fun: The Image of the American City in Popular Books, 1840–1870." *Journal of Popular Culture* 9, no. 2 (Winter 1975): 573–82.

Simpson, Pamela H. *Cheap, Quick, and Easy: Imitative Architectural Materials, 1870–1930*. Knoxville: University of Tennessee Press, 1999.

Sizer, Lyde Cullen. *The Political Work of Northern Women Writers and the Civil War, 1850–1872*. Chapel Hill: University of North Carolina Press, 2000.

Smith, Andrew F. *Popped Culture: A Social History of Popcorn in America*. Columbia: University of South Carolina Press, 1999.

Snow, Robert E., and David E. Wright. "Coney Island: A Case Study in Popular Culture." *Journal of Popular Culture* 9, no. 4 (Spring 1976): 960–75.

Somers, Dale. "The Leisure Revolution: Recreation in the American City, 1820–1920. "*Journal of Popular Culture* 5, no. 1 (Summer 1971): 125–37.

Stearns, Peter N. *Fat History: Bodies and Beauty in the Modern West.* New York: New York University Press, 1997.

Stevenson, Louise L. *The Victorian Homefront: American Thought and Culture, 1860–1880.* New York: Twayne, 1991.

Suderman, Elmer F. "Elizabeth Stuart Phelps and the *Gates Ajar* Novels." *Journal of Popular Culture* 3, no. 1 (Summer 1969): 91–106.

Sullivan, Jack. *New-World Symphonies.* New Haven, Conn.: Yale University Press, 2000.

Summers, Mark W. *Railroads, Reconstruction, and the Gospel of Prosperity: Aid under the Radical Republicans, 1865–1877.* Princeton: Princeton University Press, 1984.

Sutherland, Daniel E. *The Expansion of Everyday Life, 1860–1876.* Fayetteville: University of Arkansas Press, 2000.

Tawa, Nicholas. *High-Minded and Low-Down: Music in the Lives of Americans, 1800–1861.* Boston: Northeastern University Press, 2000.

Trachtenberg, Alan. *The Incorporation of America: Culture and Society in the Gilded Age.* New York: Hill and Wang, 1982.

Trager, James. *The People's Chronology.* Rev. ed. New York: Henry Holt, 1992.

Turner, E. S. *The Shocking History of Advertising!* New York: Dutton Books, 1953.

U. S. Bureau of the Census. *The Statistical History of the United States from the Colonial Times to the Present.* Washington, D.C.: U. S. Bureau of the Census, 1976.

Varhola, Michael J. *Everyday Life during the Civil War: A Guide for Writers, Students, and Historians.* Cincinnatti, OH: Writer's Digest Books, 1999.

Volo, Dorothy Denneen, and James M. Volo. *Daily Life in Civil War America.* Westport, Conn.: Greenwood Press, 1997.

———. *Daily Life in Everyday America.* Westport, Conn.: Greenwood Press, 1998.

———. *Encyclopedia of the Antebellum South.* Westport, Conn.: Greenwood Press, 2000.

Watkins, Mel. *On the Real Side: Laughing, Lying, and Signifying.* New York: Simon & Schuster/Touchstone, 1994.

Weil, Gordon L. *Sears, Roebuck, U. S. A.: The Great American Catalog Store and How It Grew.* New York: Stein & Daya, 1977.

Welter, Rush, *Popular Education and Democratic Thought in America.* New York: Columbia University Press, 1962.

# Index

Abortion, 33
*Adventures of Huckleberry Finn,* 113–116
*Adventures of Tom Sawyer,* 113, 114
Advertisements for war materials, 41
Advertising: bulk, 40; creative techniques in, 44; full page, 39; honesty in, 47; magazines, 43–51; new types and styles, 38; newspaper, 37–43
African Americans: in baseball, 91; music, 119, 130–133, 166; religion, 17–18, 97
African Methodist Episcopal Church, 18
Agate rule, 38–39
Alcott, Louisa May, xv, 109
Alger, Horatio, xv
*American Architecture and Building News,* 54
American Bible Society, 11
American Institute of Architects, 62
*American Railway Guide,* 158
American West, 106
Anthony, Susan B., 148
Antietam, 11
Appomattox Court House, x
Architecture: commercial, 59–61; family housing, 61–62; "gingerbread," 56; Gothic Revival, 56; private

homes, 54–57; public buildings, 57–59; Renaissance, 56; Romanesque, 56; Second Empire, 56; Victorian, 56
Army, daily life in, 9
Arthur, Timothy Shaw, 110, 139
*Atlantic Monthly,* 66, 104

Balloon-frame construction, 55
Ballooning, 161
Barbed wire, xvi
Barnard, George, 171
Barnum, P.T., xvi, 42, 148
Baseball, 90
Battery Wagner, South Carolina, 8
Beadle and Adams, xiii, 106
*Beadles' Banner,* 108
Beecher, Henry Ward, 96, 104
Beer, 86
Bell, Alexander Graham, xvii
*Ben Hur,* 111
Bennett, James Gordon, 40
Bible, 103
Bicycle riding, 95
Bird, Robert Montgomery, 104
Birthing process, 34
*Black Crook,* xv, 142
"Black Friday," xvi

Bland, James, 131
Bloomer, Amelia, 70
"Bloomer Costume, The," 70
"Bloomer Gallopade, The," 70
"Bloomers," 70
Boarding houses, low-rise apartments, 61
"Bonnie Blue Flag, The," 123
Boone, Daniel, 106
Booth, Edwin, 135, 136
Booth, John Wilkes, xv
Bradbury, William B., 120
Braddon, M.E., 103
Brady, Mathew, 169
"British Blondes." *See* Thompson, Lydia
British Cunard Line, xiv
Brooks, Phillips, 96
Browne, Francis F., 124
Bryan, Williams Jennings, 166
Bryant, William Cullen, 112
Bulfinch, Charles, 57
Buntline, Ned, 110
Burbank, Luther, xvii
Burlesque, 142–143
Butterick, Ebenezer, 66
B.V.D. underwear introduced, xvii
Byron, Lord, 103

Cable cars, xvi
Calcium chloride, 82
Camp meetings, 97, 148
Canals, 152
Candy, 84
*Carpet Bag, The,* 114
Carpeting, 57
"Carry Me Back to Old Virginny," 131
Carson, Kit, 106
*Cartes-de-visite,* 169
Cartoonists, 175–179
"Celebrated Jumping Frog of Cala-veras County, The," 114
Centennial Exposition, xvii, 66, 100
Central Pacific and Union Railroad contracted, xiv
Chamberlain, Samuel, 33
Chapman, John, 73
Chase, Caleb, 6

Chase, Salmon P., 41
Chautauqua, 135, 148
Childs, Lydia Maria, 104
Christy, E.P., 121
Circuses, 144–146
Clarke, James Freeman, 96
Classical drama, 137
Clothing companies and advertising, 48
Coates, Henry M., 112
Cobb, Sylvanus T., 110
Cody, William F. ("Buffalo Bill"), 106
Coffee, 75, 86
Colleges and universities, 28, 30
Collins, Wilkie, 111
Color tinting, 168
Colored Methodist Episcopal Church, 18
Colored Primitive Baptist Church, 18
Common schools, 28
Concert saloons, 142
Confederate Bible Society, 9
Confederate Memorial Day, 100
*Confederate Symbols in the Contemporary South,* x
Constable, Arnold, 59
Contraception, 33
Cook, George, 172
Cooking utensils, 75
Cooper, James Fenimore, 104
Corcoran Gallery, 167
Cracker-jacks, 83
Crawford, Francis Marion, 111
Crevecour, Hector St. Jean de, vii
Cropsey, Edward, 110
Croquet, 91
Cross-dressing, 144
Crusade, 4
Cummins, Maria Susan, 110
Currier & Ives, 165

Daguerreotype, 163
Daly's Fifth Avenue Theatre, 136, 138
Dan Bryant's Minstrels, 123
Davenport, Fanny, 139
Davis, Jefferson, xiv
Davis, Rebecca Harding, 116
DeForest, John William, 116
Devlin's Clothing Store, 150

Dickens, Charles, 35, 103
Dickinson, Emily, 154
Dickeson, Montroville Wilson, 164
Dime novels, 105–108
Diorama, 163–164
Divorce, 33
"Dixie," 123, 126
Dixon, George Washington, 140
Domestic novel, 108–111
Downing, Andrew Jackson, 55
"Dr. Livingstone, I Presume," 36
"Drummer Boy of Shiloh," 122
Durance, Peter, 82

Edison, Thomas Alva, 156
Edmonds, Sarah Emma, 7
Ellis, Edward S., 106
Emancipation Proclamation, 4
Emmett, Daniel D., 123
Environment, 49
Equitable Life Assurance Society, 59
"Erie Canal, The," 152
Esther, the Beautiful Queen, 120
"Ethiopian Opera," 140
Ethiopian Serenaders, 140
Evans, Augusta Jane, 110
Everett, Edward, 8

Fads, 94
Farms, 23; farmhouses, 56
Fat Man's Club, 67
Fenian Brotherhood, 96
Fern, Fanny, 109
Fern Leaves from Fanny Fern's Portfolio,
    110
Field hospitals, 9
Fifteenth Amendment ratified, xvi
First Inaugural Address, President
    Lincoln, xiv
First national income tax levied, xix
Folk culture, ix
Football, xvii
Footwear, 63
Ford's Theatre, xv, 136
Foreign-born soldiers, 5
Fort Sumter, ix
Foster, Stephen Collins, 119, 121–122
Fourteenth Amendment, xv

Fourth of July, 100–102
Fowler, Orson, 31
Frank Leslie's Popular Monthly, 43, 104,
    108, 173, 178
Franklin, Benjamin, 34, 83
Fraternal organizations, 98
Frontier, 15
Furness, William, 96
Fussell, Jacob, 84

Gaboriaux, Emile, 111
Gambling, 89
Gander-pulling, 94
Gardner, Alexander, 171
Garland, Hamlin, 133
Gates Ajar, 110
Genre painting, 165–166
Gettysburg Cemetery dedicated and
    Lincoln's Address given, xiv
Gilbert and Sullivan, 121
Gilded Age, The, 66, 114
Gilmore, Patrick, 123
Godey's Lady's Book, xiii, 56, 66, 80,
    109, 168
Gorrie, Dr. John, 82
Government bonds for sale, 36
Grand Army of the Republic, 100
Grand Union Company, 83
Grange, 99
Grant, Ulysses S. Grant, ix, xvi
Great Atlantic & Pacific Tea Co., xvi, 83
Great Expectations, 103
Great Seal of the United States, xi
Great Sewing Machine Combination,
    66
"Greek Slave," 167
Green, Anna Katherine, 111
"Greenbacks," 12
Greenough, Horatio, 166
Gryce, Ebenezer, 111

Half-Dime Library, 108
Hamilton, Gail, 109
Hayne, Paul Hamilton, 103, 108
Hardtack and Coffee, 80
Harland, Marion, 110
Harper's Bazaar, 67
Harper's Monthly, 43, 59, 103, 173

Harvey, Fred, xvii
Hawthorne, Nathaniel, 103, 110, 160
Hayne, Paul Hamilton, 113
Headen, Ambrose, 30
Heenan-Sayers heavyweight fight, 173
Hires Root Beer, xvii
"Hippodrama," 144
Historical romance, 111
Hodges, John ("Cool White"), 136
Hoe rotary press, 35
Holmes, Oliver Wendell, 90
"Homespun Dress, The," 124
Homestead Act, 14
Hone, Philip, 167
Horse racing, 89
Hospitality, 74
Howe, Elias, 70
Howells, William Dean, 114, 116
Hudson, Frederic, 34
Hugo, Victor, 103
Human rights and human liberty, 4
Hunger and starvation, 27
Hunt, Walter, 73

Ice cream, 84
Ice house, 80
Ideology, 3
Illustrated journalism, 172
Industrial Revolution, 57
Ingraham, Joseph Holt, 108
*Innocents Abroad*, 114
Inventions, x, xvi
Ivory Soap, 47

James, Frank and Jesse, 159
James, Henry, 161
James Redpath Agency, 149
Jefferson, Thomas, 166
Jerome Park, 93
Johnson, Nancy M., iii, 80
Jones Brothers Tea Company, 83
Judson, E. Zane Carroll, 108, 110

Kennedy, John Pendleton, 103
Kentucky Derby, xvii
Kittredge Cornice and Ornament Company, 56
Ku Klux Klan, xv

Laborers, 4, 67
*Ladies Report of New York Fashions,* 66
*Lamplighter, The,* 110
Lawn croquet, xv
Lawn tennis, 95
Leatherstocking Tales, 104
Lecture circuits, 148
*Ledger,* 35
Lee, Robert E., 126, 177
*Les Miserables,* 103
*Letters from an American Farmer. See*
    Crevecour, Hector St. Jean de
Lewis, Helen C., 70
Libraries, 103
*Life on the Mississippi,* 113, 115, 153, 154
*Lily, The,* 66
"Linoleumville," 57
Liquors, 86
Literacy, 5
Literature, popular, 103
Lithography, 164–165
Longfellow, Henry Wadsworth, 55,
    104, 112
Lord & Taylor, 59
"Lorena," 120
Lyceum, 135, 148

Macy's, R.H., xv, xvii, 59
Madame Caplin, 70
*Madame Demorest's Quarterly Mirror of
    Fashions,* 62
Magazines: adults, 47; children's,
    23–24
Mail order catalogues and sales, 55
Mail service, 161–162; cost of postage,
    162; private carriers, 162; Railway
    Mail Service, 162
*Malaeska, The Indian Wife of the White
    Hunter,* xiii, 106
Marble Dry-Goods Palace, 59
Mardi Gras, 100
*Marie Celeste,* xvi
"mark twain," 153
Marriage, 32
Marsh, Jordan, 59
Mass production, 55
Masturbation, 31
Mather, Cotton, 119

Maturation, 27
*Mazeppa, or The Wild Horse*, 144
McCall, James, 70
McGuffey, William Holmes, 26; *Second Reader, Fourth Reader*, 28
Medicine shows, 146
Melodrama, 138–140
Melville, Herman, 103
Memminger, C.G., 41
Memorial Day, 100
Menken, Adah Isaacs, 144
Men's dress, 67
Menus, 74, 75–77
Milton, John, 111
Mineral water, 85
Minstrel show, 119, 140–142
*Miss Leslie's New Cook Book*, 75
*Miss Ravenal's Conversion from Secession to Loyalty*, 116
Mississippi steamboat, 53
Mitchell, S. Augustus, 33
Modern America, 10–16
Montgomery Ward & Co., xvi, 55
Mormon panorama, 164
Morrill Land Grant Act, 28
Morris, Clara, 139
Morse, Samuel F.B., xiii
Mount, William Sidney, 166
Munro, George, 106, 108
Music: brass band and military, 121–123; classical, 121; western 133
*Mysteries and Miseries of New York*, 110
Mystery tale, 111

Nashville, Tenn., 83
Nast, Thomas, 173
National American Lyceum, 148
National Association of Base Ball Players, 90
National Era, 104
National Grange of the Patrons of Husbandry, 46, 98
Navigable rivers, 153
Negroes, 6, 140. *See also* African Americans
National League of Professional Baseball Clubs, 91
Nether Side of New York, The, 110

*New Cottage Homes and Details*, 59
*New York Herald*, 40
*New York Illustrated News*, 173
*New York Ledger*, 109
*New York Tribune*, 102
Newspapers, daily, 37–43
Niblo Gardens, 142
Nichols, George, 140
Nick of the Woods, 104
*Nurse and Spy in the Union Army*, 7
Nook Farm, 63
N.W. Ayer & Son Advertising Agency, 40

Obesity, 71, 75
*Old Homestead, The*, 140
Olive Branch, The, 110
Order No. 252, 177
Orphans and orphanages, 27
Otis, Elisha Graves, 59
"Our American Cousin," 126
Oyster bars, saloons, free lunch counters, 70

"Palace sleeping cars," 158
Pamela, 109
Panorama, 164
Paper-pattern industry, 66
Parades, 10
Parodies, 129–130, 137
Passenger cars, 157
Pastor, Tony, 137, 143
Patent medicines, 44
Patrons of Husbandry ("Grange"), 46
Patterson, Floyd, viii
Peanuts, 83–84
*Pennsylvania Gazette*, 37
Penny press, 37
*People's Literary Companion*, 47
*Peterson's National Ladies' Magazine*, 47
Petroleum products, xiii
Phelps, Elizabeth Stuart, 110
*Photographic Sketchbook of the War*, 171
*Photographic Views of Sherman's Campaign*, 171
Photographers, 169–172
Photography, 167–169
Physicians, 34

Pinkham, Lydia E., xvii
Player piano invented, xvii
*Pocahontas*, 124
Pocket-novels, 108
Poe, Edgar Allan, 111
Poetry, 111–113
Popcorn, 83
Population, surges in, 15
Pork, 80
Portland cement company, 62
Powers, Hiram, 166
Powers, John, 47
Prejudices, 5
Pretzel, xiv, 84
*Prince of the House of David,* 103
Prize fighting, 94
"Psalm of Life," 112
Pullman, George, 158

*Quaker City,* 161
"Queen of Sheba, The," 145

*Ragged Dick. See* Alger, Horatio
Railroads, 154–159; robberies, 159;
    track gauges, lures to passengers,
    158; workers, 159
Ray, Isaac, 31
Recruitment, 2
Refrigeration, 75
Religious revivals, 9, 17
Renwick, James, Jr., 135
Rogers, John, 167
Roller skating, 95–96
Rowell, George, 40
*Rowell's American Newspaper Directory,*
    40
Ruskin, John, 58
Russell, Benjamin, 164

Sabbath, 157
Safety brake, 60
Sanborn, James, 82
Sanitary Fair in St. Louis, 25
Sapolio soap and powder, 48
*Saturday Evening Post,* 44
Saylor, David O., 66
Schoolbooks, 21; Confederacy, 22;
    Union 23

Scoliosis, 70
Scott, Sir Walter, 103
*Scribner's Monthly,* 58
"Scrimmage," 91
Sculpture, 166–167
"Seeing the elephant," 8
Senefelder, Alois, 164
Sewing machine, 65
*Sex in Education; or, A Fair Chance for the*
    *Girls,* 32
Sexual awakening, 31
Shakespeare, William, 103, 111,
    136–138
Sheet music, 119
Sherman, William Tecumseh, 171
Shiloh, 18
Simms, William Gilmore, 103
Singer, Isaac, 65
Sketch artists, 174
Skirmishes and Sketches, 109
Slavery, 4, 10; eating habits, 80, 103;
    schoolbooks, 21
Smith Brothers Cough Drops, xvi
S.M. Pettengill and Company, 40
Sod houses, 56
Soda pop, 85
Soldiers' rations, 79–80
Solomon, Isaac, xiv, 78
Song sheets, 119–120
Songs, 112–113, 120–121, 126–129
Sons and Daughters of Temperance, 92
*Southern Illustrated News,* 108, 173
Southworth, Emma Dorothy Eliza
    Nevite (E.D.E.N.), 110, 112
Souvenirs, 21
Spalding, Albert, 91
Spectator sports, 91
"Spooning" the ball, 92
*Sports and Games,* 91
*St. Elmo,* 110
St. Patrick's Day, 100
Standard Oil Company, 40
Standardized time, 156
Stanley, Henry, 36
Stanton, Elizabeth Cady, 71
"Star-Spangled Banner, The," 119
Steamboats, 153; races, 154
Stereoscopic photography, 168

Stetson hat, xv
Stewart, A.T., 59
Stewart's Cast Iron Palace, 59
Story papers, 104
Stoddard, Elizabeth Drew Barstod, 116
Stowe, Harriet Beecher, 71, 103, 139
Strauss, Levi, xvii
Street and Smith, 106
Stuart, Gilbert, 165
Stuart, J.E.B., x
Students, 30, 31
Studio portraits, 168
"Super Fine Crown Soap," 35

Tableaux vivants, 164
Talese, Gay, xiii
"Taps" composed, xiv
Taylor, Tom, 136
Teas, medicinal, 86
*Ten Nights in a Barroom; and What I Saw
    There,* 110, 139
Tennyson, Alfred Lord, 55, 103
Thanksgiving declared by President
    Lincoln, xiv
Theater, 135–140
Thimmonier, Barthelemy, 65
Thompson, Lydia, xvi, 144
*Times,* 34
Timrod, Henry, 109
Tin cans, xv
Tousey, Sinclair, 106
Tourist trade, 149
Town, Salem, 29
Toys, 24
"Train boys," 155
Travel literature, 160
*Tribune,* 36
Trolly system, 149
Truth, Sojourner, 148
Tufts, James W., 81
Turnpikes and trails, 151
Twain, Mark, 110, 113, 114, 136
Typewriters, xv, 13, 55

*Uncle Tom's Cabin,* xiii, 104–105, 139
Underground transportation, 149
Underwood, William, 78
Uniforms, 71
Urban transportation, 150

Van Camp, Gilbert C., xiv, 82
Vaudeville, 139, 143–144
Velocipede developed, xiv, 161
Venereal disease and brothels, 7
Venturi, Robert, viii
Veterans, 10
Vicksburg, Miss., l8

Wallace, Lew, 111
Wallpaper, 57
Wanamaker, John, 59
"Wanted—A Man," 113
Ward, Artemus, 148
Water, fresh, 71
Waterfall (hairdo), 69, 70
Waterways, 152–154
Wedding ceremony, 33
Wheeler, Gervase, 59
Whiffin, Marcus, 59
Whitman, Walt, 112, 163
Whittier, John Greenleaf, 112
Woman's Christian Temperance
    Union, 98
Women's dress, 68–71

"Yankee Doodle," 119
Yankee Robinson's Opera Pavilion, xiii
Yellowstone National Park, xv
Young Men's Christian Association,
    98
Young Women's Christian Association,
    98
Youth, 18; as soldiers, 24
Youth's Companion, 110

Zion Church, 18
Zouaves, 23, 122

## About the Authors

RAY B. BROWNE is Professor Emeritus in the Department of Popular Culture at Bowling Green State University, which he founded. He is editor of the *Journal of Popular Culture* and the *Journal of American and Comparative Cultures*. He is the author and editor of over 70 books and has served as Secretary-Treasurer of the Popular Culture Association and the American Culture Association since their beginnings.

LAWRENCE A. KREISER, JR. is an independent scholar.